Storm over Stevenage

Weekend at Wilton Park

How to tell the People

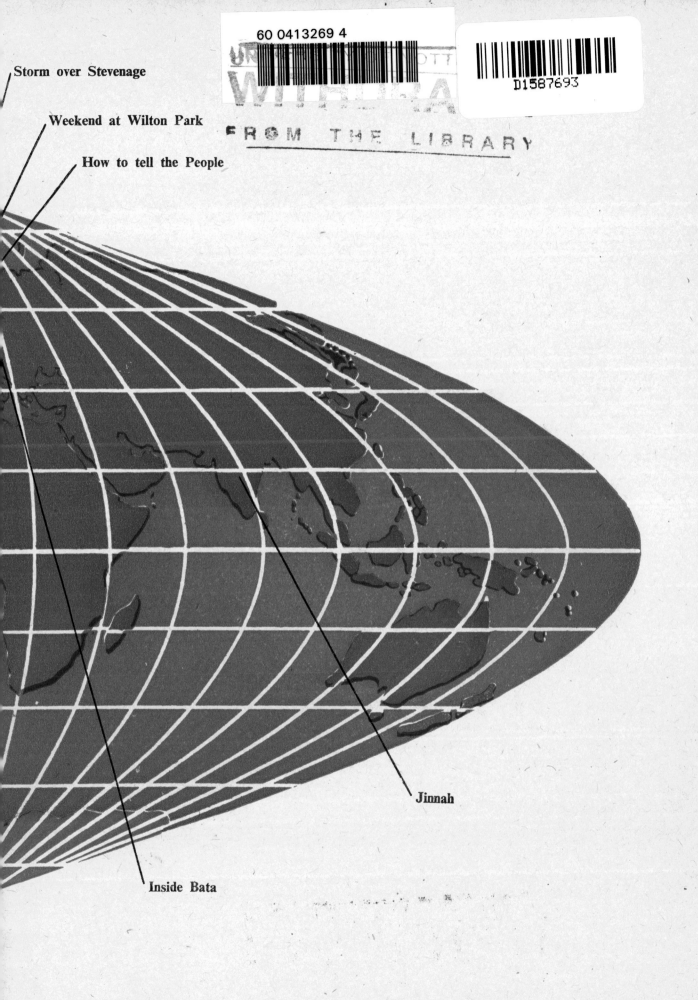

Jinnah

Inside Bata

THE CHANGING NATION

The Changing Surface of Britain

METROPOLIS IN TRANSITION
by G. M. Kallman and Hugh Casson   1
Drawings by Hugh Casson

THE RELUCTANT COUNTRYSIDE
by A. V. D. Gordon   7

THE PATTERN OF SUBURBIA
by Barbara Jones   9
Drawings by the author

THE CHANGING COASTLINE
by Lionel Brett   15

Change and the People

THE POTTERIES LOOK FORWARD
by Bernard Hollowood and Sam Pollock   18

SOUTH WALES STORY
by Douglas Jay   23

STORM OVER STEVENAGE
by Mark Benny   42

MARRIAGE AND DIVORCE IN POSTWAR
    BRITAIN
by Mass-Observation   29

GENTLE REVOLUTIONARY: A PORTRAIT OF ARTHUR
    HORNER
by Giles Romilly   36

Interchange

OKLAHOMA IMPACT
by William Sansom and Leonard Rosoman   51

WEEKEND AT WILTON PARK
by P. Gordon-Walker   79
Drawings by Walter Goetz

Reflections

THE CAUSES OF WAR: AN ESSAY
by Harold Nicolson   73

H. G. WELLS: PROPHET OF CHANGE
by Peter Quennell   87

THE SOCIAL BALANCE OF POWER
by David Mitrany   84

Exchange of Views

HOW TO TELL THE PEOPLE: A DISCUSSION ON GOVERN-
MENT PUBLIC RELATIONS between Robert Fraser,
Frank Owen and Kingsley Martin (*Chairman*)   92

IN SEARCH OF A FOREIGN POLICY: A CORRESPONDENCE
between R. H. S. Crossman MP and Anthony
Nutting MP   100

Change Abroad

INSIDE BATA
by Ernest Davies   66

JINNAH: FIRST GENTLEMAN OF ISLAM
by a Student of India   56

THE PAINTERS OF HAITI
by F. D. Klingender   60

*　　*　　*

LETTER FROM ICELAND
by Stephen Simmonds   vii

LETTER FROM AZERBAIJAN
by Christopher Sykes   xi

LETTER FROM HAMBURG
by Derrick Sington   xxxiii

A CONTACT BOOK

CONTACT PUBLICATIONS LIMITED 26 MANCHESTER SQUARE LONDON W1

COMMENT ON CONTENTS

THE OBJECT of this volume, seventh in the series of **Contact** Books, is to record some aspects of the change of life, habit and thought of this nation—and others—as the result of war and reconstruction: some of them drastic and dramatic, others gradual and barely perceptible, yet none the less significant.

The Changing Surface

of Britain comes under review in four essays by a team of architectural writers. **G. M. Kallman** and **Hugh Casson** collaborate on a study of the Metropolis in transition. Both have strong views on 'urbanism' differing from Lewis Mumford's gloomy anti-Metropolitan ideas. They are both practising architects. Casson is also an imaginative illustrator and responsible for the drawings . . . the suburb's change of appearance is discussed by **Barbara Jones**, author and illustrator of topographical books . . . the village and the open country by **A. V. D. Gordon**, formerly on the Council for the Preservation of Rural England, now a BBC Talks Producer . . . and the changing coastline is expertly surveyed by **Lionel Brett**, ' the first professional member', as he puts it, ' of a family long amateurs of architecture'. Son of Viscount Esher, the Hon. Lionel Brett has recently been engaged on the replanning of two seaside towns, Weston-super-Mare and Littlehampton.

Change and the People

First-hand reports on three communities in postwar Britain bring out significant elements of social change. There is special interest in **Douglas Jay's** account of progress in the South Wales Development Areas, for he had a fair personal share in the success of this great venture through his war-time work with the Board of Trade. From 1945-6 he was Economic Advisor to the Prime Minister, is now MP for North Battersea . . . What full employment means to the Potteries emerges from the report by **Bernard Hollowood**, broadcaster and writer on industrial affairs and himself a native of Staffordshire, and **Sam Pollock**, of the BBC. **Mark Benny** went for **Contact** Books on a three weeks' fact-finding trip to Stevenage. He investigated how people felt about becoming citizens of the first 'New Town'. Talking to many, both pro- and anti-Silkinites, he gauged the mood of a community confronted with a revolutionary decision. Mark Benny is the author of several novels marked by a strong and lively social documentary note.

Why has the number of divorces in England and Wales increased by more than 500 per cent during the past ten years? Our survey of Marriage and Divorce in Britain today attempts to answer this question. **Mass-Observation** recently conducted for **Contact** Books a survey in four urban areas, thus supplementing material from a wider survey gathered in London and Gloucester shortly before the end of the war.

Little is known about Arthur Horner, Communist miners' leader and one of Britain's most controversial public figures. **Giles Romilly** contributes his assessment of the man. He is also working on a full-length biography of Horner. Romilly, who is Winston Churchill's nephew and in his early thirties, fought in the Spanish War (on the Republican side), was captured at Narvik in 1940, and was a prisoner but escaped. He is now a special correspondent of the *News of the World*, for whom he reported the 1947 Moscow Conference.

Interchange

'Oklahoma Impact' is the record of an emotional experience rather than a conventional piece of dramatic criticism. **William Sansom,** who won early fame as a short story writer and recently was awarded a prize scholarship by the Society of Authors —and **Leonard Rosoman,** painter and illustrator, who has contributed to earlier **Contact** volumes—communicate in text and picture some of their own and a London West End public's reactions to the spell-binding vitality of American folk-lore. . . A 'German university on British soil' is how Wilton Park, study centre for German prisoners of war in England and some German civilians, has been described. **Patrick Gordon-Walker** frequently lectured there. Prewar Oxford don, wartime broadcaster to Germany and postwar Labour MP, he has always been interested in Anglo-German relations. He is also Vice-President of the British Council, and Parliamentary Private Secretary to Mr Herbert Morrison.

Reflections

Side by side with the factual survey, this **Contact** volume, like its predecessors, offers a place to the reflective essay. **Harold Nicolson** reflects on the causes of war in the light of history. A distinguished author and commentator on current affairs, he is now writing a life of Benjamin Constant . . . **Peter Quennell** reviews the work of H. G. Wells, the great prophet of social change, one year after his death. Editor of the *Cornhill* Magazine and book reviewer of the

Douglas Jay

Giles Romilly

Barbara Jones

Daily Mail, Peter Quennell is about to finish a study of Carlyle and Ruskin, which follows upon his recent volume of eighteenth-century literary portraits . . . 'Functionalism' and what it means in international relations, especially applied to the tragic misunderstanding between West and East, is the subject of **Professor David Mitrany's** thoughtful essay. As more statesmen and thinkers endorse the sane and practical ideas of functionalism, David Mitrany, its chief protagonist, is emerging as one of the most constructive contributors to modern social thinking. He is a professor of the Institute of Advanced Studies of Princeton University, and advises Messrs Unilever on international problems.

Exchange of Views

What ought the Government to tell the people, and how is it to tell its story? The Government's public relations policy and methods come up for discussion between **Robert Fraser,** Director-General of the Central Office of Information, who puts the Government's case, and **Frank Owen,** editor of the *Daily Mail*, who criticises it. Mr Fraser is Australian by origin, journalist and editor by experience, and was, during the war, responsible for some of the most successful publications produced by the then Minister of Information. Frank Owen, ex-Liberal MP, radical columnist and pamphleteer, editor of the *Evening Standard* and a war-time editor of SEAC, the British service paper, wields perhaps the most effective anti-Government pen in Fleet Street today. Chairman of the discussion is **Kingsley Martin,** editor of the *New Statesman*, whose recent book, *The Press the Public Wants*, contains his bold and original views on some of the issues debated. . . .

Summer 1947 was critical for Britain's position in the world—the dollar crisis, the Marshall offer, the Anglo-Russian trade talks. How are they to affect the future course of British foreign policy? This is the theme of a correspondence between two MP's representative of the younger forces in their respective parties. **R. H. S. Crossman** is Labour's most consistent critic of Ernest Bevin's foreign policy, one of the leaders of the 'Keep Left' group. **Anthony Nutting,** barely thirty, is well versed in European affairs, as he served with the Foreign Office as Private Secretary to Mr Eden.

Change Abroad

Half-way between the Western and the Eastern brand of 'democracy,' Czechoslovakia is working out for herself a compromise between public and private ownership in industry. The effects of nationalisation upon the Bata works, one of the biggest factories in the world, are frankly examined by **Ernest Davies** MP, economist and student of industrial organisation . . . A supplement of paintings by contemporary Haitian artists illustrates the great strides made by the artists in the undeveloped, semi-colonial areas of the American continent. **F. D. Klingender,** art critic and historian, selected these pictures from a recent UNESCO exhibition in Paris.

Pinpointing other aspects of change the world over are a letter from Iceland, by **Stephen Simmonds,** journalist and literary critic . . . from Hamburg, by **Derrick Sington,** author of the recent documentary book *Belsen Uncovered* (he was the first British officer to enter Belsen and to arrest Josef Kramer, its 'commandant') . . . and from Azerbaijan, by **Christopher Sykes,** the well-known writer of biography and fiction, who here gives a first-hand coherent account of the recent developments in Persia, decisive, in his view, to the course of postwar world affairs.

Christopher Sykes

Peter Quennell

THE CHANGING NATION

Editor

A. G. Weidenfeld

Art Editor

Vivian Ridler

Assistant Editors

Frame Smith

Nigel Nicolson

Board of Editorial Associates

H. L. Beales

Professor J. D. Bernal FRS

F. S. Button CBE

J. A. Camacho

R. H. S. Crossman MP

Lord Forrester

Dame Caroline Haslett DBE

George Lowther

Kingsley Martin

Professor David Mitrany

Hon. Harold Nicolson CMG

Stephen Spender

Professor S. Zuckerman CBE FRS

Associate Editors

Henry Durant

Ingram Fraser

A. B. Hollowood

Philip Toynbee

Published in 1947 by
Contact Publications Limited

in conjunction with
Wells Gardner Darton and Co Limited
26 Manchester Square London W1
Welbeck 8178

Published for the Netherlands by
Uitgeverij Scheffer and Sikkema
Hekelveld 16 *Amsterdam C*

Set by Cole and Company
(Westminster) Limited SW1

Printed in Great Britain by
Love and Malcomson
Redhill Surrey

How strong is a stocking?

HOW STRONG IS A STOCKING—when it is new?
Do the threads weaken after they have been
washed? What are the wearing qualities of any
fabric? What is the best method of washing,
drying and ironing it? These questions—as
vital to the manufacturers as to the public who
buy their goods—are answered every day by
the backroom boys of the Lux Washability Bureau
at Port Sunlight.

This Bureau, with its specially equipped
laboratory and highly trained technical staff, already
used by 80% of manufacturers, offers a service
which is free and confidential. The Bureau's certificate
is the Blue Ribbon of the textile trade; displayed
with goods it is recognised not only as a guarantee of
their washability, but also as an indication to the public
of good quality materials.

As a direct result of the Bureau's Testing Service, the
textile trade has been helped appreciably to improve the
quality of their fabrics, with a consequent all-round raising of
the standard of manufacture. In the immediate future that
will see the development of new materials and great improvements in old-established ones, the Bureau's advice and help will
be perhaps of even greater value. And with manufacturers
seeking new world markets while regaining and expanding the old,
Lever Brothers are happy to provide them with the continued
co-operation of the Lux Washability Bureau in demonstrating to
the world that the quality of their products is second to none.

*Among the multifarious
tests carried out by the Lux
Washability Bureau is one
to determine the bursting
strength of knitted fabrics.
A stocking is here seen
undergoing the test.*

Issued by the

LUX WASHABILITY BUREAU · PORT SUNLIGHT

LB 26-431-120

iv

THINGS TO COME FROM CREATIVE CHEMISTRY BY 'CELANESE'..

A Scientist writes his hieroglyphics on a piece of paper ... and soon your feet will sink into the silent luxury of a carpet woven from man-made fibre. More hieroglyphics ... and then comes the formula for cobweb-fine window net ...

Original painting by Doris Zinkeisen.

... And because it is man-made, each synthetic fibre created by the Celanese Scientists is destined from its very inception to specific needs. The potentialities are tremendous ... your suit, your scarf, your stockings, your slippers, your gloves — all will be made from a 'Celanese' Yarn created to suit the product. Such is the flexibility of modern creative chemistry.

British Celanese Limited

TEXTILES · PLASTICS · CHEMICALS

Choosing the Captain

How does a pilot qualify for command of a Speedbird? First, he must have at least 800 flying hours to his credit and a very high medical category. Next, he must satisfy an exacting selection board that he is, potentially, the man for the job. Then comes training at the B.O.A.C. school. Theory, thorough and widely ranged; detail, with emphasis on relevant aircraft types; and lastly, flying instruction, when civil flying procedure of every kind becomes a matter of skilled routine. And now, with a 'B' licence and a 2nd-class Navigator's Certificate, he takes his place in the Speedbird—as 1st Officer under a senior Captain. Later — much later — he'll be a Captain himself.

Speedbird Routes to: CANADA · U.S.A
MIDDLE EAST · SOUTH, EAST & WEST AFRICA
INDIA · FAR EAST · AUSTRALIA · NEW ZEALAND

B·O·A·C SPEEDBIRD ROUTES ACROSS THE WORLD

BRITISH OVERSEAS AIRWAYS CORPORATION IN ASSOCIATION WITH QANTAS EMPIRE AIRWAYS, SOUTH AFRICAN AIRWAYS, TASMAN EMPIRE AIRWAYS

By way of introduction and postscript to this volume, we publish three letters from abroad, pin-pointing the changing life and atmosphere in places as far apart as the neat capital of Iceland, the ragged frontier region of Azerbaijan, and the listless port of Hamburg

Letter from Iceland

by Stephen Simmonds

HAVE you, by any chance, ever read Auden and Mac-Neice's *Letters from Iceland*? I only read them myself the other day; I found the book in the National Library of Iceland, and it seemed the perfect opportunity to compare my own impressions of the country with one of the last prewar accounts.

On the whole, Auden and MacNeice did not like Iceland too much. Life was primitive and frugal, and much

of the landscape appeared weird and sinister to them. Also one of them, I forget whether it was Auden or Mac-Neice, caught a bad cold, and that made life seem even worse. But even so, I suppose their views were sound.

Quite a few travellers before them, though there were never many, expressed similar views. Cleasby, for instance, compared the whole of the island to a burnt-out lava field. Henderson (I read all these accounts in the Library here) considers the general aspect of the country 'the most rugged and dreary imaginable'. Baring-Gould, too, is no more cheerful when he speaks of the 'utter desolation' to be found in this weather-beaten, gale-swept land.

Of course, one could make an equally representative selection of quotations extolling the grandeur of the sky, the transparency of the air, 'the snow-capped hills, which blend and melt with ravishing reflections of ethereal pink, blue, azure, and lilac, into the grey and neutral tints of the horizon'. But I am trying to make a point, and it suits me to take Auden and MacNeice's general impression of the country while I go on to explain the change that the island has undergone.

The war has had an extraordinary effect upon Iceland. Of all the countries involved in it, Iceland was undoubtedly the only one that profited from it handsomely. Today this island, which merely vegetated in her isolation, is thriving with prosperity simply through having been

continued on page ix

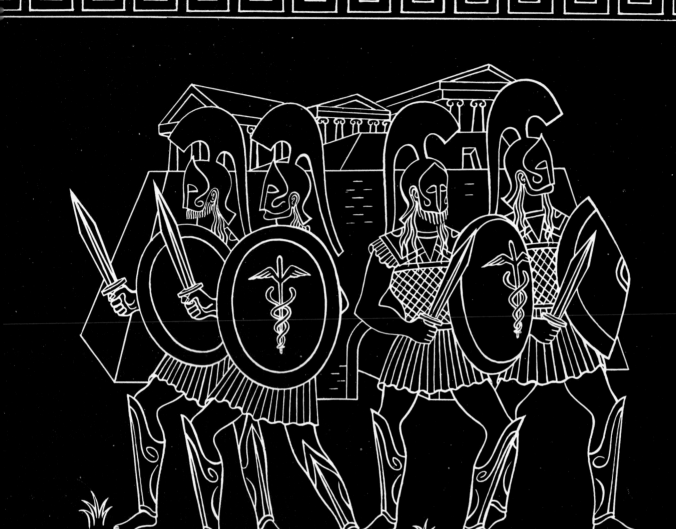

FOUR AGAINST PAIN

Seven men, so the Greek playwright Aeschylus relates, were able to hold the seven gates of Thebes against an enemy army.

In modern times, the citadel of your body can be held against the marauding hosts of pain — headaches, rheumatism, toothache, backache, neuralgia — by four stout defenders.

The symbols of these four heroes are: $CH_3CO.NH.C_6H_4O.C_2H_5$, $CH_3CO_2C_6H_4CO_2H$, $C_{18}H_{21}NO_3 + H_2O$ and $C_8H_{10}N_4O_2$. Three of them are analgesics, the fourth is a stimulant. All four are integrated in 'Cogene', prepared in the 'Genatosan' Laboratories as the proved and perfected formula for the four-way relief of pain.

'Cogene' is made up in simple tablets, to be taken one at a time, as required, with a little water. Non-habit forming, no harmful after-effects. Price 1/1½d. a tube. Supplies are limited, but your chemist will ensure that his quota is distributed fairly.

COGENE

Regd. Trade Mark   *Brand Tablets*

A 'Genatosan' Product

Letter from Iceland

continued from page vii

thrown into the very centre of world affairs. The standard of living of the 130,000 people (occupying an area the size of Ireland) is so high that it can be compared with any population of a million people. Auden and MacNeice would be astonished at the comfort of living, the many American motor cars, the efficiency of air travel, the utilisation of the hot springs for heating houses or growing bananas. I think they would like it much better this time.

The reason for this transformation is simple. The occupation troops, as if to compensate the Icelanders for the discomforts of invasion, brought with them a wave of prosperity. They put Iceland on the map, as it were, and poured money generously into her lap. But in the end, and this came as a shock to the people, it was the Icelanders who had to foot the bill with the loss of their security. The air base which the Americans still maintain near Kaflavik is the visible sign of that price, and the symbolic dilemma of the Icelanders.

For centuries they have struggled to be left alone to their natural isolation. It meant an austere life, barely paid for with the export of fish, but it also meant independence and peace in a restless world. And for a time, during the first World War, for instance, the dream seemed reality.

But then came the epoch of air travel, the discovery of Iceland's strategic importance (how the Icelanders must now curse the day Balbo's air armada landed off their shores), a short flirtation with German aviation, and finally the occupation by the British Fleet, which was later superseded by American airmen. The Icelanders resented that occupation bitterly. Maybe they would have resented a German occupation as bitterly. It is difficult to say. Hitler certainly contemplated an invasion in November 1942, but he never attempted it. In any case, the dream of 'perpetual neutrality' was shattered.

It flickered once more when the second World War came to an end. America had promised to evacuate the island when hostilities ceased. But it took two more years before the army moved out, and even then Kaflavik remained in American hands, at least for another six years. Kaflavik was the ransom.

What was the solution? Isolation and a hard life with security, proximity and comfort but insecurity? Of course, the ideal solution would have been the benefits without the obligations. But ideal solutions are part of another century. And in a way the Icelanders were perhaps fortunate in not having the freedom to choose. After all, the moment the aeroplane was born it settled their fate by killing the

continued on page xi

"Wool moulds and flatters your figure like no other fabric."

THAT HIP PROBLEM ! Of course, if your hips are perfect there's no problem at all—the moulding qualities of wool will show you off to perfection. If, however, your hips are a shade too wide do not wear a narrow skirt Accentuate your waistline and break the width with pleats or soft folds so as to give fullness to your skirt. What could be more ideal for this than wool?

New Type
Lockheed Constellation
...World's Most Modern Airliner

—Capt. Eddie Rickenbacker

" We of Eastern Airlines could have chosen any of the large airliners. After months of study and comparison, we decided on the new-type Constellations. We did so because we are convinced that they are beyond a doubt the world's fastest, most powerful, dependable and comfortable, the world's most modern airliners."

Eddie V. Rickenbacker

Leader over the Atlantic —the Constellation

Flying the Atlantic is the supreme test of airliner efficiency and dependability. For many months past, the majority of these daily flights have been Constellation flights. As on May 15, Constellations were flying 80 Atlantic round trips per week — more than any other scheduled transport.

Endorsed and chosen by distinguished airlines all over the world, this newest version of the famous Constellation brings a new kind of flying pleasure to air travellers everywhere.

MORE THOROUGHLY PROVEN. The proof is in the flying. Behind the Lockheed Constellation lie nearly 1,000 million passenger miles of commercial service plus thousands of hours of operational experience for pilots, flight personnel and ground crews. Thus the Constellation is already the most thoroughly proven of the largest modern air transports.

FIRST CHOICE OF LEADING AIRLINES and world travellers on: *Aer Lingus—Air France—American Overseas Airlines — British Overseas Airways Corp. — Eastern Air Lines — KLM Royal Dutch Airlines — KNILM Royal Netherlands Indies' Airways — L.A.V. — (Linea Aeropostal Venezolana) — Panair Do Brasil — Pan American World Airways — Qantas Empire Airways Ltd. — Trans World Airline.*

Now more than ever-World Leader
Lockheed Constellation

LOOK TO LOCKHEED FOR LEADERSHIP—YEARS AHEAD IN THE SCIENCE OF FLIGHT

Letter from Iceland

continued from page ix

possibility of Iceland's safety through neutrality.

Now the island is on the direct route between America and Russia, almost exactly halfway between the two capital cities, and whoever holds their island could effectively cut off Britain from North America. Iceland's tragedy is that one or other of the Powers would not allow the Icelanders to hold their land because, quite obviously, they *could* not hold it. No army, no navy, no fortifications: that was Iceland's pride once. But in any case, 130,000 people do not stand much of a chance. In our day it is numbers that count. And so the watch-tower of the lava-surrounded aerodrome at Kaflavik holds Iceland's future for good or evil. It has made Iceland and it is her undoing. It is a grim reminder of the unity of the world.

The aeroplane could be the means of contracting time and distance between continents; it could also be the springboard for the severance of all bonds and annihilation. Iceland's role in the world to come is, to her sorrow, linked for better or worse with the strands meeting in that tower above the barren land.

Many Icelanders would like to wish Kaflavik swept off the map, to return to their peaceful occupations of farming and fishing, and to take refuge in the Golden Ages of their Sagas. But there is no escape; and prosperity and peace have their price. Some Icelanders are slowly beginning to realise that everything in this world has to be paid for. And the price demanded is not always fair and just.

Letter from Azerbaijan

by Christopher Sykes

AZERBAIJAN is quite unlike any other part of Persia. It is the only place in that vast Empire where the Persian language is relatively little known, the normal speech of the people being a highly Persianised form of Turkish. Persians tend to be reserved and extravagantly well-mannered, but the Azerbaijanians are mostly coarse, open-hearted and jolly people. Their main political problems have for long been the same: the Kurdish problem, and the autonomy problem. More than half of the Kurds of Persia live in the south-western quarter of Azerbaijan. They have never settled down as peaceable citizens under any Persian Government, and with their traditions of hostility to the despotism of Teheran they keep the flame of rebellion ever alight and ever handy in the whole province. The autonomy problem is the same as afflicts every Persian

continued on page xiii

A cat magnified 200,000 times

THE ELECTRON MICROSCOPE enables us to see things magnified up to hundreds of thousands of times. At such magnification a cat could stand astride the English Channel, its front paws in France, its hind legs in England. So great, in fact, is the power of the Electron Microscope, that scientists can now study the secrets of organisms which, hitherto, were far beyond the limits of even the best optical microscope.

To the development of such apparatus Philips engineers and scientists have made a valuable contribution. But now, as always, they look further ahead, to even more wonderful advances in other fields of electrical development.

RADIO AND TELEVISION RECEIVERS. FLUORESCENT, TUNGSTEN AND DISCHARGE LAMPS AND LIGHTING EQUIPMENT. COMMUNICATIONS EQUIPMENT. INDUSTRIAL ELECTRONIC APPARATUS. HIGH FREQUENCY HEATING GENERATORS. X-RAY EQUIPMENT FOR ALL PURPOSES. ELECTRO-MEDICAL APPARATUS. ARC AND RESISTANCE WELDING PLANT AND ELECTRODES. MAGNETS AND MAGNETIC DEVICES. SOUND AMPLIFYING INSTALLATIONS.

 PHILIPS ELECTRICAL LIMITED

CENTURY HOUSE, SHAFTESBURY AVENUE, LONDON, W.C.2

(P298A)

Letter from Azerbaijan

continued from page xi

province. The kingdom is even more highly centralised than France, though it still largely depends on
primitive communications. This leads to misrule
against which autonomous movements are a natural
protest. When the Russians and British entered
Persia in September 1941, these movements clamoured louder than ever to be heard.

The Allies signed a treaty with Persia in 1942 in
which, among other things, they all promised not to
interfere in Persian internal affairs. For the best
part of a year the Russians interfered hardly at all;
but two years later, in 1945, they took action. There
was a 'spontaneous rising' in Azerbaijan conducted
by local bodies of rebellious troops who were armed,
officered, clothed and directed by the Russian
authorities in the province. Such authorities existed
because the Red Army, which had entered in 1941,
was still there. The Persian police and army were
prevented by the Russians from sending reinforcements to Azerbaijan, and the rebellion soon succeeded! It was followed by elections in which voters
were taken to polling booths in Russian army
trucks driven by Russian soldiers in uniform. Few
people were so improvident as to refuse invitations
to vote. A Soviet-controlled Government of Azerbaijan (owing nominal allegiance to the Shah) was
returned with an important majority.

A great many Persians who joined the political
parties inspired by Russia did so at this time from
noble motives. As with many very ancient societies,
abuses, particularly the abuses of corruption and
sloth, have crept so deep into the Persian polity that
it seemed to many loyal members of that polity that
only outside interference could begin a better age.
If they were mistaken, they were not to be despised.
In Azerbaijan most of the better elements of the
country sided at first with the Russians.

In his *Study of History*, Professor Arnold Toynbee gives a very disturbing heading to one of his
chapters: under the general title: *The Cause of the
Breakdowns of Civilisation*, he has a section called
The Intoxication of Victory. If he had witnessed the
events of 1946 in Persia he might have felt moved
to add another illustration to this part of his theme.
The Russians had enjoyed a success in Azerbaijan
so absolute that they grew stupidly over-confident.
Under this influence they made every blunder which
they could. They chose as their creatures in the new
autonomous Government leaders who were con-
temptible by the not high standards of Persian
administration. Those who had groaned under
Persian misrule groaned considerably louder under
the grosser misrule of the new tyrants. Judicial
murder was the main instrument of government.

continued on page xxiii

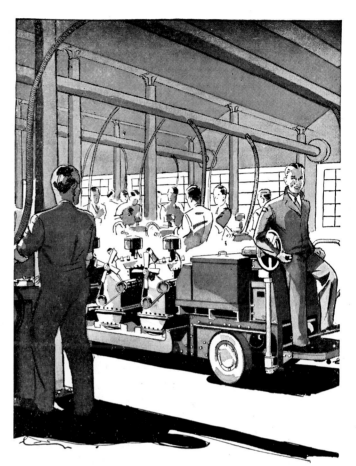

These trucks
speed production

WHEREVER manpower bears on production
problems, wherever the speed of internal distribution is important, electric trucks powered by
Exide-Ironclad can render vital service. Today,
in more and more British factories, 'electrics'
are playing a big part in the drive for expanded
production.

ELECTRICS POWERED BY **Exide-Ironclad**

THE CHLORIDE ELECTRICAL STORAGE COMPANY LIMITED
Battery Traction Department
77 King Street, Manchester 2   *Telephone : Blackfriars 4731*
V25

FIVE MILESTONES ON THE ROAD TO PERFECTION

Five milestones mark the passage of Rolex's 40 momentous years in the history of watchmaking.

೫

It was in 1905 that Hans Wilsdorf, then little more than a young man with original and courageous ideas, later the founder and proprietor of the Genevan firm of Rolex, put the first Rolex *wrist* watch on the English market. In those days the wrist watch was still a mere novelty, its future in the lap of the gods that sway public opinion. But Wilsdorf believed in its future, and time proved him right. The wrist watch first made a hit with sportsmen, then the fashion spread, first in England, and then throughout the world.

೫

By 1914, the Rolex wrist watch had come to stay. The movements were continually being perfected, brought up to date, until, on July 15th, 1914, for the first time in the world, a one-inch Rolex movement was awarded a KEW-"A" Certificate after testing in 5 positions and at 3 temperatures over a period of 45 days.

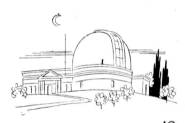

೫

In 1926, Wilsdorf took on the task of perfecting a hermetically-sealed case whereby the precision movements of Rolex watches could be protected from dirt, dust, perspiration, water, heat and cold. After long and patient experimentation, and despite innumerable disappointments, this new type of watch-case was designed and perfected. The secret of the waterproof watch was discovered, and the Rolex-"Oyster," now famous all over the world, began its brilliant career in November 1927.

In 1931, the Rolex-"Perpetual" (self-winding watch) was produced, in reality a logical outcome of its immediate predecessor, the "Oyster." Generations of watchmakers had dreamt of creating an automatic timepiece, independent of human intervention. Intricate mechanisms and impractical devices had seen the light of day in the XVIIIth and XIXth Centuries, only to be abandoned and forgotten. The wonderfully efficient Rolex-"Perpetual" was the final answer to this age-old problem.

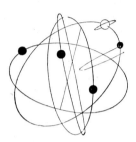

೫

1945—and in the Rolex-"Datejust" have been united all the technical perfections of modern watchmaking. Waterproof and self-winding, with chronometer movement and automatic calendar, this watch combines every invention known to horological science today. Forty years of progress are expressed in this unique model.

೫

Forty years of watch designing, too, have entered into the composition of this remarkable Jubilee model. Its distinctive case, handsome dial, upon which the date is clearly visible, its solid gold hands and numerals of classical design, are a brilliant example of traditional Genevan elegance, that ancient citadel of watch-craft.

೫

Rolex have widely contributed to the popularization and successful career of the wrist watch; they have been the inventors of the waterproof watch, the pioneers of the silent self-winding wrist watch. And now, in introducing the Rolex-Perpetual-Datejust, they have created a model perfect in form and presentation, and the most technically complete and useful wrist watch known today.

ROLEX WATCH Co. Ltd.
GENEVA (Switzerland)

A JUBILEE
OF ENDEAVOUR

"That's it!
...the car with the lowest upkeep costs

I'm going to have a

MORRIS MOTORS LTD. **N** A NUFFIELD PRODUCT COWLEY, OXFORD

WHEN A COLOUR REPRODUCTION IS DECIDED UPON the next question is one of technique ; to employ the imaginative brush of a commercial artist in water colours or oils, or crayon ? Or, alternatively, to use a colour photograph or transparency ? Because it presents the subject literally, with an accuracy beyond doubt, we use a colour photograph as an example. Our " snapshot " shows how simple it is : the colour-photographer is focusing-up : no special lighting was required and nothing especially organised. This picture shows part of the colour proofing machine-room of C. & E. LAYTON LTD. as it is on every working day. Note the narrow space available for manoeuvring and overhead girders which prohibit a bird's-eye view.

Colour Photography by Studio Jay.

The first working is Yellow.   *Then the Red plate is printed.*   *Super-imposed on both is Blue.*

*Illustrated is part of the colour proo
machine-room in C. & E. Layton's co
department.*

Intricate part of printing from colour plates i
close " register " needed to ensure the acc
super-imposition of each colour. The colou
colour reproductions of our original leave no ma
for even fractional errors in make-ready. T
illustrations show the build-up of a three-co
picture as the primary colours of the spectrum
super-imposed, one upon the other.

The production of Colour blocks

☞ *This black and white picture is printed to compare with the full colour reproduction on the page facing. There are stages of production in many plants when a similar picture could be taken and found effective in sales promotional material. Colour can give life and interest to what is otherwise a commonplace photograph of men and machines.*

The three-colour process

In 1503 the Hopfers, an Augsberg family of metal workers, took crude impressions of their work to show prospective customers. Today manufacturers show their wares faithfully produced in full colours by the tri-chromatic process, for the same three colours can now print many diverse subjects simultaneously. The other colour pages in this " Contact " publication, for example, were printed at the same time and with the same inks as the colour page opposite : such is the flexibility of the three-colour process. Many advertisers and their agents use colour for the life-like portrayal of new products ; to mark the introduction of a new pack or redesigned label ; to picture fashions and fashion fabrics as they are. There is no end to the imaginative use of colour to strengthen an advertising message, especially if you appeal to the colour-minded buyer in foreign lands.

Original drawings or photographs

Originals for reproduction by three-colour half-tone undergo the same process and no special treatment is required in the preparation of the originals. Your product itself may be sufficiently colourful to need nothing added, but often a purely industrial subject, dull, lifeless, still, can be brought to life if it is depicted in a background of colour. The composition of this original will need all the care and skill that a commercial artist can put into it, and in this your usual advertising counsel is best able to advise. The facilities and experience of the studios at Laytons are, nevertheless, available if they are required.

Filters for colour separation

To isolate the colours in their respective tone values the original is photographed through colour filters. A purple filter to neutralize the blue and red, a green filter to neutralize the blue and yellow, and an orange filter to neutralize yellow and red : thus, the three primary colours of which the original is composed (yellow, red and blue) are separated in their relative strengths. A fourth negative is made if black is used. These photographs are taken through a " screen ".

The " Screen "

The quality of the reproduction depends on the surface of the paper to be used. The better the paper the finer the screen. The screen is made-up of two optically flat glasses, ruled with parallel lines and cemented together at right-angles. Its effect is to break-up the original into a series of graduated " dots ", the actual size of the dot coinciding with the strength of colour in the original : *i.e.*, a pale colour will produce a very fine " dot " and *vice versa*. The screen generally used for high-class periodical reproduction is 133, printing 133 dots per linear inch.

The copper printing plate

After the basic colour separations, the negatives undergo several corrective processes before they are ready for " printing ". This is similar to the ordinary method of taking photographic contact prints, but instead of printing on glossy paper, the half-tone negative is " printed-down " on to a sensitized polished, copper plate. After exposure the " print " is dyed to make the image visible, heat treated to render the sensitized surface of the " dots " acid resisting and immersed in iron perchloride which eats into the exposed spaces between the dots, leaving the relief surface ultimately used for printing. The craftsmen employed at Laytons are skilled and able ; to them should go the credit for the production of many fine colour pictures in magazines and periodicals, in the trade and technical press and in countless house organs, brochures and catalogues. Laytons are happy to advise manufacturers or agents on any reproduction problem. Please address communications to the Sales Controller, C. and E. Layton Limited, Standard House, Farringdon Street, London, E.C.4.

e gives the picture depth.

Laytons

an all-embracing service for Advertisers and their Agents

COURTAULDS
IN THE UNITED KINGDOM
No. 2 COVENTRY

IN 1904, when the old-established silk firm of Courtaulds bought the British rights to manufacture viscose rayon yarn, they selected Coventry for their factory. It was centrally situated and the womenfolk of nearby miners' families needed work; moreover, the city had an ancient textile tradition. The site purchased was an old timber yard in Foleshill Road.

Here from 1905 to 1910 the firm's chemists, technologists and workpeople fought difficulty after difficulty in spinning what later became the most successful type of rayon yarn in the world. These endeavours not only founded the Company's present-day prosperity but advanced the textile industries—and the dress standards—of every civilised country. It was from these works that a nucleus of technicians left in 1909 to found the rayon industry in the United States of America.

Today Courtaulds have four factories in Coventry and district. At Main Works viscose yarn is spun and the greater part of the Company's machinery is made. At Matlock Road and nearby Nuneaton the yarn is processed for use by the textile industries, and at Little Heath cellulose acetate rayon yarn and plastics are manufactured.

In addition to rayon for clothing, the principal war-time productions of these factories were rayon yarn for tyres and industrial fabrics, engineering parts, and cellulose acetate plastics.

About 6,600 of Courtaulds' 21,000 employees work in these Warwickshire factories, which employ nearly twice as many men as women. Among the senior staff are many of the most able technicians in Britain's rayon industry. They set a high example to young people seeking a progressive career and regular employment at good pay.

The purpose of this series of statements is to inform the public of some part of the contribution made by Courtaulds' industrial enterprise to economic well-being in various districts of the United Kingdom.

Issued by Courtaulds Limited, 16 St. Martins-le-Grand, London, E:C.1

The Changing Surface of Britain: Sometimes a new suburb or a Peacehaven violently scrawls its signature across a pleasing landscape; sometimes changing agricultural methods etch a new pattern gradually and harmoniously on our fields. Each of the four writers in this symposium deals with one aspect of the subject—the Metropolis, the Countryside, the Suburb and the Coastline—showing, as we move outwards from London to the sea, how the physical changes depend ultimately on changes in the social and political landscape

METROPOLIS IN TRANSITION

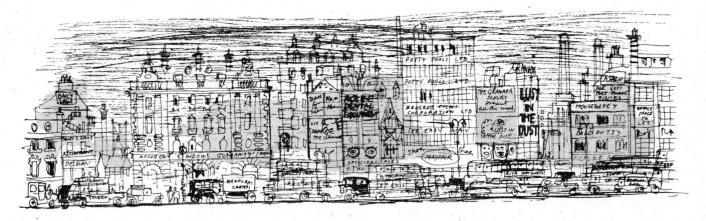

by G. M. Kallmann and Hugh Casson

THERE is a building in New Jersey USA which, it is said, bears the sign: 'This is the largest laundry of its size in the world'. Here is the voice of the modern Metropolis—muddle-headed, clamorous, bizarre —the mother-city, shouting through the megaphone of the show-ground barker. Yet for all its boasting and fantasy, both traditional qualities of city life, the voice still has the power to bemuse and allure. Look at the figures.

Roughly one-fifth of the population of Great Britain lives in the Metropolis—a good proportion of them presumably by desire. For most people, success, social advancement, all the apparatus of what the ad-men call 'distinction' can still only be found in the big city. Something like eighteen thousand immigrants flock every month into London in search of it. They flock to London, to a big city, to (if you like) the largest city of its size in the world, but no longer to a true Metropolis. London, the Metropolis, or what has been called Vintage London, was once comfortably confined within the County of London. Aided by building societies and the BBC, by chain stores and 50-shilling suits, by cinemas and the Green Line, non-Vintage London stretches over most of SE England. Metropolis has become Metroland. Every county town tries to become a miniature London, and sports the panoply of metropolitanism with the awkward bravado of an adolescent in a hired dress suit. With the melancholy fate of these towns, once the proud centres of their own trades and regions, we are not here concerned. It is not the spread of metropolitanism that

we must deplore—for this is inevitable and to some degree desirable—but its swift disintegration before the assault of our changing society.

It is important to remember that the Metropolis is not simply an enlarged county or industrial town. It has its own special functions, its own laws, character and destiny. Unlike the 'producer towns', the Metropolis does not depend for its existence on the region in which it is situated. Placed at the crossroads of the nations, it is linked to the international network more closely even than to its own hinterland. Here the country's produce is bartered on the markets of the world. Here national wealth is expressed in terms of finance and political power, and is enjoyed in luxurious spending. At the metropolitan centre congregate the consumers of material and culture, the millions needed to man the machinery of commercial and political bureaucracy, and the service industries necessary for the welfare of such numbers of people.

Thus metropolitan activities, in contrast to regional activities which are concerned with the soil, with raw materials and crafts, are largely of the mind. They are concerned with the abstract notions of business and finance, with the ramifications of politics, with fashion, entertainment and learning. The carrier of city culture is the intellectual, the aesthete, the professional man, the financier, and the politician, or, as Mr J. M. Richards calls him, the C (consumer) man.

Regional culture is a product of local ethnological and climatic differentiation. It is a magical peasant culture.

All the elegance and pageantry of smart metropolitan life can be seen in Dicky Doyle's portrait of a West End square

That of the city is universal, emancipated, intellectual. The arts of the region are traditional, linked with crafts and local idiom. Those of the city are classical and international. The rhythm of regional life is tuned to that of nature. City life is remote from primeval elements and formalised in an artificial routine. City culture thus represents the true antithesis of regional culture, and its increasing predominance clearly reflects the trend of present-day civilisation.

The ideal setting for metropolitan pursuits could still be found in the big city up to the beginning of this century. The narrow, companionable streets based on the informal mediaeval pattern, the precincts set aside for various professions and crafts, the Georgian residential terraces and squares, the carefully landscaped open spaces, were all suited for the enjoyment of gregariousness. The consumer was well catered for by ample amenities, as least so far as privileged society in its still manageable size was concerned. Local charm and individuality were not as yet extinct, and the cosmopolitan influence in an expanding world invested the metropolitan with the stature of a world citizen.

Gradually, however, with the rapid growth of population, the metropolitan scene was liquidated by its own negative vitality, a process of which we are at present seeing the final stages. Conditions in the Metropolis rapidly deteriorated. An externalisation of urban life, with emphasis on show and distraction, became more and more evident. Yet the glittering lights, the streets paved with the proverbial gold, continued to attract its many willing victims. The metropolitan myth retained its allure, although statistics proved that extinction threatens those who seek their fortune in the Metropolis. Mumford has reminded us that the big city is the least successful environment for reproducing men, and that the greater the portion of a country's population that is retained in big cities, the surer becomes its biological doom. The big city's record for vice, poverty, ill-health and failure is equally unquestioned. But the price, heavy as it was, still seemed worth paying.

In return, the Metropolis offered the spectacle of an international fair in continuous operation, with its side-shows and freaks, its foreign quarters, historical pavilions, amusement parks and bazaars, its wealth, squalor, bustle and glare. Here the communal rites were staged, and also the less conscious but equally exciting drama of social contrasts; the slums of Pimlico huddling to the gates of Buckingham Palace, the rookeries of 'spivs' behind the smart shopping frontages, respectability cheek to cheek with degradation. The height of the metropolitan spectacle, staged in front of an appropriately gay, if garish decor, was attained in the Edwardian era. The privileged class, not yet drably clothed, disported itself on adequate pavements. The thoroughfares were pleasantly crowded with elegant carriages and well-groomed horses. The lower orders obtruded upon

St Paul's Churchyard and Manchester Square still retain that quality of intimate enclosure so essential to genuine city life

the eye just sufficiently to form a picturesque contrast. The stucco façades, well-painted, beamed down on the pageantry, and the crisply pointed brick, the gleaming windows and gilt paint provided the necessary sparkle.

The metropolitan scene of our day has retained very little of this past splendour. Sullen crowds queue outside the cinemas in Leicester Square, are herded along the narrow pavements, or touted into the joyless pin-table saloons. Equally dispirited are the more fastidious, seeking the exile of the French Soho pub, following without much conviction the routine of the Café Royal, pursuing the shades of past privilege at the Cavendish, in nostalgic clubland, or in the twilit consolations of the 'Four Hundred'. The heart has gone out of the metropolitan spectacle; it is now little more than elaborate pretence, a slickly painted drop curtain behind which the heavy scenery is almost invisibly, almost inaudibly, being changed. Swiftly but surely the old fabric is being torn up, the familiar furniture removed. This transformation is a continuous process. It is accomplished not by the sudden surgical destruction of the war, but by the steady inner workings of our changing society.

The increase in the population of London, settled in a suburban area equal in size to that of the former city, has had a devastating effect upon the Metropolis. These new metropolitans are different people from the old city inhabitants, different in their activities, their outlook, and their culture. By force of their numbers they have changed the characteristic social picture of London.

Just as the country dweller represented the producer, and the former town dweller the consumer, the new type of metropolitan represents the distributor. The activities in which he engages are those of business. He is the liaison man. Mr Richards calls him the D (distributor) man. Mr John Betjeman has immortalised him as 'Percy Progress'. Remember his record?

'*Born*: Anno Domini 1906. *Educated*: Carshalton. *Occupation*: Company Director. *Recreation*: Platinum Blondes. *Favourite Author*: Dornford Yates. *Address*: Olde Chimneys, 142 Maconochie Way, Iver, Bucks. *Phone*: Dial IVE any old time and ask the girl for P.P.'

Remember, too, his occupation?

'Chairman of Back Numbers Ltd; Managing Director of Tudor Bungalettes Ltd; on the board of Art Stone (Condensed Milk) Products Ltd; Director of Tinned Carrots Ltd, 'Hoots Waha' Synthetic Whiskey, Beautisite Billposting Co, and the Take It and Leave It Building Society'.

This type of man who represents the social ideal aspired to by the myriads settled in Metropolis, is an extrovert, a materialist, a good mixer. His requirements are different both from the producer and consumer type. He is neither of the country nor really at home in the city. He settles in suburbia, in houses that are neither rural nor urban. For his entertainment he demands large-scale spectacles, sports enjoyed from the

3

An impenetrable fence of motor cars cages the greenery of St James Square (left) and the urbane movements of Harley Street (top right). Architecture, good or bad, vanishes beneath the weight of advertising (bottom right)

grandstand, roadhouses, cinemas or the dogs. He has as yet to create his own type of environment, being at present invader on both the producer's and the consumer's territory. This new type of suburban man, now representing a majority in metropolitan society, uses the Metropolis in a new way. He daily invades it for the purposes of work, entertainment or learning, and withdraws at night to his dormitory. Under this rhythmic assault, carried out with the forcefulness of a mechanised division, the old city fabric is gradually being shattered. For Londoners, every workday is D-day, with all the familiar logistic problems of a major military operation. It is as if a pleasantly cluttered Victorian drawing room was invaded by a gang of healthy school children. The results are immediate and in no way surprising; there is not enough room to move around, and things get broken.

The first noticeable change is the destruction of social space. The streets and squares, once the scenes of concourse, promenade and social gathering, are now choked with mechanised transport. The atmosphere is heavy with fumes, the pavements are dangerously overcrowded. Progress along them is unpleasant and at peak hours almost impossible. Shopping is carried out under disagreeable circumstances, except where it is still accommodated in those remnants of the former consumer city, the pedestrian arcades. Public buildings, once linked to each other by continuous social space, are now islands within a stream of traffic. The former residential squares yield their seclusion to the demands of transport, or conceal their greenery behind an impenetrable fence of parked cars.

Inevitably, the visual scene shows signs of rapid deterioration. With the traffic comes all the paraphernalia of its own ill-designed apparatus, and the blight that accompanies the D man wherever he intrudes, the advertisements blocking the façades and clamouring for an undue share in the city picture, the garages, the chain stores, dance halls and milkbars. Architecture is the main casualty in this assault. The changeover in central areas from residential to commercial use destroys the fine domestic scale of the old Metropolis. Georgian buildings are either converted to business use, for which they are not particularly well suited, or mercifully demolished. Everywhere the new element is parasitical upon the old. Nowhere does it create any new standards of its own. Its outcrops of new commercial buildings, its cinemas, bars and chain stores do not even aspire to architectural significance, but pander blatantly to the lowest standards of popular appeal. Like an obscene film, this type of development penetrates everywhere, covering all traces of local character or individuality.

Wherever the new element intrudes, it is followed by the same visual deterioration. Already much of London's character has been destroyed, in particular the spontaneous individuality of its many areas dedicated by tradition and convenience to particular functions. Only

4

' The word for progress is Odeon '

The monstrous club-foot of the Odeon towers over Leicester Square where all the visual horrors of the modern metropolitan scene can be found in their most degraded form. Against this fantastic scenery of neon and hoardings, even the trees seem an unwelcome intrusion and the patch of trampled grass, hemmed in by the circling traffic, becomes a corral for morons instead of a promenade for citizens

1

2

3

Results of the internal combustion engine

Gradually the intimate bustle proper to city life is disrupted by the demands of the internal combustion engine. Quiet residential streets like Queen Anne's Gate (**1**) become short-cuts for the ingenious driver; architectural monuments like the church of St Mary-le-Strand (**2**), ludicrous and lonely in the tide of traffic, are no longer safely accessible; shopping, once a pleasant social occupation, becomes a dangerous nightmare (**3**). Only occasionally is the eye reminded, as by the tiny café wedged impertinently among the Fine Art dealers of Mayfair (left), of those sharp social contrasts which have always been characteristic of metropolitanism those fortunate enough to be protected from intrusion—such as the lawyers' precincts of Lincoln's Inn Fields and the Temple, the Tower, or the Whitehall precincts, are still perceptible. Others, such as Covent Garden, Soho and Fleet Street, which lack such clear architectural definition, are gravely endangered. The Howard de Walden professional quarter and Bloomsbury are fighting a losing battle.

The price paid for the lack of physical adjustment to social change is a heavy one. Urban activities are carried out under increasingly hostile conditions. At the peak hours the congested streets present the spectacle of a stricken and paralysed organism. Overcrowding and queueing are the symptoms of insufficient amenity. The destruction of individuality and character and their replacement by a monotonous, equalising and worthless visual scene are the outward expression of maladjustment.

What then is to be done? Obviously the problem demands more fundamental treatment than the usual cosmetics of road-widening and more open spaces. The social forces now causing havoc in the city, and represented in particular by mechanised transport, demand a new conception in city planning. Time and speed must be introduced as the new dimensions. It must be realised that the consumer aspect and the distributor aspect of city life are today proceeding at different speeds, and along separate paths. The one calls for a different sort of environment from the other. For this purpose a segregation of social space and transport network must be attempted. Social space must be planned to form one continuous system, linking the various building blocks to each other. These should be grouped in the form of cellular areas, serviced by transport, but not invaded by it, and, wherever possible, a pedestrian network of an intricate nature should be developed independent of the fast moving vehicular system.

The first step towards this pattern can be observed in the present one-way systems put into force in various parts of the city. These are attempts to segregate through traffic from access and service traffic. The next development will be towards the discriminatory classification of roads envisaged in the London Plan, by means of which traffic can speed along the arterial and sub-arterial roads and be drawn off them at intervals to serve the various consumer cells. The city area itself can then be grouped into functional zones based on those which have come to develop spontaneously in the past. The various quarters can each be developed in accordance with its own character, with open spaces and buildings inter-related as in the collegiate environment of the past. The result of this will be a much improved condition for city requirements. Both accessibility and a condition of enclosure, so necessary for concentration on communal tasks, will be provided, and the improved visual effect will be tremendous.

The new metropolitan element will no longer be able to destroy local character, and yet will be able to produce its own form of development. The speedways, as the example of New York has shown, can be, when finely landscaped, an attractive addition to the city picture. Engineering structures at intersections, such as fly-overs, will present their visual drama in contrast to stations, shelters, garages, which will no longer be accommodated in makeshift buildings, and can be designed to possess their own type of aesthetic appeal. Within this framework of communications the city area will be left to develop its own architecture, tall city blocks for administration and commerce, long horizontal shopping arcades, large span halls for the market, and, in contrast, the animated shapes of concert halls, cinemas and theatres.

No speculation, however, as to future metropolitan development would be complete without taking into account the deeper implications of the social changes that are occurring at present. There are many who believe that the vast Metropolis of our day is destined to disintegrate finally, and will give way once again to the small or regionally orientated city. It is, of course, quite possible that the new era of distribution will produce its own decentralised pattern, aided by the speed and ease of modern communications. The Metropolis as a specific city type does not rely solely on the many millions which at present inhabit it. A large number of metropolitans will no doubt be attracted away to the new towns, where the varied opportunities of work, the planned amenities, and easy access to the country will offer them all the advantages they vainly sought in the Metropolis. New industrial estates will be built, planned as balanced communities, and linked to the Metropolis by a network of efficient communications. Furthermore, metropolitan functions can be delegated to other localities—learning to university communities, and government to others. (Already one of the Ministries is located outside London.) There are signs, too, of cultural *nuclei* being established all over the country on the system of a power grid, fostered by such bodies as the Arts Council. Such a general decentralised form of environment is well within the realm of possibility, and may indeed prove to be the solution of the metropolitan problem. For within such a system the Metropolis will be free to develop its own specific character even more distinctly as a highly artificial, intellectual organism, truly representative of city culture. Smaller in size, but more intensely developed, it might regain the conviviality which existed in the narrow streets of the mediaeval city and in the architectural urbanity of the Augustan era.

Against such a background the social spectacle of our modern metropolitan society would regain its health and purpose.

THE RELUCTANT COUNTRYSIDE

by A. V. D. Gordon

'THERE were cheers in the House when the Postmaster General announced that a television station would not, after all, be placed on the summit of White Horse Hill. Another site would be found.'

A paragraph like this appeared in most of the British newspapers one morning in early May. It was a good beginning to spring, which was at last finding its way above ground. A small number of people who had protested vigorously at Mr Paling's proposal opened their paper, rubbed their eyes, and rejoiced. They wrote congratulatory notes to each other, and were very surprised at their success. Many more of the citizens were just as pleased. But, at the same time, we were worried too. Worried because progress must proceed. But we were comforted by reminding ourselves that, after all, the Victorians had already spoilt our villages.

But the Victorians did nothing of the kind. In their treatment of the open country and the villages, they followed the grand tradition of their predecessors, who made the English countryside literally out of bog and heath and forest. It is true that the Victorians made their towns so vile that their descendants fled from them as soon as they had the money and the means to do so. But it has been left to us of the twentieth century to destroy the little towns, the villages and the open country that we had come to see. The Victorians were more careful, and more stately. They did not split the land asunder, like an atom, and hope for a better beauty spot out of the remains. The country estates of the Victorian magnates and the great Jewish families were generally models of the best rural economy of the times, and their owners respected the traditions, and the limitations, of the English scenery, despite their shocking attitude towards the social conditions of what, to them, was still the peasantry. The architecture of some of the lodges may have been a trifle odd and in the villages and round about some necessary extra cottages may have looked plain, but no worse. Bad taste was still a rich man's toy, and he kept it for his private use, not squandering it before the general.

For the rest, the simple countryman and his plot of land were allowed to grow and develop in their own momentum with plenty of good Victorian money to help things along. Towards the close of the century the English countryside had become a lovely framework for the lives of simple, honest men.

What happened next is commonplace. Victoria died almost as soon as the motor car was born, and the next generation of city dwellers, we, the children of the age of wonders, burst forth from our dreary streets and demanded the refreshment of the countryside. We must be entertained in this new way. At once. We must have beauty spots, with facilities for getting there, and other facilities on the spot. We must have roads, quickly. We got them. We also got the hoardings, the drifts of litter, the tin teashops, thatched petrol pumps, a tangled skein of arterial roads each with its fringe of ribbon houses with the laundry hanging out behind.

One thing is certain; if the Common Man and his Government do no more in the next thirty years to change the countryside for the better than their predecessors have done in the last thirty years, there will be no more need to bother, for the thing will have ceased to exist. Unfortunately the balance of current legislation on the subject, such as the Town and Country Planning Act, seems heavily weighted in favour of the financial aspects of land value. It seems probable that the values inherent in a pleasing landscape as a framework to men's lives will have to continue to take their chance, and will be realised only if the executors of plans pay full attention to the 'amenity' clauses of the Act. This has not happened before. National parks seem to be definitely on the way, but these will consist mostly of stretches of wild land of a kind not discussed in this article.

What, then, are the changes today in rural England, what are they likely to be in the coming years, and what powerful factors are likely to alter the modes of country life? First let us define the countryside, or rather define what we believe it not to be—for there are, in this harsh age, many sensitive and despondent escapists for whom the country ends and suburbia begins directly any sign can be observed in the surroundings of a feature more recent in date than 1840, including the railway line. For them the country is a series of picture postcards peopled by amiable eccentrics. The attitude of these people and the kind of countryside, ever receding, that they believe in, attractive though it seems to most of us some of the time, can have no place in this survey, since their very object is to avoid contact with the life of today except in matters of comfort and hygiene, and in the satisfaction of an unfashionable intellect.

So far from being a retreat where one can murmur of a rural peace, an ancient village scene, the countryside is a rough, tough place to live in, where the people are fundamentally hard and thrifty. It is an agricultural economy at work, trying hard to make ends meet, at present with considerable success. At times it offers a life of harsh and bitter disappointment, so hard that it seems possible that the drift to the towns would be much greater were it not for the beautiful precision with which the landscape is designed, with one eye on its looks and the other on its uses. The value of a well-planned landscape cannot be exaggerated. It is an eternal truth.

The country scene and the life of its people are constantly changing; growth and decay, and men's efforts to control both see to that. But it is also very vulnerable to careless and hasty attempts to modernise it by bringing along, haphazard, what is left over of the wonderful inventions the townsman has made for himself. The rate of growth and change in the country is so much slower than the tempo of city life that great care must be taken, in making improvements, to place them in their setting, delicately balanced, and not to hack down the frame and stride across the canvas. The most urgent requirements of rural housing, water and electricity supplies, road improvements, the development of secondary industries can all be achieved without spoiling the effect of man's unique control of nature, which can be seen nowhere else in the world in so complete a form. Some things, and some people, are bound to be upset, but there need be no wholesale savagery.

Social improvements and the modernising of environment in rural life are often thought of as a kind of bait to farm workers to stay on the land, to the advantage of the farmer's bank balance and everybody's digestion. These are very worthy ends, but the base materialism of the means can be decently cloaked.

But it is not only necessary to devise a pattern of rural life that will encourage the men and women already there to stay in the country, that will enable them to live there without feeling that the townsman has a better time of it, and is looking down his nose at them. The great need, for agriculture and its associated pursuits, is for more people. This additional population must be drawn from the overgrown towns and it must be housed. The future appearance of the countryside depends very much on how these new houses are built and where they are placed. The politics of the housing programme—Mr Bevan's four to private owner's one—indicates that most of them will be found in groups, or small estates, tacked on to the edge of villages, a tendency noticed in local authorities' building before the war. At the same time, as these new peripheral houses are built, there is a danger that the old centre of the village will decay, partly because the Government grant for reconditioning rural workers' cottages is a thing of the past.

There will be a tendency in housing towards a sameness of design and materials in all parts of the country, brick and timber taking the lead. Shortage of materials, high prices and the system of building by contract make any widespread return to the traditional use of local materials a preservationist's dream. But most of the new designs are tasteful without being ghastly, and there is every chance that they will mellow pleasantly with their surroundings if they last long enough. There seems little likelihood that traditional designs will give way to any flat-roofed, concrete type of thing, although shortage and experiment may bring about a few lively examples of the kind. Only in the farmsteads themselves do modernity and utility strike a different note. Here silo towers, concrete sheds with shallow pitched roofs will be increasingly found, grouped with the older buildings, and

by some extraordinary magic making a not unpleasing compound. But in general nothing seems to emerge in contemporary rural building—where it can be found—to which one can point a joyful finger and roundly declare: 'That is the style of tomorrow.'

At the same time there can be no real hope for rural England if the farming economy is allowed to fall back into the doldrums of the 'twenties and the 'thirties. The war and its aftermath have given farming an enormous impetus; the shortage of food all over the world and the present Agriculture Act bid fair to keep farmers on their feet for some time to come. The effect of this has been a noticeable improvement in the landscape, despite the needs of aeroplanes, which take up broad acres of the best land, and the surface winning of minerals—chalk, ironstone and coal. But in general this wartime lifting of the farmer from his economic depression has been also a most modern beauty treatment, which came just in time. There is now much arable land amongst the green meadows, formerly endless in some counties, with a consequent demand for better draining of the land. Everywhere hedging and ditching has been done. Mature woodlands have been cut, instead of being left to rot, and there is even hope of a policy of planting and afforestation that will look beyond the next crop of pitprops.

Only in the demesnes of the great houses is there marked deterioration, for that world has passed, and of its remaining representatives some live in a wing, some go to Ireland, now becoming the last refuge of English Conservatism.

In the lives of the country people there is more confidence. They have taken the impact of prosperity with a certain stubbornness, and are all entirely prepared to remain prosperous. Toil is still hard, but there is some reward; there is no talk of a 40-hour week, although many young men leave the land for the factories because they resent the necessary weekend duties on a farm. But despite this, there is a refreshingly large number of young people in the villages. The only villages that continue to decay for lack of youth are those without a bus service. This desire for mobility forms the most important demand of any for improvement, more even than houses, water and electricity. It seems not to be connected with any drift to the towns; it is more due to a healthy demand to be able to move about when you want to.

In ten years' time the economic conditions of today should have ceased to be the main cause of rural prosperity which, being based on abnormal circumstances, cannot have any permanence on that account. Meanwhile a whole mass of legislation promising developments and improvements in the countryside should be gradually taking the strain when financial crises and food shortage ease off. If all the Government's new plans succeed, let us hope they will succeed in a manner which will enable us to say of the English countryside, without a trace of cynicism, that the more it changes the more it stays the same.

THE PATTERN OF SUBURBIA

by Barbara Jones

It's easy to be funny about the suburbs. Like Wigan or marriage, it's always good for a laugh. But, as the following survey points out, for the majority of Englishmen suburbia has become the ideal way of life, and its contribution to our architectural heritage is incalculable. For these reasons it merits the most serious attention from students of the English scene

Terra-cotta dragon for gable ridge King's Lynn c. 1920

THERE is no doubt: the suburbs are winning, at least around London and the biggest cities; they are engulfing the outlying villages, they have become the way of life for millions. They are the children of the railway and the buses and the tubes; they are one of the main contributions of the last hundred years to our architecture. A long and highly destructive war has thinned the villa ranks comparatively slightly; no miracle will clear them all away, and, whatever is done now to curb or quell suburban building in the future, we still have thousands of acres of suburb already on our hands.

Some of the acres are enchanting. When the suburb began, it was an affair for the well-to-do, the keepers of carriages, since poor men could not afford to live more than walking distance from their work. The rapid increase of population had overcrowded the cities, and the smoke of the rising industries was making them black with soot; how natural, then, that the wealthy middle classes in search of family homes should discover that most of the cities were encircled by ranges of clean and empty hills, conveniently untouched since the town began its career as a village sheltering beneath them.

The houses that began to cover (but not to overcrowd) these hills were the beginnings of a new architecture—and of one not merely new but revolutionary. The old, expedient forms of building had only provided safety and shelter for the needs of various lives. Endless panoramas and histories of English domestic architecture show how it developed from a utility into a major art, with periods of excellence in different spheres, so that while the fifteenth century probably produced the finest houses for God, the eighteenth century built superb houses for men and planned them into excellent towns. From the palace façade via the market hall to the smallest implement of cottage industry, logic and exquisite taste informed design; almost nothing was bad.

After this short period, the main tradition wilts away, lingering last in the stucco terraces and villas just away from the town centre—perhaps the last outworks of the old unit, perhaps the first circle of suburb.

Meanwhile architecture burst out in a host of vigorous new forms, most mixed in quality; the architecture of the early railways, the prefabricated and demountable Crystal Palace, the bridges, the factories, our whole seaside, endless admirable new architecture for new needs. And for the old needs, mostly revivals of this, that, the other and the kitchen stove, separately, consecutively and altogether, some of the most awful and wonderful nonsense ever built. Notion and emotion had replaced logic and taste.

Alone of the eighteenth century impulses, the desire to impress remained unimpaired. One of the best early suburbs to see is Sydenham, on a hill to the south of London, where, clustered round the new and curious beauty of the stark and shining Crystal Palace, there arose a wealthy suburb of the highest fantasy. The gardens are shady and so large that they are almost grounds, the winding roads are lined with trees, and everywhere there still hangs the atmosphere of the vanished Palace.

By no means were all the nineteenth century suburbs wealthy ones, however, since public transport grew so efficient and so cheap that even badly paid workers could live outside the city centre. Maps in G. M. Trevelyan's *English Social History* display the rapid spread of one

CROYDON 1882

city (London), although there is no indication of the nature of the enormous spread and, indeed, the word 'suburb' does not even occur in the index, while 'seaside', 'town' and 'village' all have their several references. The suburbs await their historian.

After 1920 came the great pink brick flood and most of it was bad. The older mellowed suburbs or those of the well-to-do 1930's are often lovely; they offer as much pleasure to the visitor as anything that can be found, and they are full of material for the painter and writer, and so make their contribution to the arts. But the houses in even the nicest suburb, if isolated from their pretty bosky gardens and viewed coldly as pieces of design, can very rarely be regarded as works of art themselves; nor can their general plan.

Take a bus out from the centre of any large town or city and you will probably, at the end of two, four or six-pennyworth, find yourself in a suburb. The bus will stop at a Parade, Green or Quadrant, at something which will give a classy or period flavour. The pavement is very wide indeed. This is the shopping centre. For specialised shopping (and for cheapness) the inhabitants will have to go into the town, but here are the shops for day-to-day needs. There are one or two bakers, several

grocers and butchers and greengrocers, a florist, a stationer, a gent's outfitters, hairdresser, baker, ironmonger, newsagent, electrician, bank, estate agent, draper, shoe-shop and so on. There may be a Model Gown Shop, with a Christian name sprawled like a signature across the sun-blind. If the colony is large enough and far enough out, the local gas and electricity companies will have their rival showrooms and all the ordinary shops will be multi-plied exceedingly. The bakers usually provide morning coffee with biscuits, and afternoon tea with bread-and-butter-and-jam and cake, but often a café serves tea-cakes and pastries eaten with a fork. A startling number of these cafés are still decorated with old-world bottle-glass in one or two window-panes; they also sell art-and-crafty bits and pieces, and embroidered fire-screens of crinolined ladies in careful profile, so that the easy poke-bonnet hides the difficult face.

Above the shops, at least along the Parade proper, planning and urban manners have their little fling—all above the ground floor is uniformly ferro-concrete with steel windows, or bogus Tudor with gables, or brick mock baroque. The ground floor is devoted to private enter-prise and each shop front fights hard for individuality; but, going from one suburb to another, it can be seen

SYDENHAM 1867

that tradition already tends to assign certain types of front to certain trades, so that hairdressers are very modern and chromium while opticians are rather chaste and Georgian. Not too far from the centre is the cinema (a big suburb may have several). This, like cinemas everywhere, is gaudy in front and ghastly behind, though here it is more exposed than usual, because the surrounding houses are so low.

The houses, the snug enclosed homes, are the real heart of the suburb and have an air of being the hub of things which the High Street never acquires. Village, town and city all centre where the shops or markets are. The suburb is utterly decentralised and diffuse, the heart of life being for each family in its own home; no corporate heart has a chance at all.

Some of these houses will have cost, between the wars, from two to five thousand pounds. The brickwork is sound, the enamel paint rich and glossy, and there will be a parquet floor in the lounge-hall and kitchen and bathrooms. Thick, coloured carpets fit the floors, and velours curtains hang to the ground from fringed pelmets. There will be a servant, and certain elegancies observed. They are very comfortable to live in and are said to be architect-designed; certainly, no two are alike.

Very many more of the houses will have cost something over £1,000. Any one of them may be a 'Distinctive Elizabethan-type house complete with veranda— the house you will be proud to own!' or it may be an 'Attractive modern four-bedroom residence replete with a host of unique features. Spacious garden and liberal room for garage'. Most of the houses will have cost only six to eight hundred pounds, and are then 'Compact semi-detached six-room houses, ideal for small family, cleverly planned, tastefully decorated, adequate space for garage'. To get a 'residence', you had to pay a thousand.

They are all arranged in haphazard Avenues, Ways, Gardens, Closes or Drives, most horrid to look at on a map, and the whole area belonging to one builder is known as an Estate, or more rarely a Garden Village. But each brochure points out that here monotony does not exist, that here each house is different in style, different in plan, different in elevation, while the site is both exclusive and accessible, surrounded by old woodlands but yet within a few minutes of shops and station.

Now let us look at these elegant houses in the brick instead of the book; the first thing that we notice is that they are much smaller than the pictures, then that they are very pink, and then that in spite of the advertisements they do all look very much alike, and sit on the ground instead of rising from it. They are pathetic. All the features favoured by Victorian mercantile wealth are still here, cheapened, mass-produced, and minimised almost to nothing, but all still recognisable. The Regency bow-windows were still a fairly new fashion when the first suburbs adopted them, squared them up and added a lot of heavy mullions and stanchions for solid worth and to show that they could afford plenty of carpentry. The new suburb, wishing to retain the look of weight, will not return to the old thin glazing bars which looked elegant and admitted light, and as it cannot afford really fine woodwork, compromises with plenty of unseasoned pine.

Stained glass was useful to give to the oriel window of the massive oak staircase a look of ancient riches and even of monastic foundation. The modern villa usually has a little bit of coloured glass or diamond paning in the hall and maybe at the top of the bow-window as well. The massive staircase is now vestigial and most of the heavy carving is reduced to a turned newel-post at the bottom; but even so it is too heavy for the tiny hall.

Some sort of fancy porch remains over the front door and here sometimes survive little heart-shaped loopholes and art-nouveau traceries. A very tall chimney adds further picturesqueness and there are endless possibilities in gables and dormer-windows.

For some reason, the most joyfully derided feature of suburban architecture is the Tudor beam. What is usually wrong with this is not that it is sham but that it is shoddy. In the richer suburbs some fascinating variations on fancy woodwork can be seen, but they are solid. It is very difficult indeed to think of *anything* which is nice if it is shoddily made; such airy trifles as the tiny Japanese paper umbrellas that used to be in crackers were charming as much for their incredible craftsmanship as for their size; but anything which is even a little skimped will, however well designed, look worse than the same thing made properly from cheaper materials. The larger and more permanent the thing, the more painful becomes this obvious but neglected fact.

Huge numbers of suburban houses were built not as dwelling places, but first to catch the eye of the gullible with glass and glazed tiles, and then to have just enough guts to stand up while the hire-purchase payments were being made. But if they had been beautifully made, we could have seen in them very much the sort of charm that a ghost book-front has on the concealed door of a library.

Inside the villas are a vast number of objects of which one can but heartily disapprove, and at which it is pleasant to jibe wittily. Objects which come in for heavy attack are the cumbersome three-piece suites covered with clipped moquette, and the moulded china ornaments—a brightly coloured ragged boy standing by a glass fish-bowl fitted into the china meadow, which appeared to remain in production throughout the toughest days of war scarcity. But is the thing really any worse than, say, the weak fag-ends of the Staffordshire dogs, now eagerly bought, however blunted the mould or slapstick the colour?

Snobbery still mildly governs much in England, and few people furnish their homes logically. In the eighteenth century, the envied ruling class had logic and taste in plenty and could be safely followed. Today, the models copied are more rich than cultured and dare not trust their own judgment on new productions. So they mostly

BIRMINGHAM 1930

Time-lag in taste

The usual time-lag between the modish domestic styles of the fashionable architects and the jerry-builder's later versions of them varies between ten and fifty years. There are still traces of Norman Shaw and Ernest George in Birmingham 1930 (*right*) *thirty years after their hey-day, but* Modernismus (*below*) *followed only a few years behind the continental experiments of the 'twenties'. All stylistic whimsies, however, inevitably vanish beneath the discipline of the £1,200 limit and the shortage of timber* (*bottom*)

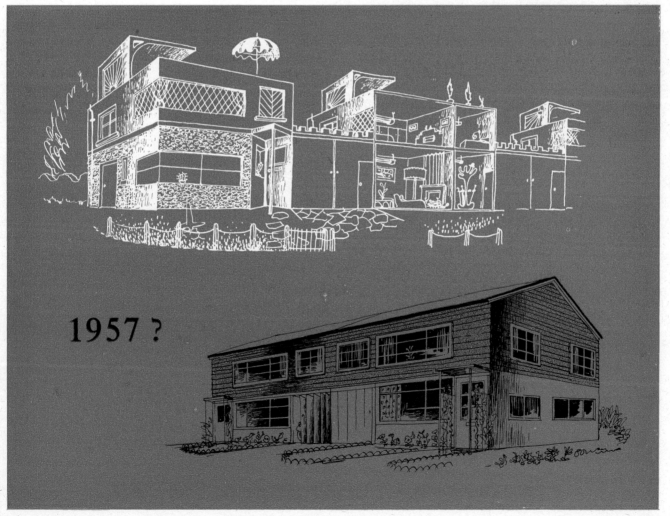

1957 ?

buy antiques, which the suburban dwellers cannot afford. This reduces the suburbs to reproductions, which reach their zenith in the dining-room, which can be Jacobean right down to the pendant centre light's dripping candles. If not reproductions, they had little alternative (till Utility) except manufacturer's modern, a style which, though superficially twentieth century, remains spiritually Victorian in its lack of logic and its naïve belief that a bit of applied moulding makes furniture nice to look at. The only difference is that today the moulding is Jazz where eighty years ago it would probably have been Gothic or Natural History (and much better made). Pray that the present enhanced value of even the grimmest secondhand furniture and the elevation of good nineteenth century objects to the status of antiques will not lead to a surge of indiscriminate reproductions in mahogany-stained deal of the weightiest and worst Impressive furniture.

Two general possibilities suggest themselves for the future. One is that authority should intervene and allow only carefully designed houses in the twentieth century idiom to be made, as convenient as a pre-fab, sometimes with scope for enlargement from a little house to a medium-sized one, and as labour-saving as possible. No fake decoration of any period to be allowed, neither black Tudor roses nor white Georgian acanthus. Now it can be argued that anything is good on some grounds, or at least that it amuses poets and painters; but if you compare a cheap Estate villa with the smallest gardener's bothy carefully designed to be used but not to impress, the villa goes down badly. It is shoddy.

What is wrong with imposing firmly from above a style of absolute simplicity, with woodwork, tiles, concrete, plaster and bricks plain but of decent quality? Provided that the proportion is sound, the simpler the design of a small house, the better. If it is well enough made, it will stand till it mellows; picturesqueness is not ornament but accident; it is moss and weeds, wind and rain, lichen and creeper. It cannot be made from plastic and added with tintacks at trifling extra cost.

Inside the home, however, there can be no interference. Some people will buy pretty simple tea-sets which are easy to wash up, some will buy old ones which look lovely on the table, and nothing need be done to stop those other people who will buy a teapot made rhomboid or pancake merely because it is new and sold as 'smart'. For myself, I am simple-minded enough to believe that the market for cheap nastiness will end one day, and that just enough of it will remain unsmashed to make quaint bits for later connoisseurs.

The other possibility is that when there are enough houses in England to contain the population, the speculative builder will manage to get his head again and start persuading stupid people that his little horrors are more desirable than the little horrors round the corner. And they will be so badly built that they will be slums and rubble before they have attained even the first shadow of picturesqueness.

Several changes of plan would be desirable in future suburbs: they must not spread so far along the main roads and they do need more communal amenities—good libraries, for just one thing, are very rare in the suburbs. And it is very difficult to believe that a small theatre could not pay in Suburbia as well as in the centre of a provincial town. But first let us have the little houses well built and pleasant to see. Then, in the course of time, the junk suburbs can sink into dust.

Gabled or flat-roofed, the suburban house proclaims its monotonous individuality

THE CHANGING COASTLINE

by Lionel Brett

ENGLISHMEN can theoretically use the coastline of their island for the greatest good of the greatest number. To appreciate this situation is not easy for those who have grown up in days when irresistible forces decreed that the great downland spaces should contract Peacehaven and that the swans of Abbotsbury should be the first bombed-outs. It is particularly difficult to realise the change while the armed forces still make their enormous demands which few civilians have the technical knowledge or the courage to resist, and other official bodies blunder about under their screen of secrecy and procrastination. It sometimes seems that for a cloud of midges with their irritating little bites we have substituted a herd of elephants doing more spectacular damage. Yet there has been a change, perhaps the most unequivocally useful work done by our postwar Government. Large numbers of people are now employed in deciding and enforcing the best use of land, and though they will make mistakes they are likely to do better than their blind predecessors, Chance and Profit.

They have already made their preliminary survey of the 2,750 miles of coastline in England and Wales and must have been struck by its diversity. For it is the cut in the cake, and its appearance depends on what the cake is made of. Geological diversity produces agricultural and ecological and architectural diversity, and if to all that you add economics and war and the incurable whimsies of human beings, you begin to decide that the coastline cannot be thought of as an entity. Nobody can write of Looe and Liverpool, of Butlin and Bamburgh, of Margate and Mousehole, under a single heading. Quite early on, one needs to differentiate.

WILD COAST

Not only wild in the Hebridean sense, but lonely and birdhaunted like the flat East Anglian shore, or nobly ceremonial like the chalk cliffs—these are the coast where nobody could bear to live. Protected by howling gales, they keep their primeval shape, and now offer themselves as potential national parks. How shall we use them?

The preservationist has his answer pat: 'Thus far and no farther'. What has been saved from the shacks and the services is too precious to lose now. Need there be any qualification to our enthusiastic agreement with him? I think there must be, if only because the blank negative is the negation of planning. For one thing, if we ban 'development', how will the lover of scenery approach his love and how will he live when he gets there? Or is he to be fenced off altogether? Variations in solitude are indicated, from the inaccessible bird sanctuary to the trackless but open waste, thence to the national park specially designed for holidays, thence to the private holiday camp with all its controversial paraphernalia. Of course the more trackless and open waste we can save the better. Coastal national parks, if they are to be created, will presumably be compact areas rather than narrow strips, if only because coastal contours, and the paths and roads that follow them, have a way of running at right angles to the sea. One may therefore hope that long stretches of unorganised lonely coast will remain to the seaside farmer, the shepherd and the coastguard.

These are the places that will always, as in the past, attract two kinds of invader. The first is the training branch of the Fighting Services. To each his own opinion of the merits of this particular case, of the nature of the next war and the value of training for the last, of the uses of a conscript army thus trained, and of the fitness of this island as a training area in the atomic age. Whatever one's views, the fact remains that these reservations, though they may deny some places to some people of a generation or two, are not likely to do permanent damage to the wild coast. If he would avoid the breeding grounds of rare birds and plants, this particular invader would make fewer enemies.

The second invader of the wild coast is the shack builder, from the first discoverer of the unspoilt sandy cove to the last man in the rear rank who completes the spoliation. This, presumably, is not going to be allowed any more. You rent a plot in the planned and planted colony at Portmeirion or get no plot at all. We still have the miles and miles of seaside slum in Norfolk, Sussex and North Wales to liquidate at an expense which hitherto has been quite beyond the means of the poorer local authorities within whose areas this kind of squalid exploitation has taken place. But the job is under way.

TOY HARBOURS

How dull the shining sands of new continents that have no Clovelly or Portofino or St Tropez! Yet these toy harbours have their own problems of readjustment, not unlike those that face the twentieth-century village—more difficult in the sense that the farms are still there whereas many of the little ports have lost their fishing fleets. With the decay of local industry appears that devoted and faithful undertaker, the minor artist. From stage-coach to sailing-ship, from sailing-ship to windmill, from windmill to coal mine, the artist (if he will forgive this death's head analogy) pursues the dilapidated apparatus of obsolete technics. Just now St Ives and Polperro enjoy a St Luke's summer of prosperity brought them by a swarm of Christopher Woods (for each camp-stool attracts its little crowd of gaping spectators). But for how long? Not for ever, because sooner or later (and the toy harbour has had a long innings) fashions in the picturesque change.

The yachtsman must come to the rescue. Yachting has the distinction of being the most beautiful of all sports, making the most generous contribution to the pleasures of the eye. And it must increase—fewer Liptons and Sopwiths, maybe, but more crews of friends jointly owning and manning yawls and ketches, and coasting arduously from port to port. This traffic, if they exploit it imaginatively, will save the toy harbours in the same way as the motorist has saved the coaching inns.

The prosperous expand. Then comes the problem of adding to these little places without violating them. How few architects (I know only one) have the feel of the nautical style. Miniature scale, rock-hewn solidity combined with a slapdash attitude to paint, tar and whitewash —these are the obvious attributes. And if mistakes are made there is no hiding behind monumental elms. Along our bare coasts they stand four-square on the skyline or are displayed like fish on a slab, the all-electric bloodless houses of the twentieth century.

BIG PORTS

The big ports of Britain are a bitter disappointment. All great ports are frightening places. Built to the super-human scale of modern ships, there is a surrealist emptiness and desolation about them; black water covered with floating refuse makes death too easy, the vast spaces make life insignificant. One expects all this and, knowing some history, one allows for the special shoddiness of British industrialism. Yet if one thinks of Glasgow, Liverpool, Bristol, London, Hull and Newcastle, and then of Hamburg, Rotterdam, Lisbon, Barcelona, Marseilles and Genoa, the contrast is humiliating.

What seems to have happened is that the picturesque squalor and kaleidoscopic bustle of the mediaeval port was effectively ironed out by the heavy metal of Victorian industrialism (so that there is no British Marseilles) yet never replaced by the monumentality of Victorian town-planning (so that there is no British Hamburg). Our ports are neither gay nor solemn. As most people's first glimpse of Britain, they are a fitting prelude to the station waiting-rooms and commercial hotels that loom ahead.

The remedies, involving the whole apparatus of post-Abercrombie town-planning, are beyond the scope of this survey. But one medicine is worth taking anyway, as soon as it can be got: paint—blue, white, black and yellow— thousands of tons of it.

'THE SEASIDE'

A great deal of clean fun has been poked at our British seaside resorts and it is only fair that we should recognise what we owe to them. Their creator was the railway, which made it possible for the urban middle class first to escape in really large numbers from the squalor of Victorian town life to the places discovered not long before by the great of the Regency (Hastings, Brighton, Weymouth, Scarborough), and then to create their own resorts (Eastbourne, Worthing, Bournemouth, Torquay). It was the sheerest luck that the railway, which deposits people at fixed points and encourages the nuclear growth of towns, arrived before the motor car, which encourages random dispersal and ribbon development. If the car had come first, before control of development was dreamt of, we should now be in a far worse way than we are. As it is, the great resorts have canalised the torrent that pours every summer to the sea and back and left the wild coast high and dry.

What the railway did for the middle class of the nineteenth century, holidays with pay are now doing for the industrial population of the twentieth. It in turn has invaded the 'select' resorts of earlier generations and added its own favourites (Southend, Margate, Weston, Blackpool). On the whole, it feels happier in a crowd, likes a cheerful rather than a quiet holiday, and has *so far* not tried very hard to avoid the embraces of the now ageing, dowdy and secretly apprehensive seaside resorts.

Why apprehensive? Because the traditional resort, still organised for 'respectable' people, is not physically equipped or mentally adjusted to provide the cheap and gaudy and frankly vulgar pleasures that are wanted just now. The hand of that sterling British character, the seaside landlady, lies heavy on its amenities, when what are wanted are multi-storied cheap hotels (our great caterers must surely have their eye on this), gay open air cafés, more and better music and dancing and drama, and death to the licensing laws. Not everyone's holiday, but the other kind is already too amply provided for.

The more imaginative resorts, aware of the way the wind blows, aware too of the coming threat from across the Channel and our grievous handicap of the English climate, are making plans. These, having the social and civilised amenities that no draughty holiday camp can rival, have a bright future if the second half of the century realises our hopes and belies our fears. The others, the grey treeless esplanades lined by grey cheerless boarding-houses, will go to the wall.

CAMPERS

They will go to the wall because there is an enemy in the Camp. The rise to well-organised notoriety of the holiday camp is the most significant holiday innovation (new here, not elsewhere) since the discovery of the seaside at the beginning of the nineteenth century. It is an attempt to break with the makeshift and wholly obsolete arrangements hitherto made for mass holidays and to think out the whole problem afresh. Like all such attempts, it is an immediate functional advance yet at the same time an aesthetic relapse, having thrown over the cosy traditions that gave the lodging-house sand-in-the-hall holiday such childhood romance. These things can only come with time. Meanwhile, the holiday camp is notable in other ways. It assumes (and this is unheard of since the eighteenth century) that the English are sociable, or at least capable of being made so. It is designed to bring people together, not to foster the illusion that they are separate. Its buildings are frankly ephemeral, here today and gone the day after tomorrow. How much easier it will be to deal with the physical remains of Skegness in 2047 than it is in 1947 to modify the too too solid masonry of (say) Weston-super-Mare.

But though it will not last for ever, it will last long enough to be remarkably offensive to the eye unless its aesthetics are taken in hand. The problem is the indefinite repetition of the tiny units of which it consists. Arranged informally, one gets the irritating not-quite-straight inconsequence of the chicken-farm. Arranged formally, the little chalets are just not important enough to sustain the axial traditions that have come down to us from Imperial Rome. Aware of this dilemma, the architect's obvious escape is to group his chalets in long low terraces—if his client allows it. Otherwise it seems that only one remedy remains: trees. Dumped in open seaside fields, the separate chalets are a plain eyesore. Hidden among trees, as in several German examples and as in England at Langdale, there is privacy, shelter, and the feeling of campfire solidarity that is presumably what the camper goes camping for. This implies the siting of seaside camps in sheltered places where trees exist or could be persuaded to grow. And these surely—and not the wild coast—are the places for them.

But the more thought one gives to the siting of settlements and the zoning of land for this and that, the more one realises that it is dangerously misleading to generalise. The holiday camp in open fields at Corton, near Lowestoft, seems perfectly satisfactory. The romantic colony at Portmeirion obviously makes that lonely estuary more beautiful, not less. Rows of brilliantly painted bathing huts are a decoration in some places, a sacrilege in others. For the fact is that no amount of planning by rule-of-thumb or Ministerial directive can take the place of the lost art of landscape design. It might seem splendid, for instance, if the edict were to go out from St James's Square that the whole coastline to a depth of two miles should be protected from all forms of building unless in compact settlements. But what is the effective visual depth of the coastline? For fenlands and salt marshes it could be anything up to ten miles. On the channel cliffs, where the ground may fall inland from the cliff edge, a house a hundred yards from high-water-mark may be quite invisible. One may carefully protect the skyline as seen from the sea, while violating the sea horizon as seen from inland. One may with great éclat found a New Town on some of the few remaining seaside agricultural acres, and leave an unregenerate Victorian resort to rot. These things happen when general principles are given authority over the genius of the place.

To think about landscape design has been pure escapism ever since the Industrial Revolution. With the Town and Country Planning Bill of 1947 it ceases to be so. Some day, of course, the sea may lose its holiday magic as suddenly as it acquired it. But until that incredible event the coastline is the one place where appearances must come first, and where there is now power to see that they do. To power must be added vision. With the people's car will come centrifugal forces and problems of control beside which the still compact and train-fed holiday camp is child's play. Concrete roads, hostels, restaurants, car parks, trailer camps, will have to be fitted into the coastal landscape, and can be fitted in if the job is done by lovers of that landscape. The English School of Landscape Design, which closed down a hundred years ago after a period of unique productivity, must be reopened at once. There is more work to be done than ever before, from Lands End to John o' Groat's inclusive.

THE POTTERIES LOOK FORWARD

by Bernard Hollowood and Sam Pollock

The industrial region of the Upper Trent Valley is known throughout the world as the Potteries—or the 'Five Towns' of Arnold Bennett's novels. Before the war they were afflicted by unemployment. Since then full employment has meant a great change in the lives of the people. Bernard Hollowood and Sam Pollock report on the present state of the pottery industry, on the changes brought about by machinery, and on the hopes and fears of masters and men

1 Stoke Revisited

by Bernard Hollowood

OUTSIDE Stoke station the panorama of the Potteries slowed up and stopped, wide open for inspection. Below the embankment a row of mean houses grovelled in steam and smoke and the deposited grit of a century. Behind them lay more mean houses and mean factories, right away into the distance. A depressing scene. Washing hung from window-sills, bleaching in the hot sun and collecting smuts from the railway.

The train moved into the station.

First impressions of Stoke are deceptive: across the street stands the blackened image of the great Josiah Wedgwood, and behind him the pleasant façade of the North Stafford Hotel. But to left and right, to Hanley, Burslem and Tunstall, to Fenton and Neck-end or Longton, stretches the grim smile of the Five Towns. The smile is miraculous: the grimness almost completely unrelieved. In the whole of this city of three hundred thousand people you will find inanimate beauty only by the merest chance. J. B. Priestley found the Potteries unbearably dreary, '. . . for nothing that you will hear or smell in these six towns [Arnold Bennett preferred the more euphonious "five"] will raise your spirits'.

Yet it is in this super-provincial string of towns that the world's best and most beautiful pottery is made. And, one must add, some of the world's worst and ugliest pottery. If North Staffordshire produced nothing but electrical porcelain, sanitary ware, glazed tiles, cheap cellulose vases and shooting gallery crockery, nobody would be surprised; that it turns out delightful tableware and handsome ornaments in fine earthenware and china is something to wonder at.

The secret, of course, lies in the people, for there are very few families in the district without some direct connection with the craft of potting. Today, only a quarter of the working population is engaged in the industry—some 50,000 compared with 66,000 before the war—but the quality of the labour and skill available is first-rate. A great tradition, a long apprenticeship in a craft that has proved exceptionally difficult to mechanise, and (possibly) the fact that males and females are employed in roughly equal numbers—these things help to explain the potting skill of the region, the 'green fingers' at work in every one of the two hundred and more factories.

These factories are like no others on earth. Most of them are small, no taller than the adjoining houses. Their brick walls are coated with grime, splashed with slip (liquid clay) and usually scribbled over to a height of four feet with chalk. 'Chalk' is plentiful in the Potteries—old moulds of plaster-of-Paris can be picked up on any shard-ruck or refuse heap—and the children *must* express themselves.

From a distance the potbanks reveal their location only by their ovens and kilns. These are the great brick structures, shaped like bottles with sloping shoulders, in which the clayware is baked hard. They stand in clusters, dominating the skyline and dwarfing the factories and houses like so many Gullivers.

But these familiar landmarks are gradually disappearing; they are coming down to make room for continuous tunnel ovens fired by gas and electricity. Many of the larger factories have already switched over to the new method, but further progress is hampered by bottlenecks in the engineering industry and by uncertainty about future supplies of fuel and power. This region, the North Staffordshire coalfield, produces about seven million tons of coal a year, and yet its major industry is working well below capacity through lack of fuel. That doesn't make sense to most potters.

I chatted with a young master-potter on his 'bank' in Fenton. He has recently taken over an old and well-established china-manufacturing business from his father. It is all *bone* china at this end of the city—china made from clay containing calcined animal bone—not the hard-paste porcelain of Worcester or the soft porcelains of the Continent. English bone china, delicate tea-sets with hand-painted or lithographed floral decorations (for export only) made in a ramshackle bungalow by about 200 workers, most of them women.

I asked whether he intended to install a tunnel oven.

'If you put one in', he said, ' you've got to keep it going to get your money back. And that means a steady demand for your pots and a steady supply of gas or electricity. Frankly, I'm not too happy about either. With the old intermittent oven we know where we are; we stoke up when there's enough ware to make an oven—not until. And we don't burn fuel when there's nothing to fire.'

'But I thought that tunnel ovens were economical?'

'So they are. They save time; you get better heat control and, of course, you don't have to wait for the oven to cool before you can get at the ware again. They're all right for the big potters.'

'What's your worry about demand? I thought you were all booked up for years and years ahead. Didn't your manufacturers' federation refuse to take new orders at the British Industries Fair?'

'True enough, we've plenty of work on paper—but exactly how many of our orders are firm and how many are duplicates, appearing in other potters' books, we just don't know. We were concentrated, during the war, and lost sixty per cent of our skilled labour. And now that we've got the capital, or a chance of borrowing some to buy new machinery, it isn't available.'

'Are you afraid of competition?'

'Not if we can get our reconstruction and rebuilding done in time. Before the war we were losing trade to the cheap mass-producers of Japan, Czechoslovakia and the USA, and we'll lose the ground we've recovered if we don't reduce our costs. You see, British prices are too high. Our quality is supreme—and, I think, our design—but it's not so *much* better that foreign buyers will go on paying such a big difference. Our prices are as much as 25 and 30 per cent higher than USA prices in spite of the fact that American wages are nearly three times as high as ours.'

'What's the reason?'

'Transport charges, the tariff and, in my view, poor marketing and excessive distributive margins.'

'Nothing wrong on this side?'

'Of course there is. We're operating with a lot of out-of-date equipment, and that means out-of-date shop practice and organisation. We don't want mass-production—our markets are too varied for that—but we're on a quantity production basis already without getting any of the advantages in costs.'

'So it's chiefly a matter of getting new plant and machinery quickly?'

'And labour, and materials and fuel; they're all in short supply. We could sell twice as much as we're making today, and we could turn out twice as much, if the shortages were removed. . . .'

After inspecting the works (I blushed repeatedly at the remarks hurled by the 'paintresses' at my foreman guide), and trying unsuccessfully to cadge an export reject tea-set decorated with pink roses, I set out for Burslem along a derelict strip of ribbon-development which is the main artery of the Potteries. Burslem is the mother town of the district, a very decrepit old lady obviously none too pleased with her brood. I looked in at the Art School (which works in close collaboration with the industry and tries to supply it with a stream of ceramic designers and artists), studied again the handsome frescoes of the old Wedgwood Institute (Oliver Lodge was once a student here), and crossed Waterloo Road to the famous Doulton works. Here I found an old friend, an employee. He gave me the worker's angle.

'In the old days', he said, 'this district had only one industry—potting. This meant low wages and long bouts of unemployment for nearly everybody. Now, there's much more to choose from—coal, engineering, rubber (the Michelin people are at Stoke and another large rubber firm is about to build there) and several other industries. We've got decent wage agreements now. Wages in potting compare well with those in most other industries and we've got a guaranteed week and one week's holiday with pay. Men get 75 shillings a week if they're labourers, up to 93 shillings if they're skilled; women get around about 50 shillings. The men's wages compare with 80 shillings a week in agriculture and about 90 shillings in shipbuilding and engineering.

'But I don't think the industry will ever get enough new recruits of the right type until conditions have been improved. Potting used to be one of the most dangerous trades in the country—lead-poisoning and silicosis—and they've made a lot of improvements and lead-poisoning has been wiped out. But there's still a lot of silicosis, and they'll never get rid of it altogether until we get better workshops.'

'Is there any fear of unemployment?'

'Yes, it'll take many years of full employment to remove that. Besides, we don't think the industry is properly equipped to meet foreign competition. Two years ago the National Society of Pottery Workers drafted its own recommendations about reconstruction, and some of them were followed up in the Working Party Report, but we'd like to see more control, not less. We'd like the potteries combined into larger and more efficient units with enough capital to rebuild on the scale of the new Wedgwood factory at Barlaston. We'd like to see more standardisation and mass-production, even if it means less work for craftsmen. Anyway, what's the use of having an old craft at your finger-tips if the world

Processes in Pottery Making

Pottery is no longer a craft, but the great tradition of craftsmanship remains. The hands of the thrower are less active than in the days of Josiah Wedgwood —they have been superseded by intricate machines —but clay remains as intractable a material as ever and at every stage of production needs careful, sympathetic handling

The designer *is a key man—even more so as quantity-production processes dominate the industry*

The thrower *has not everywhere survived the development of auto-matic making processes*

Plate-making : *a semi-automatic process in which the clay takes its form from plaster moulds*

Placing : *the ware being stacked ready for firing*

is too poor to buy it? We want to see the utility idea improved and carried on for the home and export markets—with the Government buying in bulk.'

'But wouldn't all this reduce the quality of your pots?'

'Why should it? The quality of modern pottery is chiefly a matter of having the right body (clays), the right design, machines and organisation. That means the right types of ceramic chemists, engineers, designers and so on. We want better educational and training facilities and more opportunities for the employee to reach the board-room. We want to sell more pottery to all markets —not just to the expensive American market—so we've got to compete with the mass-producers. I don't see why we shouldn't keep our quality *and* get all the economies of modern production methods. . . .'

At present the industry is exporting ware to the value of about ten million pounds per annum, and none of this is what Mr Dalton would call unrequited. In other words, the industry costs virtually nothing in imported raw materials. It is a native industry, relying on domestic

Photographs by courtesy of the Central Office of Information

supplies of clay (china clay, ball clay and Cornish stone from Devon and Cornwall, flints from the Channel coasts, gypsum from Derbyshire and elsewhere, coal colour-chemicals and so on). And, of course, it deals in much more than tableware and ornaments. The other branches of the industry, those making electrical porce-lain (insulators, etc), sanitary earthenware (pipes, wash-basins, lavatory-pans, etc), and glazed tiles (for walls and fireplaces) are important ancillaries of the building programme. And in general they're much more modern and efficient than their older neighbours in the tableware section—partly because they're not so handicapped by old restrictive sites and premises, partly because their technical problems are less complicated, and partly because their executive and administrative control does not usually depend on the health and strength of a single family tree.

The family concern is all very well when the strain of genius or ability-plus-enterprise continues as in the case of the Wedgwoods, Adams, Spodes and so on, from root to branch without a serious break—when the skill, zeal and acumen of the pioneer remains with successive generations. But, unfortunately, there are many businesses which languish because they are in the hands of un-progressive owner-managers—men content to draw a small salary from the business year by year, men without training or inclination for risk-taking.

This industry has its problems, but there is no industry in Britain with greater opportunities. So far the export market for pottery has been extremely limited; sales outside the Dominions and Americas have been in-significant. Now, if the Geneva talks come to anything, we may expect a gradual expansion of the world's trading territory. If the pottery industry gets a square deal from the Government and puts its house in order with all possible speed, the boom of the eighteenth century may well be repeated in the twentieth.

walk-out by a key worker who can walk over the road and write his (or her) own ticket.

This keen sellers' market in the outside world has naturally had its effect on internal relations. Like the workers in most of our undermanned industries, those in pottery now work in an atmosphere of security such as was seldom found in the inter-war years outside a Government office. And the outlook for years ahead seems equally 'settled'. But the fashionable complaint that the British worker is not as good a man as his father is seldom heard in the Potteries.

Among the vacancies advertised in the *Sentinel* I noticed more than one offer of starting wages of 37s 6d to 47s 6d a week for boys of fifteen and sixteen—one indication of the industry's urgent need for young blood. Wages throughout the industry stand sixth in the national

Handling: *fixing the handles to the cups and jugs*

The Kiln: *electric and gas kilns are replacing the old-fashioned bottleneck oven*

Decoration *is reproduced mainly from lithographs or prints, though hand painting still employs thousands of women*

2. The Hands of the Potter

by Sam Pollock

THE best place to study the labour position in the Potteries is in the vacancy columns of the Stoke *Evening Sentinel*. 'Pleasant working conditions', 'Air-conditioned shops, best class factory conditions', 'Good wages and canteen, sports and recreation facili-ties', 'First-class conditions with canteen facilities.' Column by column, and evening after evening, the master potters of the Five Towns conduct their search for hands. Eight years ago an abrupt 'Wanted, caster . . . or sponger, or dipper or saucer-maker' was enough: the mere rumour of a vacancy drew applicants by the hundred.

A pottery manager's life today (so one of them told me) is spent hurrying between his office, where he has just struck three noughts off the latest overseas order for a million pieces, and the shop floor, where he has been summoned to avert a threatened one-man (or woman)

scale—much higher than those of some of the industries which are competing successfully for the scarce workers.

The industry's chief handicap—as with cotton 'and coal—is its grim past. Apart from memories of unemployment and insecurity, every other public bar in the neighbourhood seems to have its corner seat reserved for an old boy who, between gasps and coughs, will tell you what pot dust has done to his chest and that he will let no boy or girl of his run the same risks.

In their quest for labour the Pottery manufacturers now have to face the competition of the light engineering and other 'clean' manufacturing industries which have opened factories in the neighbourhood. The layout and working conditions of the new factories are in strong and favourable contrast with the majority of the potbanks, most of which are dirty and ramshackle. What it amounts to is that 'the Potteries' has become more than ever a mere geographical expression: a 'balanced economy', the target of every other 'Development Area', is well in sight. And with the present scarcity of workers, the process of balancing involves scaling down for somebody. Tens of thousands of potters were directed into light engineering during the war and many of them show no inclination to return. There has been no 'drift' away from the potworks—the workers were taken away and only large-scale unemployment after the war would have sent them all back again. As for the young people leaving school, they have—what their fathers never had—a choice: and they're taking it.

Few people at the head of the industry see much hope of solving the labour difficulties by mechanisation. Clay, they insist, is not wood or steel: it is queer fickle stuff that needs handling—*manually*. Even a non-expert like myself is entitled to demur at this: the answer I was given was that America manufactures cheap ware in large quantities for a market in which we could never hope to compete, and that in any case our strong suit is quality, and for quality we need craftsmanship. But why should craftsmanship suffer when a machine is brought in to assist and speed up a dull repetitive job—like sticking handles on cups? Has the industry a sound answer?

In any case, if you have a girl whose job it is to stick handle after handle on cup after cup, at a piece-rate per hundred, craftsmanship will not suffer much if you give her a machine to help. As it is, she sits there paring at the clay with all the craft and precision of someone sharpening matchsticks for a cribbage board. And there are scores of jobs of equal monotony and drudgery. I asked one of these girls how she would view the displacement of her craft by a machine. 'Oh, I expect we'd all get our "books"!' was her first reaction. Yes, but supposing she was kept on to work the machine? 'I'd get used to it,' she said. 'Might be able to earn a bit more that way, too.' Where it exists, the opposition of workers to machines has a foundation of pure bread and butter: they know too well that the attitude of the average British employer to such mechanical aids in the past was more 'How many hands can I pay off?' than 'How much can I boost up production?'

If any branch of pottery work can justly be called a 'craft', it is 'throwing'. My friend Harry is what an American newspaperman would call 'ace' thrower to one of the biggest firms in Stoke. He's been with them for forty years. All visitors are steered towards Harry's wheel, and stand there in gaping astonishment and delight as the clay on the whirling disc, under pressure of his cunning hands, takes as it seems, a fresh shape every second—jug, bowl, egg-cup, vase of every shape and size, slender beaker. No illusionist could equal the wonder of the display.

I watched two young ex-Servicemen at work in one of the larger potworks: one was turning and decorating a vase at a lathe, and the other 'throwing' plates on a plaster-of-paris mould—a partly mechanised operation now. You recognise the watchful but confident stance, the slick easy control: you last saw them, perhaps, by a milling or grinding machine in an aero-factory—machines which work to a ten-thousandth of an inch, and their operators are no mean craftsmen. In the development of further 'buttons and levers' lies the future of British pottery. Harry's kind of cunning will perhaps die with him and his generation: and British pottery, as an industry, keep them company to the grave.

And craftsmanship will stage its last rally—even when the thrower has been mechanised—in the decorating department. Here I found eager young men and women from the local Art Schools, people really in love with their job who wouldn't care for any other. To them no other industry could offer cleaner or more attractive surroundings to work in, more enjoyable work, or I believe much better pay.

I believe that if the industry mechanised—or at least reorganised—those parts of the work which are manifest drudgery, it would still exhibit enough quality to satisfy both the creative artist and the discerning customer.

SOUTH WALES STORY

by Douglas Jay

In at least one sector of industrial Britain, it has been possible to translate economic theory into visible reality: today, in Britain's Development Areas, the full employment policy on which this country's future depends is being worked out. New factories are being built, new industrial estates laid out, slag heaps and derelict iron foundries cleared for working sites, for parks and playing fields, and for houses. Here is an account of the progress of development in South Wales

IN South Wales today, and in the other Development Areas, you can see being worked out the full employment policy, on which the economic future of this country will depend. Fine, modern factories are being built on a large scale. New industrial estates are being laid out. New factories built during the war for munitions are coming into full civilian production. Slag heaps and derelict iron works are being cleared for new industrial sites, and for parks and playing fields. And, incidentally, a great number of new houses of all types are being built. This translation of economic theory and planning into visible reality is all the more fascinating because of the extreme human distress which prevailed in South Wales, the north-east coast and south-west Scotland before the war. It is human life itself which is being transformed through the realisation of an economic plan.

The 'distribution of industry' policy which is being followed by the present Government is designed, above all, to raise the national output and standard of living by setting the whole available manpower of the nation to work. That is the purpose of the intensive and success-

ful effort to revive South Wales and other areas, and that is why this effort must be given a first priority in the national economic plan. Unless everybody is at work, our national output will be insufficient; and unless the 500,000 people who were chronically unemployed in the prewar distressed areas are given new industries and factories, we cannot all be at work. For that reason the revival of South Wales is as necessary for the standard of living of the rest of Britain as of South Wales itself.

This simple truth has been obscured by a great deal of muddled thinking, which even now prevails in some quarters, and represents the Development Area policy as somehow ancillary to, rather than the heart of, economic recovery. I believe this confusion is due to three particular fallacies, all of which spring from the myopic old-time habit of looking at all economic problems from the point of view of a private profit-earning producer. Hence much stupidity and many tears.

The first fallacy is the belief that if there are, say, 150,000 unemployed persons in an area such as South Wales, representing 35 or 40 per cent of the local working population, these workers can somehow be rapidly transferred to another area where there is a labour shortage. The main reason why this is economically impossible is, of course, that houses, roads and all the other physical capital necessary to modern living cannot be improvised overnight. It requires far less building labour—probably only one-tenth as much—to build a factory for 1,000 people than it does to build the houses, roads and sewers for the families of 1,000. That is one of the most important of all the economic facts of life in conditions of full employment. Another reason is that the family is as much an economic unit as the factory. The daughter of a postman in Blaenavon is a potential worker in Blaenavon. But since she has to help in the house and mind the baby in the evenings, she is not a potential worker anywhere else. Therefore, if there is no work for her in Blaenavon, a potential worker is lost to the nation. That is why the lack of work for women in coalmining towns has been a fantastic drag on the national output in the past.

The second fallacy is the belief that if one economic unit is closed down under a system of private enterprise, the workers will necessarily be absorbed into another. If this were true, the closing down of an 'uneconomic' concern such as a high-cost coal pit, or an old-fashioned shipyard, might be expected to increase the national output. But if the greater part of the labour is simply left unemployed, the national output is, of course, diminished. And, in certain areas, where there is no authority with the power to close down the one unit and at the same time to start up another, according to a deliberate plan, the released labour will almost certainly be unemployed.

The third fallacy is the failure to observe that the houses, roads and services outside the factory gates are as much an element in the overhead costs of production as the machinery and factory buildings themselves. It is only the blind habit of looking at things from the point of view of the private enterprise unit which has obscured this underlying economic truth. If you look down from a South Wales mountain-side and watch the workers from one of the new factories going home to their cottages in a mining town, you will see clearly enough that the costs of production do not mysteriously stop at the factory gates. The roadway outside the factory gates is just as necessary to its working as the roadway inside; and the bricks which make the workers' homes are as necessary as the bricks which make the canteen or tool room of the factory itself.

It was genuine failure to understand these simple economic truths, probably more than malice or greed, that was the real cause of the prolonged scandal and waste in the prewar distressed areas, which cost the nation the lost output of 500,000 workers annually over a period of twenty years—an output which would more than offset today the whole loss of our foreign investment income due to the war, and would, for example, have provided us with enough merchant ships and defence materials to have put defeat in 1939-42 out of the question. And it was recognition of these truths that inspired the Distribution of Industry Act in 1945, as an essential part of the economic and employment policy set out in the White Paper on Employment Policy of May 1944.

The Distribution of Industry policy is thus economic, and not primarily just social. It is not mere town-planning. Its essence is that a central authority—actually the Board of Trade, working with the other departments —should influence the geographical distribution of new factories over the whole country, with two objectives: first, to see that a new and sufficient demand for labour should spring up where there is surplus manpower; and, secondly, to prevent waste of materials by the building of new factories where there is already manpower shortage.

In each individual Development Area the central Government is now influencing industrialists all over the country by a steady process of consultation and persuasion to place their expansions where labour exists— which is, of course, as much in their own interests as that of the nation. The fantastic prewar process, by which almost all business men were simultaneously seeking to expand into West London, Birmingham and a few other places, in ignorance that others were doing the same, and without any real economic justification, resulted in houses, roads and so forth already existing in the North and West having to be reduplicated in London or the Midlands on a vast scale. It was one of the most flagrant examples ever seen of a number of people unconsciously frustrating each other's private interests by all blindly seeking their own.

The method by which the Distribution of Industry Act proposed to carry out the general planning of industrial location was very simple. It ensured that industrialists throughout the country should notify the Board of Trade of any intention to erect new factories, and it gave the Board power to schedule as Development Areas any areas where unemployment was threatening. In these the Board itself, through certain chosen instruments, might build factories, clear sites, run trading estates and generally promote useful productive employment. It is sometimes thought that the abandonment of the clause giving the Board of Trade restrictive powers conditionally in certain areas has weakened the Act. But this is a total misconception. Under the building licensing system now in force until the end of 1950, the Government has absolute power to stop the building of any factory; and this has been made permanent by Clause 12, Section 4, of the Town and Country Planning Act. Few people have noticed this important fact.

Although the purpose of the whole policy is thus primarily economic, it will, of course, exert a profound and revivifying effect on the whole human and social life of the districts actually scheduled as Development Areas

A fine view of the pioneer Government trading estate at Treforest, probably the most successful enterprise of its kind today

under the Bill. The present Development Areas are industrial South Wales, the north-east coast, industrial Scotland, west Cumberland and parts of south Lancashire. There can be no question that real poverty reached its extreme form before the war in the areas like Tyneside and the South Wales valleys, where genuine unemployment often ranged from 50 to 80 per cent; or that the greatest economic hardships of those days fell upon the children of unemployed wage-earners in the areas of heavy depression. For the children in the mining valleys of South Wales in those years, fresh milk was almost unknown, malnutrition continuous, and boots and shoes very seldom seen. Today these children are as well fed and well clothed as those in London, Oxford, Luton or Leicester. Perhaps the most vivid commentary on the entire story is the fact that the consumption of liquid milk in the whole of the north-east coast and South Wales today, in spite of world food shortages, is three times what it was in 1938.

Here are some of the figures for the drop in infantile mortality since before the war, which show that the greatest change has been in the old distressed areas like Newcastle and Liverpool, compared with the old prosperous areas like London and Oxford:*

(The figures are per 1,000)	1938	1944
Old Distressed Areas		
Newcastle-on-Tyne	66	51
Liverpool	74	58
Fully Employed Areas		
London	50	43
Oxford	23	25

*These figures are from the Report of the Chief Medical Officer for 1946.

All this is true of the Development Areas as a whole. But it is worth while illustrating it further by the story of South Wales since the war ended. Before the war, unemployment seldom fell, in what is now the South Wales Development Area, below about 150,000—or 30 per cent of the working population. During the war a number of Royal Ordnance Factories and other munitions factories were built in the area, mainly by the Ministry of Supply. As a result it was found possible, by working double and treble shifts, and by carrying many thousands of workers 20 and 30 miles from their homes by bus and train, to reduce unemployment almost to zero by the end of the war. In the last few months of the war there were about 250,000 persons on war work in South Wales; and if such work had simply been shut down without any plan (as in 1918), unemployment would have risen to at least 150,000, and probably more, within six months. Before the end of the war, therefore, the Board of Trade, which had been given this responsibility under Hugh Dalton, set itself to counter a threatened unemployment of about that figure, and to introduce sufficient new industries to provide another 130,000 or 140,000 new jobs, about 60 per cent of them for men and 40 per cent for women.

The first line of attack was to ensure that the existing new factories should be turned over to civilian production at the end of the war. This was most vital in the case of the two great filling factories (each embracing more than 100 separate buildings): Bridgend Royal Ordnance Factory at the south of the central valleys (employing 30,000 people in war-time) and Hirwaun at the north (employing 11,000). Within a few weeks of VE-day the

Board of Trade put into operation a previously prepared plan for these two Royal Ordnance Factories to be handed over to the South Wales Industrial Estate Company—the Government concern originally set up under the old Special Area Acts—and run as a trading estate, with the numerous separate buildings let to separate firms. The next line of attack was to give licences freely to private firms from England, Wales and elsewhere to build new factories in the Development Area. Some of these were actually begun before the war ended.

Next, the Industrial Estate Company began to build new factories and clear sites both on old and new trading estates and on individual sites, which private firms could lease. Naturally the precise location of all these schemes had to be agreed with the proper town planning authorities.

By such means, sufficient schemes have now been approved to cover the whole of the prospective unemployment in the area; and a large number are built or are building. Actually thirty-five new factories have now been completed, and are in production; another hundred are already building; and a further hundred are approved. The whole plan thus provides for the building of about 250 new factories over the three or four years from the end of the war. The actual rate of building will depend on the supply of steel, timber and other building materials, which at the moment are exceedingly short, and on competitive claims of housing and other reconstruction plans.

Even more impressive than these figures is the fact that some scheme or other, of the appropriate magnitude, has now been started or approved for almost every community in the area, including those upper mining villages and towns which only a few years ago were thought to be beyond hope of revival. The narrowness of the valleys makes it impossible for everybody to be given a factory job within walking distance of their homes; but all will be able to find it within reasonable daily travelling distance. The main centres of employment will be:

(1) In the east: Newport, where a whole series of schemes are going forward; Glascoed Royal Ordnance Factory; and the new British Nylon Spinners Factory, both near Pontypool. At Glascoed, 3,000 persons are now employed as direct Ministry of Supply employees, making parts for Airey houses, concrete sleepers and ceramics, as well as some defence materials. The British Nylon Spinners factory near by, which is being designed with great architectural care in an exceedingly beautiful stretch of country just east of the Pontypool mountains, will be the main nylon plant in the British Isles. It will cost about £10,000,000, require over 10,000 tons of steel for construction, and by the middle of 1948 should be turning out enough nylon to make 60,000,000 pairs of stockings per year.

(2) In the central area: Cardiff has a large number of

New work for South Wales : from the foot of the old valleys and housing estates rises a zip-fastener factory at Dinas

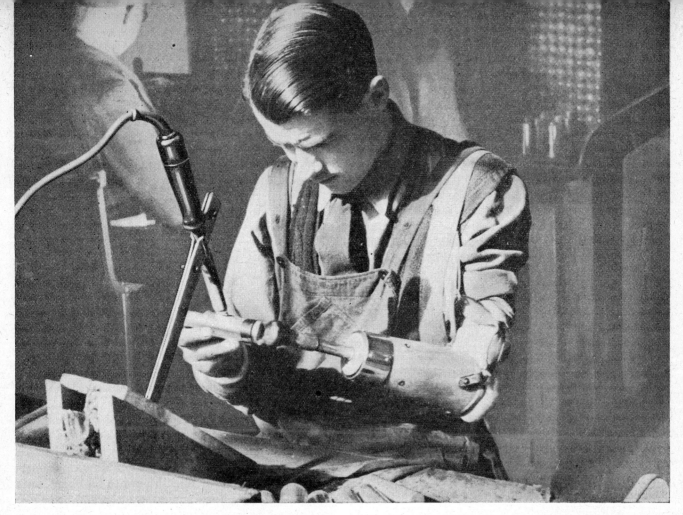

A rehabilitated ex-Service man at work in the new 'Remploy' factory for disabled men on the Bridgend Estate

new factories as well as the Inland Revenue Establishment decentralised from London; it is now a prosperous city, despite the temporary disappearance of coal exports. Cardiff Royal Ordnance Factory is actually being maintained by the Ministry of Supply, but is at the moment making machinery, ceramics and atomic plant as well as guns. North of Cardiff in the Taff Valley, the pioneer prewar Treforest Estate—probably the best designed in the country—has been completed with a number of additional new factories, and is giving employment to the populations of the tributary valleys of Rhondda, Aberdare and Merthyr.

Merthyr itself, which suffered heavy unemployment in the immediate postwar recoil from war work, has four large-scale new factories already completed, and several more building. Its future as a prosperous town is now, I believe, assured. The firm of Kayser Bondor, which had the enterprise to go to Merthyr before the war, is now making fully-fashioned hosiery and clothing in two new factories finished since the war, and employing 1,500 people, which will rise to 3,000. Lines Brothers of Croydon have taken over the other largest new factory in Merthyr, and already have 800 persons making prams and toys. At the Hirwaun Estate, only a few miles away, which caters mainly for the Aberdare and Mountain Ash Valley, despite many physical difficulties and delays in conversion, more than 2,000 people are at work on radio

sets, clocks and various other products. In the Rhondda Valley itself, sites are very difficult to find; but the Gramophone Company now have 750 persons producing electrical goods, mainly for export, at a very large new engineering factory at Treorchy. Farther down the valley, as at Merthyr and Aberdare, slag heaps are being cleared by the Government Estate Company and standard factories built. At the new Bridgend Estate, which caters for the valleys a little to the west and south, employment has now reached 4,000 on all manner of products. This, be it noted, is in a converted filling factory, which many technicians during the war thought would be no use for anything but scrapping—the fate, South Wales recalls, of similar factories after 1918. Now the Government is drawing large rents from numerous firms; goods of all kinds are being produced; and 4,000 people are at work who would otherwise be concentrated in idleness in the neighbouring valleys.

In the western area—Swansea, Neath, Port Talbot and the valleys behind them—unemployment never disappeared even in the war. The decline of the tinplate industry and the simultaneous disappearance of coal exports have made this area one of the two or three greatest economic problems in Britain. There is unemployment there now, and the immediate future will be difficult; but schemes are now going forward which should assure its revival in the not far distant future. Far the biggest is the £50,000,000 Richard Thomas-Baldwin scheme for a new steel and tinplate strip mill at Margam, on the coast between the mountains and the sea, near Port Talbot. This is the most important new industrial project in Britain, and, so far as I know, the biggest now going forward in Europe. Bulldozers have already started work on this site; and the decision of the Government to nationalise the iron and steel industry will ensure that the scheme is carried right through.

Besides a number of other small new schemes in the western area, many of them designed in particular for silicotic ex-miners, the two chief centres of employment and revival will be the new Swansea Trading Estate, and the new clock industry at Ystradgynlais, twelve miles up the Swansea Valley. The Swansea Trading Estate has been planned by the Board of Trade, the Swansea Corporation, the South Wales Industrial Estate Company, and the private firm, Slough Estates Limited, all working together. It will be at Forestfach on the western side of Swansea, so as to cater also for the people of Gowerton, Gorseinon, and Llanelly. Four new factories are already completed on this estate, and a number of others building. But it is designed on a big scale to employ more than 7,000 persons eventually, and will take several years to complete.

At Ystradgynlais, in an exceedingly beautiful part of the upper Swansea Valley, in an anthracite miners' community between two steep mountain slopes, is the beginning of Britain's new watch and clock industry, now already coming to life in what was a private landowner's park up to 1945. Anybody who wants to see how the new industrial Britain is being created in these once derelict areas should visit this particular project, which is being operated by Smith's Clocks in a series of factories built by the Government. It is a venture which, among other objectives, will help to make the country less dependent on clock and watch imports in peace-time, and will assure us of a reserve of fuse-making capacity in war. The first factory, which is a model from the architectural point of view, is already turning out watches, and employs 350 persons. If you want to understand the spirit of revival in South Wales today, you could not do better than listen to the factory choir at Ystradgynlais practising in the canteen on a sunny Sunday afternoon.

So far, what has this enterprise by the Government and industrialists amounted to in terms of total employment? The total of unemployed before the war was usually more than 150,000 in the present Development Area; and something not much less than this would have occurred after this war, if there had been no Government plan for South Wales. In fact, owing to the first recoil from war work, unemployment in the Development Area rose from the minimum of 12,000 in June 1945 to 69,000 in February 1946. Then the effect of the plan began to tell; and unemployment fell steadily to 45,000 in December 1946. The fuel crisis pushed it momentarily back to 68,000 in March of 1947, but it has now dropped again to under 45,000—or only 8 per cent of the insured population, compared with the 30 per cent which was normal before the war.

These statistics are conclusive. They are a great tribute to all those—Civil Servants and industrialists, trades unionists and local authorities—who have been carrying out the plan in face of great and inevitable physical difficulties, shortages and delays, as well as a number of other unnecessary difficulties caused by the ignorant if understandable impatience of those who wanted everything to happen overnight. It has not always, I think, been realised what great efforts the Government planners had to make to induce English firms to set up in South Wales at all, and how careful the authorities had to be to dovetail the needs of the new industries with the needs of the now publicly owned coal mines.

More telling even than the statistics, however, are the faces and clothes of the people, especially of the children, the goods in the shops and the general atmosphere of the South Wales communities today. Before the war there was no hope, because there was no work. During the war there was work, but also fear—fear of the unemployment which everyone expected to follow the almost dreaded coming of peace. Now there is work and hope as well. Exasperating as are the day-to-day delays and difficulties of getting this or that building finished, the people know not merely that they and their children are better fed and better clothed than between the two wars, but that month by month unemployment will continue to fall, and that their lives will improve in the years that lie ahead.

Photographs on pages 23 ,25 and 27   om 'This Modern Age' by courtesy of the J. Arthur Rank Organisation. Photograph on page 26 by courtesy of 'The Board o 'Trade Journal'

MARRIAGE AND DIVORCE IN POSTWAR BRITAIN

by Mass-Observation

One marriage in every five now ends in separation. In part related to the war, in others unrelated,

the last ten years have brought decisive changes in the attitude of Britain's men and women to

marriage and divorce. This Mass-Observation survey, especially conducted for Contact Books,

throws new light upon a vital aspect of change in contemporary British society

'It has been discovered experimentally that you can draw laughter from an audience anywhere in the world, of any class or race, simply by walking on to a stage and uttering the words: "I am a married man".'

Ted Kavanagh, creator of ITMA

'Oh dear, I don't know *what* we have in common. I like a good laugh, but my husband is serious.'

Working class wife, married for 25 years

'It is desirable that the facts should be seen in their proper perspective, the more so in view of the ignorance which prevails concerning them.'

Registrar General

BEFORE the war, the divorce rate in most of Western Europe was from three to eight times higher than in Britain, and in the USA it was nearly 13 times as great. The accompanying table shows the rates per 10,000 population in 1936, the end of a period of comparative stability in this country.

In considering the factors which have led, during the past decade, to a more than fivefold increase in the annual number of divorces in England and Wales, these facts should be borne in mind. Before 1938, divorce in Britain was either exceedingly difficult, or exceedingly costly, or both. Legal and financial sanctions reinforced the moral one. A. P. Herbert's Matrimonial Causes Act (1937) broadened the grounds, and increasing use of the Poor Persons Procedure has lessened the average cost. In recent years the majority of all divorce suits have been brought under this Procedure, which means that the majority of those seeking divorce have been people with an income of less than £4 a week, and whose possessions are worth less than £100. The Services Department alone has been faced with some 50,000 divorce cases, a number equal to six times the total petitions filed in any one year prior to the Herbert Act.

Out of 100 married people of all social classes questioned, only 22 recalled having been separated from their spouse for a month or more at any time during their married life, apart from compulsory war-time separations.

Nearly half had never been apart for as much as a week, and the majority of these said they had never been apart at all. Yet nearly three-quarters of these same people, asked whether or not they would consider divorce if their own marriage went wrong, were prepared to contemplate it, verbally. Asked their views about unmarried people living together, about half expressed more or less unconditional disapproval. While only a minority expressed approval in general or positive terms, half made it clear that they would feel no strong objections under given circumstances, or felt it was a private matter, up to the people concerned.

Although grounds for divorce have broadened, and it is probable (though unproven) that the moral sanction has weakened, too, the heavy sanction of cost remains for the majority. There are no exceptions to the £4 a week level of maximum income for cut-price divorces. Above this level, a minimum expenditure of £50 has to be considered. More normally, costs are between £65 and £85; and a defended suit is likely to cost £150 or more. A defending husband has to bear in mind that he will have to pay his wife's costs as well as his own. Divorce is 'easy' only for the rich and the very poor.

Any inclination to see in divorce statistics a decline of

DIVORCE RATE IN 1936	
Country	*Per* 10,000 *population*
United Kingdom	1.0
Norway	3.5
Holland	3.5
Belgium	3.7
Sweden	4.5
France	5.2
Germany	7.5
Denmark	8.6
USA	12.9

the esteem in which marriage is held by ordinary men and women, or even an increase in the number of broken marriages, must be critically inspected. Many of those who now seek divorce would, only a few years ago, have followed the simpler course of legal separation, or merely have separated, with or without mutual consent. This change in working class custom no doubt partly accounts for the fact that separations have not increased proportionately with divorces. Nevertheless, a numerical increase of 10,000 a year, as between 1923 and 1943, represents a substantial, if less startling rise. Less publicised separations remain more frequent than divorces, though in a diminishing ratio. Taking the year 1943 as a norm preceding the rush when the pressure of war relaxed, we find an aggregate of divorce petitions filed, and Separation and Maintenance suits commenced, of roughly 38,500. In that year, for every seven couples who married, one called in the law formally to sanction the dissolution of their home.

How many more separate informally, and how many who do not separate live together in mutual sufferance under the same roof?

Mass-Observation asked 787 women whether there were any disadvantages about married life that they hadn't foreseen when they got married. More than a third confessed to some unforeseen snag. Discounting all difficulties which could be attributed directly to the war, three in every ten of those who were married between five and ten years ago admitted some disadvantage. This is the peak period for the commencement of divorce proceedings, but few of these couples will finally break up. Like the woman of 27, married at 18, who said of her husband: 'He don't talk much. He just says hello and good night', the majority will continue to make the best of a not very satisfactory job.

We also asked these wives and mothers whether they felt they were right or wrong in their reasons for getting married. Between one in twelve and one in twenty among all groups except the most recently married said positively that they were wrong. If we add one half of those who were not certain enough to say definitely that they were right, then about one in ten of these unbroken marriages must be considered, at best, a disappointment from the wife's point of view.

The reasons why people marry are notoriously arbitrary. Much public discussion has followed the Registrar General's recent report showing that, by 1939, nearly 30 per cent of all mothers conceived their first child out of wedlock. One in seven of all children born are now the product of extra-marital conception; and the illegitimate birthrate, rising steadily from a stable peace-time norm of 4 to 4½ per cent of all live births, reached more than double that figure in 1945. 82,708 children were born out of wedlock in 1946, an increase of over 20,000 on the previous year, and 57,000 more than in 1939. However, 1946 was a record year for babies altogether, and the actual percentage of illegitimates has declined since the D-day peak.

Some of these facts, as the Registrar General permits himself to say, are 'sufficiently startling to render the matter of more than statistical significance'. It is very easy, however, to read more than their just measure of *social* significance into such statistically startling data. More divorce does not necessarily mean more broken homes. Nor, since no comparable data has ever been assembled before, can the high rate of illegitimate conception be assumed to indicate a major change in social values. It may equally well represent the discovery of a hitherto unsuspected social norm. All we know for certain is that society is now willing to look certain aspects of its behaviour in the face, and to incorporate into a logical public pattern of law and acknowledged social custom matters which were previously regarded as private and law-less. The Population (Statistics) Act of 1938, which enabled data on pre-marital conceptions to be collected for the first time, is itself, perhaps, a more significant contemporary social symptom than the facts now disclosed through its operation.

During the past decade, from the Registrar General's new birth-registration form, to the recent Nuffield Report on Old Age, the Curtis Report and many others, previously unacknowledged facts about social life in Britain have been docketed and documented and presented to the public on an ever-increasing scale. Because the descriptions are novel and often startling, there is a strong temptation to believe that the phenomena themselves are new and scandalising. But all that is indisputably new is the will to acknowledge social realities. Stimulated by the major social problem of the Western world today— a declining birthrate and threatened decline in population —the state of matrimony has become the subject of investigation, discussion, therapeutic treatment, education and advice from Press, pulpit, pioneer, racketeer and Government Department. In discussing this, the undisputed social change, we must not confuse a growing awareness that marriage is a problem with a purely conjectural increase in problem marriages.

AWARENESS OF PROBLEM

Among several organisations now working to assist in solving marriage problems, the Marriage Guidance Council (Presidents: The Lord Bishop of London and Lord Horder) numbers among its aims:

> That it is a public duty to do everything possible to prevent the tragedy of the broken home, and the train of evils which it initiates, by the provision of sympathetic and expert treatment for the prevention and cure of marital disharmony.

Since the foundation of the parent body in 1938, some sixty Councils have been formed throughout the country. The London Council alone has dealt with between 5,000 and 6,000 cases in the past five years, and the number is increasing. Dr David Mace, one of the Council's Secretaries, writes a regular and serious feature in the London

Star, dealing with specific and intimate matrimonial problems put to him by correspondents.

The Council's aims centre round orthodox Christian ethics. At a meeting in June 1947 of the North-West Kent Marriage Guidance Council, the Bishop of Rochester announced the appointment of a specialist in sex education to the Diocese, who would 'help to prepare young people for marriage'. Such an innovation by the established Church would have been so startling as to be almost inconceivable only a few years ago.

Dealing with a rather different, but widely overlapping, aspect of marital disharmony are the numerous 'birth control' clinics which now exist throughout the country. An important, though less publicised aspect of their work, is the pro-baby side, as it is known in Dr Marie Stopes's clinics: the provision, that is, of advice and practical assistance to childless couples desiring children. Of the larger voluntary organisations formed since Dr Stopes's pioneering days, the Family Planning Association now has 61 clinics in rural and urban areas throughout the country, dealt last year with 33,000 new attendances in England and Wales, and reports a ratio of old to new attendances of roughly 2 to 5. The Association recently opened a new clinic in London for the treatment of infertility in men, and, since its opening, attendances have increased by about 100 per cent a month. The Family Planning Association believes that among the most important causes of marital maladjustment are fear of pregnancy on the part of the wife, or involuntary childlessness with each party secretly blaming the other.

These are some of the symptoms of a growing self-consciousness about marriage in Britain. Organised voluntary effort deals mainly with the solution of problems once they have reached an acute form. How do these problems arise in the first place? Let us look at some aspects of marriage as they appear in the words of ordinary men and women at various stages in their progress from desire to divorce or golden wedding.*

SEX EDUCATION

The great majority of people look back to some time before the age of 20 for memories of their first real love affair. About a quarter remember their first affair before the age of 16, and a not insignificant minority look back to an age earlier than 14. Should these boys and girls, accumulating memories which they will carry with them through their adult lives, learn solely from experience the sort of relationship they will need to develop to make a success of marriage; or should this be the subject of instruction, in schools, through parents, or through voluntary organisations?

* Mass-Observation results quoted from now on refer partly to an investigation among married women in London and Gloucester conducted on a sampling basis shortly before the end of the war, and partly to a smaller sample survey in four urban areas carried out specifically for **Contact** Publications in May and June 1947.

The landmarks among official efforts to encourage some form of education for marriage are of very recent date. The Board of Education's 115-page volume on *Health Education,* published as recently as 1939, makes no mention of education for marriage, or in sex, though it contains a section on mothercraft and three pages on mental health. In 1943 the Board published a pamphlet on *Sex Education in Schools and Youth Clubs,* and today such education is recommended, but not obligatory. In the Church, Convocation adopted a resolution in 1944 urging upon teachers and parents the need for more definite teaching on the permanence of Christian marriage.

When Mass-Observation asked people what they felt about the idea of sex education in schools, the great majority showed approval, often of an emphatic kind. Several referred spontaneously to their own experience:

'I think it's very important. I never had any myself. I went out with chaps older than myself and learnt from them and I don't think that's right. It *must* be taught in schools' (*married man, artisan class, age 25*).

'I think you should know something. I often make remarks. Mother says I shouldn't, but she never told me anything' (*single woman, same class, same age*).

The minority, mostly older people, either took the view that 'that sort of thing comes naturally to you' or believed that instruction would lead to immorality:

'Let it come to them. Better that way. Let life take its natural course' (*married man, working class, 60*).

'It's unnecessary. You get to know things instinctively' (*widow, working class, 70*).

'They hear enough. That's the trouble with young people today. They know too much' (*married man, working class, 60*).

There was notably little suggestion that such instruction was the parents' responsibility, but some spontaneous comment from married people that teachers would be better fitted to give it than parents.

The desirability of some sort of formal education for marriage is thus fairly widely accepted today, and through such agencies as the Central Council for Health Education it is being put into practice on a widening scale among groups of young people or adults who ask for it. But only a minority are yet covered by such means. Most still pick up the threads as they go along. Here are further indications of their progress towards marriage.

ENGAGEMENTS

Engagements, in the old formal sense, are less frequent than they were. As one woman put it: 'They went out with Queen Victoria, didn't they?' But nearly one in four of the married people observed, both men and women, had reached a stage which they looked upon as 'being engaged' to at least one other person before they met their present husband or wife. Engagements were broken mainly by mutual agreement, and though men complain of unilateral action more than women, women's pride rather than actual fact may well be responsible for the difference. A comparison, among the same group, of the length of time people consider an engagement *should* last, and the length of time they knew their own final mates before marrying them shows that, on average, these people knew their future husbands or wives a good deal longer than they feel it essential for an engaged couple to know one another, and two out of five had been acquainted for three years or longer.

MARRIAGE AGE

Asked what they considered the best age to get married, married and single people gave virtually identical answers. Two-thirds of the women considered ages under 25 ideal, while a similar majority of men were fairly equally divided between 20 to 25, and 25 to 30. Many of the rest, among both sexes, were rather vague, but these mostly favoured getting married young. About one woman in twenty and one man in seven considered the age of 30 or over ideal.

The most frequent age at marriage in Britain is between 21 and 25 for spinsters, and between 25 and 30 for bachelors. This fits fairly closely to the pattern of women's wishes—not so closely to men's. Among our study group, nearly two-thirds of both sexes got married within two years of their ideal age. Of the rest, most of the women were married within two to five years of their ideal. But a quarter of the men were over five years wide

of their own target, the majority of these marrying older than they would have liked.

FIRST MEETINGS

We asked people where they first met their present husband and wife. Twenty-five per cent were introduced through friends or family, the others at their workplace (10 per cent), at dances, on holidays, or just 'in the park'. First meetings which develop into marriage take place anywhere and everywhere. A notably high proportion of marriages arise from chance encounters:

'We met in the pictures. Threepenny touch it was then. There were two girls sitting with a space on either side of them when my mate and I were shown in. My mate married the other girl' (*man, 50, working class*).

'Really by accident. I went to live in lodgings. I lived upstairs and she lived downstairs. The funny thing was I wasn't anxious to take those digs. I didn't want to go there' (*man, 30, artisan class*).

'I went to work in a Picture Palace, and he used to live next door and come to the pictures there' (*woman, 23, working class*).

'I went with his friend for six years. Then one day he introduced me to another fellow getting off a bus, and after that I went with him' (*woman, 45, working class*).

'In the park. I was out with my friend, and we two girls met these two fellows and I stuck to mine' (*woman, 50, working class*).

'At a hotel. He passed the salt at breakfast' (*woman, 50, working class*).

From such accidental circumstance, after months or years, marriage develops. Immediately the man and

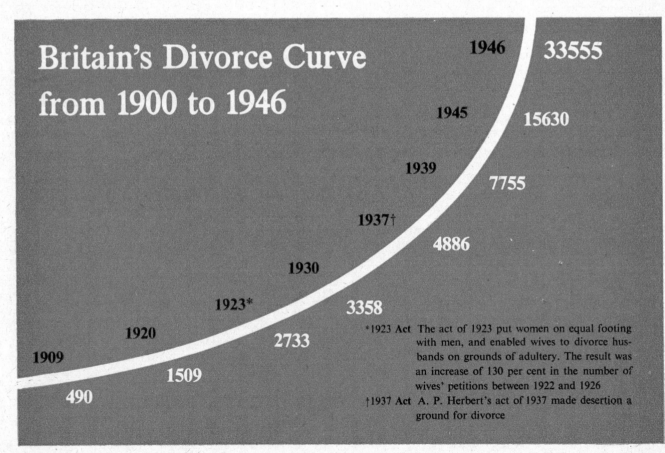

Britain's Divorce Curve from 1900 to 1946

1909 — 490
1920 — 1509
1923* — 2733
1930 — 3358
1937† — 4886
1939 — 7755
1945 — 15630
1946 — 33555

*1923 Act The act of 1923 put women on equal footing with men, and enabled wives to divorce husbands on grounds of adultery. The result was an increase of 130 per cent in the number of wives' petitions between 1922 and 1926

†1937 Act A. P. Herbert's act of 1937 made desertion a ground for divorce

woman have agreed to marry, the first matrimonial argument may arise. What is the wedding to be like? Nearly every woman can answer that question, and overwhelmingly they come out in favour of making it a dressy affair. More than half want a white wedding, and three-quarters specifically say their ideal wedding would be in church. This, too, despite the fact that, among our sample, half said they were not religious and only one in five said they belonged to any particular Church or sect.

Men are vaguer, more inclined to say the type of wedding doesn't matter, but are much more often in favour of a quiet affair, whether in a church or registry office. Among the group studied, three men had the sort of wedding they wanted for every two women who did so. The difference was mainly in the high proportion of women who wanted to be married in white, but weren't; for many, a compromise with cash or coupons as much as with their husband's wishes. As one woman put it: 'If you have a costume wedding you've always got something nice to wear afterwards. The majority of brides have their wedding dresses dyed.'

Mr E. L. Packer, an experienced probation officer, in an interesting article in *Pilot Papers* (March 1947) has drawn attention to the effects of the double bed in contemporary working class marriage: 'The double bed', he says, 'has contributed to the failure to achieve sexual harmony', and he instances several examples to this effect. Mr Packer has marshalled much of the limited available evidence about the sexual side of marriage, frigidity, frequency of intercourse and the like, which we do not propose to re-discuss here. The tradition of the double bed, however, is a matter of some importance in considering the changes in social outlook surrounding marriage today. Among those with definite feelings on the matter, we found a majority of both sexes favouring double beds, and little difference between the proportion of married and single people favouring them. About one in three, however, said single beds were best. The reasons for these preferences, in rough order of frequency, were:

Prefer Double Beds	Prefer Single Beds
Should be, this is marriage	Healthier, more hygienic
Sexual spontaneity, etc	Less disturbance, more sleep
Makes for happier marriage	Cooler
Habit; always have used one	Modern idea
Keeps you together (psychologically)	More privacy
	More comfortable
Warmer	More freedom
More friendly, more intimate	
More comfortable	
More fun	

Double beds are preferred because they are 'the emblem of married life', because single beds 'don't seem like being married', or, as an older working man put it: 'Because in my days it was only double beds—we had none of these fancy notions'.

The reasons for preferring single beds, on the other hand, bear out Mr Packer's suggestion that varying temperamental needs can often make double beds the source of unnecessary contention. People speak feelingly of quarrels for the bedclothes, of being frightened to move, of being too hot, or too cold, and so on, in double beds. But there are many whose preference for a double bed is quite positive and personal, and who object to single beds on grounds of artificiality, a feeling of separation, etc, based on experience:

'I definitely think double beds, although we have single. I think with singles you grow apart—you know, if you have a quarrel—what is that saying about the sun going down on a quarrel?' (*middle class woman, 25*).

While, on the one hand, it is no doubt regrettable that many couples should use double beds for no other reason than 'it's the normal thing in the East End', the opposite trend towards using single beds for no better reason than that it is done in the West End also has its potential repercussions among the well-to-do. As one working class husband enigmatically put it, with single beds 'the husband and wife might get suspicious of one another'.

SETTLING IN

The Love Test Machines in amusement arcades and fairs settle your partner's character for a penny in one word: Red hot; Platonic; Passionate; Flirty; Bashful; Naughty; Fickle; Genuine; Ardent; Brand new; Amorous; Jealous.

When we asked single men and women what sort of a person they wanted to marry, only 4 per cent mentioned physical qualities, and their acknowledged verbal requirements were largely utilitarian, partly characterological. Men wanted their future wife to be home-loving and a good housekeeper. Women's ideal husbands had well-defined character and personality traits: they were men able to give their wives comfort and security; considerate, thoughtful and loving. Single people's ideas of the worst thing about marriage included prominently the dread of nagging wives or husbands, general disharmony or infidelity, and of being tied.

Asked what they thought were the best things about being married, single people ranged the top five factors in this rough order of precedence: children; freedom; a home of your own; companionship; having a house; and security. The stress was quite similar among married people, but they laid more emphasis on companionship, less on having a house, and spoke more of sharing things and helping one another, a factor which seldom occurred to the unmarried.

'Having a house' these days is a very long-term ideal. A survey in eight London boroughs and in Gloucester towards the end of the war showed the following relationship between the place in which families were living, and the length of time they had been married:*

	Percentage in each place		
Place	Five years Married or Less	5-10 years	More than 10 years
With relatives, sharing, etc	56	19	10
Flat, maisonette, self-contained part of house, etc	38	58	48
House	6	23	42

It is not surprising, then, that unmarried people's ideal of a house to themselves occurs less often after a few years' married reality. It is one of the best things about being married while marriage is still a dream, but the majority of couples today have many years to wait before they can achieve it.

We asked numerous married women for their main reason for marrying. Their answers ranged from love, a desire for a home, for children, for companionship, to less personal reasons like 'the war'. Their answers also showed the interesting varying stress as the years pass by. The longer people have been married, the less they are inclined to say they married for love; indeed, the less inclined they are to say why they married at all. Children seem most important in the middle period; and among the younger couples special war reasons account for the often hasty marriages of about one in nine.

In Poplar, Bermondsey and Shoreditch women said they married to have a home considerably more often than that they married for love. In Hampstead, Chelsea and Marylebone, the emphasis was reversed. In poorer districts the reasons for marrying which loom largest in people's minds are often profoundly negative ones. They want to escape from intolerable home conditions, of overcrowding or unsatisfactory relationships with parents:

'To get out of my Mum's house more than anything. My Mum and Dad were always squabbling; he's fond of his pint, and he used to have more than was good for him, and that used to set them off. I wanted to get married and have a home of my own and a bit of peace' (27, *married at* 18).

'Well, my mother died when I was three and my father married again and I had four step-sisters and one step-brother, and though my step-mother was all right, I always felt I was in the way. I suppose it was that more than anything' (27, *married at* 23).

SNAGS

Among the uncatered-for snags of married life, the most mentioned were: loss of freedom; too much work; too little money; difficulties with the children; other domestic friction; nagging; selfishness; and ill-health.

* These figures have comparative validity since they refer to couples living in the same parts of the areas covered, married for varying periods. They are not intended to have absolute validity, though they probably give a fair rough indication for urban areas. Gloucester showed more newly married couples sharing than the London districts covered.

This question was approached in two different ways in separate surveys, which produced rather different stresses, but similar complaints. The main difference between the sexes is that the wives complain of hard work, while the husbands complain of nagging; two aspects, perhaps, of the same problem?

Throughout our work on marriage and family life, the recurrent grumble we have found has concerned the wife being tied to the house, loss of freedom of movement, and an inability to take part in the outside pleasures and amusements of single life. A diminishing number of husbands agree with the one of sixty-five who, when asked what he and his wife had in common, replied simply: 'A wife's place is indoors.' But wives still stay indoors, because out of the married women questioned, about a third said they rarely or never went out in the evening at all.

CHILDREN

These observations bring us to the basic marriage 'problem', the underlying problem of national survival out of which, in the last analysis, our public interest in the private relationship between members of the smallest and most intimate unit in society has primarily arisen. 1946 was the year in which, had war not disturbed the trend of half a century, the population of Britain was due to start shrinking. The trend has been disturbed, and the postwar birthrate has soared. But a rising birthrate for a short while after the war had been predicted, and it will be some time before any indication of any permanent change can be assumed.

Despite cumulative publicity on the national need for larger families, three polls by the British Institute of Public Opinion during the past nine years show little difference in the number of people favouring a two-, three- or four-child family. The family of two heads the poll, with 39 per cent of votes; and only 4 per cent of British people today consider more than four children an ideal-sized family.

While a cross-section poll is valuable as an indication of the social trend, Mass-Observation found that people's ideas on the ideal family were strongly coloured by their own achievement. Those who have large families often say that large families are ideal, and indeed sincerely believe that they are, *once they have got them*. But existing evidence, strongly reinforced by the recent data on extra-marital conceptions, shows that knowledge and efficient use of contraceptive techniques is still very far from universal. We are left, as the Registrar General has cautiously put it, with a 'strong impression that a large proportion of our children continue to arrive other than at the conscious and deliberate intention of their progenitors'. Or, in the words of a mother of eleven children: 'I wanted two or three, not all the crowd I've got. I suppose we weren't of the same mind, and it takes two to be careful. You never know what will happen along in another nine months.'

BIPO's* results showed a steady diminution in the number of children in the ideal family of the old, middle and younger generations. On average, the national ideal worked out at nearly three children, an adequate replacement figure if it were achieved. Mass-Observation's results sought to eliminate the effect on people's expressed ideal of large families, 'ideal' once they exist, but often conceived in error and against the couple's wishes. This procedure reduced the average ideal family substantially, and produced, among couples married less than five years (the group to whom family-size is an immediate practical problem) an average of 2.5 children desired per family. Assuming that a substantial minority would, through infertility, sickness and other causes, be unable to achieve their ideal, if all families were effectively restricted through contraceptive control, the number of children would not be sufficient to replenish the race.

BIPO and Mass-Observation agree in finding only very slight differences between different income and educational levels in the number of children *desired*. Here is a further indication of the extent to which even our present limited supply of babies can be attributed to accidental conceptions and plans which have gone wrong. Among the working class, *coitus interruptus* is still among the most frequent means of birth control, and the women are frequently quite unaware of any contraceptive measures which they can use themselves.

CAUSES

The causes of the declining birthrate, and the measures which may be taken to increase it, are now under discussion by the Royal Commission. While married women themselves are quite prepared to give valid-sounding reasons for not wanting more children, their 'reasons' must not be taken too literally. For what they are worth, here they are:

Reason for not wanting more Children	Percentage of Women giving this Reason		
	Married 5 years and under	*5-10 years*	*More than 10 years*
Money	23	29	17
Work, responsibility	15	17	13
Children's chances (specified)	22	12	10
Inability to have more	2	7	19
Health	2	7	5
Future security	4	4	2
Housing	2	5	4
War reasons	2	3	4
Fear of childbirth	2	1	2
Husband trouble	0	3	1
Age	6	5	16
Other reasons	4	4	6
Vague	25	11	11

* British Institute of Public Opinion.

Dr Innes Pearce, of the Peckham Pioneer Health Centre, discusses the bearing on the birthrate problem of the fact that, among members of some fifteen hundred ordinary suburban families admitted to the Centre, nine-tenths were found on admission to be suffering from some pathological disorder, and of these seven-tenths were unaware that anything was wrong with them. She says:

'This unawareness does not mean that such persons are unaffected by the presence of their disorders. Quite the reverse is the case, for the body's very high endowment of reserve capacity to meet the day-to-day exigencies of living is, in the presence of pathological disorder, diverted to compensate for that disorder. But while this process of compensation masks the disorder and averts suffering, it nevertheless robs the individual of the use of his natural reserves for living. This fixation of reserves that should be fluid undermines the individual's natural confidence and spontaneous courage for adventure, and saps his zest for living. To meet this diminished capacity for action, he becomes an individual who all unconsciously retreats from his situation. In so doing, he is acting very properly in view of his condition, but being unconscious of why he is so acting, he now begins to rationalise. And as he casts about for reasons, there is no dearth of personal and general circumstances undesirable enough to become "rational" explanations, or "motives", for the avoidance of children. Such reasons or "motives" as he now gives for his action are not, however, the motivating *cause* of that action.'

From further analysis she draws the following conclusions:

That alleged 'motives' must be regarded as unreliable indications of the springs of action—no matter in what good faith they are given.

That a decline in fertility is a symptom of devitalisation—affecting rich and poor alike.

That external changes—better housing, children's allowances, etc—devised to remove alleged 'motives', will not, in fact, bring about a desire for children, so long as the populace is held in the grip of an intrinsic condition of devitalisation.

Peckham's conclusions are very similar to those reached almost contemporaneously by Mass-Observation from a quite different level of field experience. They may be compared with the plea of Dr James Halliday† for a consideration of the birthrate decline as a problem of psychosomatic medicine. Halliday links the declining birthrate to a weakening sense of community, and a resulting increase in individual social anxiety. Among several fascinating pointers to further study, he instances the fact that bottle-fed puppies develop a more nervous temperament than breast-fed puppies from the same litter. He queries the effect of increased bottle feeding among human babies and the withdrawal, on grounds of hygiene, of the old-fashioned 'dummy'.

Sense of isolation; nerves; social anxiety; lack of adventurousness; unwillingness to have children. This is the sequence suggested. If it should be proved correct in its application to the birthrate, its formulation will have repercussions upon the whole pattern, not only of marriage in Britain, but of contemporary social values in the Western world.

† *Psychosomatic Medicine and the Declining Birthrate* by James L. Halliday MD Glasgow (*Lancet*, May 12, 1945).

GENTLE REVOLUTIONARY

A portrait of Arthur Horner

by Giles Romilly

BIG drops of rain were falling on the grass, on to the heads of a crowd of thousands, who looked towards a florid-faced, pink-thumbed, open-waistcoated, showmanlike figure, gesticulating from a platform. The gestures became extravagant, the quips outrageous; and gradually those stolid miners' faces, immunised to Yorkshire climate, broke into delighted grins. For Mr Emanuel Shinwell, the Minister of Fuel and Power, having already handed out his speech-text, was having a lovely time saying whatever came into his fertile head. He cajoled. He paused. Then, with an air of comical distress, exclaimed:

'Where's the coal? Give me coal! Don't give me resolutions! I can't burn resolutions—though some of them ought to be burned!'

They chortled toughly; and a co-operative smile appeared on the face of a very small fellow, encased in a brown overcoat, who sat beside him on the platform. This little brown man, rather like a tiny brown wren, was Arthur Horner. He had said his piece; the meeting was obviously a success; the miners, who had let their output fall after the first flush of five-day enthusiasm, were simultaneously reproached and encouraged; and everything appeared to be straightforward. But it was not quite like that.

For near by was a bandstand-platform, with another eminent pair of speakers—the Right Honourable Clement R. Attlee, Prime Minister, and Lord Citrine. According to printed programmes, which the miners held, Shinwell and Citrine were to speak together on one platform, and on the other, Attlee and Horner. At the last hour, as the Prime Minister's party, with Horner in it, were speeding towards Doncaster in a reserved coach, the Labour Party Chief Whip had reshuffled the pack. For it had been decided that Attlee should make a foreign policy speech, developing a gloved attack on methods of government in Russia and the Eastern European satellite countries; and if Horner, speaking directly afterwards, had challenged this—as he would have—then the situation might have become embarrassing.

The incident is slight. Yet it piquantly characterises the career of Arthur Horner who, at 53, holds the dominant position of General Secretary of the National Union of Mineworkers, and is at the same time a leading Communist, with a seat on the Central Committee of his party; the first to wield such power in British affairs. Ostracised from the secret councils of the Labour leaders,

discouraged even from posing with them in photographs, after they have all been speaking together, but necessarily consulted, and independently powerful as leader of 700,000 miners, this sparrow-sized person is a man with many enemies, all of whom like him. Behind amiable blue eyes, shielded by an owlish pair of thick brown spectacles, sits both a gentle character and a ruthless doctrine. His enemies, detesting the doctrine, cannot find harsh words to describe the character. Baffled, some take refuge by accounting for him as a 'split personality'.

Split or not, three features principally distinguish him from the utility pattern of a British Trade Union leader. The first is coal. The second, Horner himself. The third, Communism.

The enormous circumstantial importance which coal confers only partly accounts for the interest, not to say fascination, which Horner's name arouses. Had he not risen through coal, he would have risen through something else. Elliptically shaped, fast-moving, the person with whom he instantly suggests comparison is Lord Beaverbrook. Nor does he mind being told so. He admires the vigorous ruthlessness by which, during the Battle of Britain, Beaverbrook got aircraft; his capacity to sacrifice the nearer to the farther good; his certainty that his perspective was correct. But, differences of principles apart, his personality has none of the aggressiveness of Beaverbrook's, though equal in courage. Both are first-rate talkers.

For anyone who is a natural parasite on a good conversationalist, Horner provides sustaining, humanly-seasoned and well-varied dishes, served hot and fast. This surprises at first. A homely-looking fellow, apt to the urban background as a London sparrow, he starts off with the homeliest kind of chat. His voice never rises above its natural easy pitch, and he never laughs—contrast the formidable Beaverbrook rasp!—but the mobile features express engaging animation, breaking frequently into likeable smiles. This surely is a person you have known for a very long time, though you never saw him till five minutes ago. Then comes a shock. The homely chat 'fades' through unperceived, incredibly rapid transitions, into dazzling fireworks. It's some trick, sleight of hand, how's it done? Impossible afterwards to put the pieces together again.

He is a first-rate reminiscer. Whether talking about the day before yesterday, or the Spanish War, or the personality of A. J. Cook, or the General Strike, or prison, or the Army, or Russia, or South Wales, his stories, covering a range of experience which seems to embody the entire social history of the last thirty years, have a masterly clarity, pith and sense. They are spotted, too, with vivid physical detail. He cuts a cameo at the same time as he makes a point. Remembering how, at Benecassim, in the high Spanish summer of 1937, he won back a gathering of deserters from the International Brigade by avoiding exhortation, and giving them instead a round by round account of Tommy Farr's 15-round stand against Joe Louis, he remembers also that this audience were all in bathing shorts. Such fusion of the analytical and the pictorial, characteristic of Horner, gives his conversation a distinguishing charm.

From the personal to the general, his mind moves with electric speed. Like a juggler's hands, it is as hard to follow. 'Collectively,' a member of the National Coal Board said once, 'we are no match for him individually.' He can step down the current when necessary. Pushing one hand back and forth through his brown hair, the other holding the telephone, he will repeat for the seventh or eighth time, in tones of exasperated and decisive but altogether friendly reasonableness, to some slow-witted crackle out of the depths of Monmouthshire or Clackmannan:

'Look, Bob! Will they ask for a ruling? Never mind about its being joint. Just tell them to ask for a ruling. That's all.'

Or, on some issue of shillings and pence:

'You're still selling labour. Bound to try and get the best price for what you're selling. We haven't yet got a Socialist society.'

And having at last hung up, will comment grinning: 'These fellows won't let go the bannisters for fear of falling downstairs.'

Horner shares, with Churchill, Beaverbrook, Napoleon, and most successful men, that indispensable attribute, a co-operative physical and nervous system. Athlete when young, he cannot remember ever having been ill. With ceaseless smoking, perpetual long journeys, speeches, conferences, meetings, a mass of complex business, coupled with exhausting conviviality, he puts a strain on his constitution, which it stands apparently. Next, mental speed and power, aided by a potent memory. The clarity and coherence of his mind, when coping with practical issues, are of the first order. He never falters for a word or an argument, returning the service almost before it has crossed the net. He is a pointed gun; multiple pom-pom. This accounts for a formidableness in debate, which all opponents concede. From Aneurin Bevan, with whom he clashed in the death-agonies of the 1926 strike, to Sam Watson, the 'orthodox' Durham miners' leader, chief foe of Communism inside their National Executive,

all testify to his power of stating a case, expert marshalling of facts, and 'closely-linked' arguments.

A Marxian theorist, Horner is also an exceptionally practical and realistic man. Marxists would claim that the theory moulds the practice; there is truth in that; but his practical roots are sunk very deep. His extraordinary knock-about life, association with every class, and immense Trade Union experience have given him a refinement, a sort of sixth sense, in practical judgment, which is beyond that of the 'Schoolmen' of his party. If a thing is desirable, but not possible, he will waste no time in thinking about it. At the same time—here the theory gives strength—he will advance to the absolute limit of what is possible. When the National Coal Board pleaded for a six months' postponement of Vesting-Day, urging their difficulties, their unpreparedness, Horner said: 'No'; he would only agree to 'note their difficulties'; but the thing was right, and possible, and must be done immediately. (They have twice offered him a £5,000-a-year job on the Board.)

Horner is also a courageous man. He has never been afraid to risk a decision, and to take the responsibility. When this leads to trouble, forensic skill extricates him. This year at Margate, with the entire Labour Movement gathered for its conference, he made a statement on behalf of the Communist Party which included a list of miners' claims. Wrathful at thus having their clothes stolen while they were out bathing, his own Executive summoned a special meeting, in order to repudiate him. That they did repudiate him is known; less known, that he turned this meeting, its atmosphere ominous with an 'at-last-I've-caught-you' spirit, into personal triumph; as he unfolded his case, proving point by point that he had said only what was already in the Miners' Charter (itself his creation), resolutions of disapproval, which had been brought prepared, were scrunched-up and dropped under the table; ears were scratched with pencils, jowls rubbed, heads averted; repudiation eventually couched in much milder form, reflecting no slur on his integrity.

'You object to this', he perorated, 'not because of what I've said, but because I've said it as a Communist. Yes, I am a Communist. Was there any doubt of that, when you elected me? If there was, or is, any, let me clear it up. No inducement, and no threat, will ever make me into anything different. Twenty years ago'—thus this Dimitrov!—'I watched your predecessors doing the same thing to A. J. Cook. Breaking his spirit. But there are two differences, which you may forget, between A. J. Cook and myself. Cook did not have a Communist Party behind him. I have. Cook was dying of cancer. I'm not.'*

Within his Union and among the Coal Board; before the war, with the suspicious South Wales coal owners; during the war, with the Ministry of Fuel and Power; Horner has enjoyed a reputation for performing promises, whether or not divergent from his own views. Individuals, who regard him as politically irresponsible, trust him

* This account is not from Horner himself.

industrially. He fought against the recruitment of Poles, but was defeated; and the Coal Board say he has done, and is doing, his best to honour the agreements.

On the personal side, he is good at making friends. He can win the liking of, say, a reserved man, whom others find difficult, by sympathetic reference to some personal misfortune. Arguing with a political opponent, he will be patting him on the knee, quite unselfconscious—never having seen him before! A well-known Labour MP, to whom 'totalitarianism' seems a worse danger than the Tories, commented after a fierce argument: 'Gosh! That's a charming fellow.' And these are not tricks; if they were, they would be detected. Behind them is a genuine sympathy with human beings. Horner is a naïve person, and the people who deal with him feel this, underneath his phenomenal cleverness. His close friend, Alf Davies, leader of the South Wales miners, says of him: 'Arthur is like a child.' It is true. He has the simplicity of a child. Not a widely-read man, outside his Marxist sphere, he nevertheless strikes one, because of this, as having the roots of culture in him. He is not narrow in the sense of those revolutionaries who say of art that it is 'what the average man likes' or 'a weapon of the struggle'. His is a receptive, non-excluding, sensibility. He listens; takes account carefully of a mental experience unfamiliar to him, and makes no crude comment. No doubt, he tries to understand everything; and values things, also people, not as instruments of the class war, but for their own sake, rather in spite of himself sometimes; the human being will conquer the professional revolutionary. He is also very good company, giving a great deal of himself, and quickening the pulse of life in sluggish companions. Such personal assets have more than a slight bearing on his success.

Horner gets hard qualities from his father, a rugged old English Liberal, for whom he has great respect. A retired railway supervisor, and Secretary of the local Co-op, James Horner is also the genius of the Independent Order of Rechabites, sworn to teetotalism and the observance of a strict moral code. From him, Horner learned that moral injunctions, as that you musn't tell lies, have to be practised literally; his father, he says, would 'never tell a lie, never compromise, never twist'. From him, too, Arthur learned tolerance. So did his brother Albert. A miner once, but now a near-capitalist, running a big oil depot in Nottingham, Albert is nearly a 'progressive'. But he handles his elder brother's dangerous politics with affectionate concern. 'Be on your guard, Arthur,' he says. 'They'll get you if they can.'

Born in a poor part of Merthyr Tydfil, Glamorganshire, on April 5 1894, second in a family of three boys and four girls, Arthur's earliest memories are of mining. At four, he watched miners breaking stones with hammers in Rhydycar Field, in order to earn their relief. His mother's father, black-bearded John Lewis (no relation of John L.), was blown to pieces in a pit. His mother was a milk-maid; small and gentle, but inflexible in her class pride; resisting ferociously her husband's occasional efforts to cut a genteel figure. Once, hearing her son broadcast, she exclaimed: 'Switch it off. That's not Arthur. That's an educated man.'

Bright in class, Arthur mounted to higher grade, but failed to win a County scholarship. He soon had to be earning shillings out of school. First, he turned a butcher's sausage-machine for 1s 6d a week. Then he was in a barber's shop, lathering 'dirty drunken faces', till he ran out screeching. Then came the grocer's shop. The twelve-year boy was harnessed to a truck running on little wheels. The Nicolls brothers, owners of this shop, were lay preachers. They became interested in Arthur, and began to wrestle for his soul. Chapel was then, for those wanting self-improvement, chafed by their narrow bonds, the only resource. But the brothers had some struggle. 'We've got Arthur, Mr Horner,' they would cry, hopefully. Then, doleful: 'He's gone again, Mr Horner.' At last they triumphed. 'Brother Horner', fourteen, became a missionary for the Baptist faith. Clothed in white samite, mystic, phenomenal, he travelled the Welsh valleys, preaching the Word of Christ in plain stone Temples. First raptures subsiding, the business-minded elders began to doubt whether this angel-child was, in fact, quite what was needed. It irked shopowners to be told, in accents clear and pure, that the Sermon on the Mount entailed payment of a minimum wage.

'I was eloquent,' says Horner, 'and a little objectionable, because I always materialised the questions.'

At fifteen, the Baptist boy had joined the Independent Labour Party; Keir Hardie was at the House of Commons, in his cloth cap, as member for Merthyr, and the Nonconformism of South Wales fermented with the yeast of radical politics. Then war came, the elements split. Horner denounced the war. He wrote for the *Merthyr Pioneer* on 'Christianity and Socialism' and 'The Cult of Hate'. The deacons, furious, set about censoring his sermons, so he abandoned his mission, and started discussions with some advanced Marxists in the Rhondda; from these emerging, after weeks of argument, a convinced Marxist.

Thus, when Horner started talking politically, he had already had many years' experience of stating a case. His life thenceforth became an argument, the argument a fight. Words, books, ideas, had only a polemical function. Through the 1914-18 war it was a fight against the war, involving aliases, sudden changes of address. Afterwards began the long fight for the miners. He was in Carmarthen jail for refusing to obey military orders when the Mardy colliers elected him checkweighman; and got out by a hunger and thirst strike. Mardy was 'Little Moscow', Horner, (incongruously) the 'Little Tzar'. He was in and out of prison. He visited revolutionary Russia. When, in 1919, the Communist Party of Great Britain was formed out of some small Left groups, he became a foundation member. This period reached its climax in the General Strike of May 1926, when the working class first tested its united strength, in an effort to save the hours and wages of the miners.

The General Strike was called off after nine days, but the miners held out for seven months. Horner was one of a contingent of delegates from South Wales to the conferences of the Miners' Federation, held in London, in the Kingsway Hall. Aneurin Bevan was another. They were both young, and neither yet nationally known. But their abilities and clear policies marked them out, and they were as horse-flies on the sluggish body of the meetings, and especially of old Herbert Smith, the Federation's tenacious and ox-like, but inflexible, President.

Mr. A. Horner (*South Wales*): The resolution that I want to submit to the Conference . . .

Chairman: Had you not better let us submit our resolution, and then you can give us some stick if it does not suit?

Mr. Horner: I thought you asked for one.

Chairman: No! We will submit one, and if you want to move a resolution, if you want to go outside and try to condemn somebody, then I shall be Mussolini for the time being . . .

Afterwards the arguments were continued in the National Hotel, Russell Square. Horner and Bevan formed themselves into a kind of spiritual bodyguard over the pathetic genius, A. J. Cook, heart and voice of the miners' movement, who was liable to issue embarrassing statements, and to swerve from firm policy. As the months dragged on, and the resources of the Federation dwindled, hope also sank; groups of miners, who overnight had promised to stay out, next morning drifted back; more and more delegates urged acceptance of the owners' terms; and at last only Horner and Bevan were for prolonging the fight. There came a day when these two diverged. Aneurin Bevan rose up in the Kingsway Hall, and urged the Conference to order district negotiations. Bitter argument followed in the National Hotel that night. Aneurin cried that they must retreat in order to preserve the 'homogeneous miners' Union'. 'In no circumstances', Horner contended, 'must a revolutionary be associated with a defeat.'

That was twenty years ago. But it poses the issue of Horner's relationship with the Communist Party. Critics claim that he allowed his practical good sense to be overridden by the theoretic preconceptions of Marxism. The charge, repeated in many later instances, amounts to this, that Horner, because he is a Communist, cannot be relied upon to pursue a sensible policy, adjusted to changing needs. 'A practical knowledgeable,

Arthur Horner: family man, Communist, miners' leader—*but not much of the traditional revolutionary to be seen in the merry, benevolent features of 'this little brown man, rather', as Giles Romilly says, 'like a tiny brown wren'*

empirical, British worker,' one critic calls him, 'with his feet on the ground and his head in the Russian clouds.' Anxiety is increased by the influence, in Communist inner circles, of certain intellectuals, remote from Trade Union obligations. Furthermore, even when apparently sensible, is the policy ultimately a patriotic one?

To some, these objections make Horner's name anathema; they hate his present power, and dread the use they think he will make of it; the fact that he is a likeable man, disarming, and apparently also patriotic, makes it worse. Those who have dealt with him directly, in national negotiations, concede his far-sighted practical judgment, and find no indications of a hidden subservience; they nevertheless suspect, regretfully, that he must be 'under some measure of duress', and that a situation might arise which would oblige him, having never yet mentally faced this 'dualism' (they say), to choose between the practically patriotic, and the theoretically Communist; in which case, though strongly inclined to give him the benefit of the doubt, they can't be certain what would be his choice.

The answer? First, Horner *is* a Communist. Secondly, the patriotism or otherwise of Communist policy is a matter for argument, but not here. Thirdly, the theoretic and the practical are not necessarily in conflict. The practical man may at some moment not know what to do next, when the man of theory, who is also practical, does. It is the mere theorist who makes faulty practical judgments; and critics, who point to episodes in Horner's life as examples of a conflict between theory and practice as such, have, I think, got it wrong. It is not, in these cases, that he has abandoned theory; but that he has backed his own judgment, against that of other theorists, in the application of it.

Consider two instances:

The Communist Party, during the depression of 1929-31, placed emphasis on the 'role' of unemployed workers; even Unions, owing to the remoteness of their higher bureaucrats, were regarded with some distrust. Horner opposed this, describing it as a 'glorification of negative features'; the organised employed working class was still, he said, the 'decisive element'. Called upon to admit himself wrong, he refused. The Party, through the *Daily Worker*, attacked his policy, christening it 'Hornerism'. He looked up the constitution of the Communist International, and discovered that any member could appeal to it, in defence of the 'correctness' of his doctrine. He did appeal, and so came about the unique spectacle of Horner, with the intellectuals of the Party, travelling to Moscow, in order—as someone says—'to be fumigated!' Kuusinen, Dimitrov, and others, sat on the case; and pronounced after many months that Horner had been guilty of indiscipline, but that his ideas must be considered.

Secondly, in company with Harry Pollitt, he did not accept the Communist reversal of policy which overnight in 1939 converted the war against Hitler into an 'Imperialist War'. He said that it was a war against Fascism,

and never wavered from saying so. Consequently, when the *Daily Worker* was sued for libel by Lord (then Sir Walter) Citrine and George Hicks, on account of an article accusing them of leading the workers to death in the interests of imperialists, it was obliged to call Horner into the witness-box—to prove that Communists were fighting the war anyway!—since he, leading the miners, was the only one of them, apart from Harry Pollitt, who was. At the same time that the defence wanted proof of that, it also wanted him to avoid saying anything against the Party Line—which condemned the war! Indeed a difficult situation. And not the only one. For Horner, supporting Britain's war against Hitler, simultaneously supported Russia's war against Finland, when Russia was Hitler's ally. Pro-Finnish feeling was dominant, in the Labour movement as elsewhere; Citrine and Philip Noel-Baker themselves travelled to Finland, in order to discuss means of sending the Finns help. The Trade Unions were raising money. Among them, the South Wales Miners' Federation voted £100. Horner, then their Secretary, refused to sign the cheque; he was violently attacked. For him, ostracised by his own party because he wanted to fight the war, cold-shouldered by the Labour movement because of Russia, and branded inside his Union as a 'Dictator', this period, until the Russian invasion, was a lonely and difficult one.

All this points to a character which has preserved, in the face of various pressures, the right to think independently; which therefore will never become, in the full sense, that of a professional revolutionary. On the other hand, it was his judgment, *as a Communist*, which was correct, against the judgment of other Communists. It is therefore probable that his particular brand of undoubtedly sincere Communism, tinged with national pride, will involve him, at some future date, in yet more testing troubles; that the 'dualism' of which his critics speak will yet confront with terrible decisions a man who never yet has been afraid of decisions.

On the day that he landed in England, following his 'fumigation' in Moscow, Horner was arrested, and shortly afterwards tried, convicted and sentenced by Lord Branson to hard labour for fifteen months; since, on the day before leaving England, he had prevented seizure of furniture from an unemployed worker's home; and that itself was the day after he had unsuccessfully fought a Parliamentary election. A sequence altogether characteristic! Leaving Wormwood Scrubs in 1918, where he had spent six months for refusing to obey military orders, he found himself resisting recruitment for the war of intervention against revolutionary Russia, and was immediately again charged; two years this time, and to be drummed out of the regiment.

'An error, Mr Horner, I'm sure!' cried General Sir Godwin Reade-Austen, Chairman of the Coal Board's South Wales Division, when he was told about this.

'No, no, General,' said Horner, 'they were perfectly right.'

All that, and much else, is behind him now—for the time being. His Secretaryship of the Mineworkers can only be terminated, according to their constitution, by death or 'misconduct'—which doesn't mean Communism. His working day, a heavy one, starts at seven in bed with a cup of tea and a cigarette. Supine, he reviews impending problems, then puts them out of his mind. This technique was acquired from a novel by Jack London (a favourite author), called *Straightjacket*, in which the hero, pushed into a straightjacket, 'dies'—and lives another life. 'If you can concentrate,' says Horner, 'you can shut out the rest of the world'.

He likes to have either a great deal to do, or nothing. Usually it's a great deal. After a breakfast of tea and toast, he hurries down his suburban road, indistinguishable among shopowners and minor civil servants, to a tube train. He has the Welsh time sense: mentally punctual, physically late. As soon as he has reached his leather chair, in decayed ground south of the river, overlooking a Salvation Army hostel, he seems to have been there hours already, so instant is the resumption of many-branched activity. In this office, where wall-charts show the Dolomite shapes of rising coal-output, with sudden precipitous drops entitled 'Oaks' or 'St Leger', one is reminded abruptly of Nationalisation, the Five-Day Week, the Miners' Charter; of silicosis and pneumoconiosis, death by fire-damp or roof-fall, rehabilitation, compensation, day wages and piece rates, slum valleys and subsiding houses, pit-head baths, clubs, amenities; of the hard base of struggle and uncompleted achievement on which this career rests; of the miners themselves, commenting: 'Horners don't grow on every tree!' There is, for different reminders, a cream-glazed head of Lenin. But such, among these intensely practical issues, are as a far-off echo.

The telephone rings: Lord Hyndley. A point about five-day 'anomalies', a point about Poles. A Coal Board car will call for Mr Horner; in half an hour. Meanwhile, he has just time to prepare some speech notes, for a discourse on the economic situation to the 'League for Imperial Defence', at the invitation of General Sir William Slim. The secretary will buy his ticket for the night train to Scotland, for a Labour Relations conference. Here are some legal notes; and Alf Davies on the telephone from Cardiff, reporting about colliery clerks; needing instruction. The car is waiting. But the notes? Five minutes. 'Right you are!' Then away, over the river, through the traffic, to a conference with Lord Hyndley and Sir Arthur Street; with whom, as with Emanuel Shinwell, Horner works closely and cordially. Note here, he has always got on best with men who, absolutely antipathetic to his politics, can ignore them altogether, and take him on his merits as a negotiator; it is so with Hyndley and Street; was so, during the war, with Major Gwilym Lloyd George, with Lord Portal

and Sir Andrew Duncan; and before the war with Jestyn Williams, then Secretary of the South Wales coalowners, now, under Ebby Edwards, the Board's chief labour officer. With such, politics in abeyance, he enjoys crossing swords. The more Machiavellian, the more he likes them. Thus swallowed-up, his friends won't see him again until, after waiting perhaps more than an hour for a promised 5.30, in the kaleidoscopically-activated dazzle of the hallway of a huge popular hotel, they spot suddenly a small figure, advancing on them at great speed, firing from the hip a volley of explanations, happenings and excuses. And there may be one man there, who stands watching this exhibition with grave brown eyes; who consults pointedly his wrist-watch; nods; refuses to smile; in front of whom, eventually, the engaging voice falters, the stream of excuses dries up. That grave fellow, with the calm, inquisitorial eyes, firm-closed lips, and high, able forehead, is the only man in England who can twist Horner's easy smile into an uneasy grin, like a guilty schoolboy's; the only man also, apart from his father, to whom Horner, in whose nature exists this need for loyalty, accords his unreserved esteem. He is Harry Pollitt, boilermaker, and General Secretary of the Communist Party of Great Britain.

As for Mrs Horner, massive, serene-tempered, she has long since ceased to hope for early evening returns.

'We moved from South Wales,' she explains, in musically calm tones, 'so that Arthur could be more at home. But he's more away now than ever'.

Away, but present, for this pocket-dynamo has the knack of seeming to be simultaneously in all places. Just now, he is a junction-point in British affairs; the hub of a wheel, whose spokes radiate out to the Coal Board, to the Ministries, to his Union, to the Labour and Trade Union movement generally, and to many important centres of industrial and commercial life. As such, he is exactly adjusted to circumstances. His talents are just those which the situation requires. He advances his two-fisted policy, of getting the miners their rights, and the country its coal; fights unofficial strikes, absenteeism and restrictive practices in the interests of production and of recovery; and checks the dreams of millions by a rock-steady regard for facts. In this situation, where not only his political hopes, but his aspirations for the miners, are able to be in accord with the wider needs of national policy, he can function effectively. But this situation is itself a point of suspension, holding him up. The greatest national difficulties have not yet been reached. Divergences of policy, masked at present, have not yet fully declared themselves. Furthermore, Horner himself is a developing character; a man whose zenith has not yet been reached; whose full stature circumstances have not yet measured.

He raises, therefore, questions, economic, political and more widely speculative, which cannot yet be answered; and will not be, until his own actions are obliged to answer them.

STORM OVER STEVENAGE

by Mark Benny

The suburban sprawl, sterilising good farmland and defacing Britain with an ever-spreading rash of bungalows, is piling up acute social problems. To control it, the Government has undertaken to build eight new towns at a suitable distance from London. In this study of the birth of a satellite town, the conflicts of private and public interests take vivid form, and the author emphasises the very great importance of psychological as well as physical planning

A YEAR ago there were few places in England, outside the walls of Dartmoor, where the litanies of hatred and violence were mouthed so roundly as in the charming little Hertfordshire town of Stevenage. In farmhouse kitchens and Queen Anne drawing rooms, in the gaunt Council Chamber and the discreet lounge of the Cromwell Hotel, the same hoarse and heady splutterings were heard. ' I'd willingly do a month just to lay my hands on him ', a modest young corn merchant assured me. A distinguished local squire, pausing thoughtfully as he opened his front door, asked: ' D'you think it'd be any good if I planted a time bomb in his office?'

It is difficult, for those who have met him privately, to equate the volume and intensity of this hatred with the shy, glum, incurably cautious figure of Mr Lewis Silkin, Minister of Town and Country Planning. In England it normally takes a more histrionic politician to arouse such outsize emotions—a Dizzy, a Lloyd George or a Churchill. Instead we have a hard-working solicitor of

sedentary habits, who eats hearty meals, masks his social timidity in an ill-fitting bluffness, and limits himself rigidly to one cigar a day with three on Sundays. Yet it is this man whom the no less mild citizens of Stevenage abhorred more intimately than they have abhorred any public figure since the demise of Hitler. His unexceptional character reminded them only of the more sanguinary figures of the French Revolution, of Dr Crippen and Lenin, who also had their sober bourgeois aspects. They saw him as the more dangerous because he is so like them —a kind of political *doppelgänger* stalking them quietly in their own image, pervading their ordered lives with a dark casual lawlessness.

For a town set plumb on an arterial road within thirty miles of Charing Cross, and with its own four-track railway station to boot, Stevenage has remained remarkably unaffected by the successive waves of migration towards, and away from, the Metropolis. Since the turn of the century, Stevenage has added only two thousand

The Great North Road divides the Stevenage of today, dominates its economy. A convenient coaching-sta

to the four thousand inhabitants it started with. Through the steam age and the petrol age it has carried, almost unscathed, the characteristics acquired in the days when Macadam laid a new surface on the Great North Road and gave a fresh impetus to the stage-coach business. The broad High Street, with its charming early Georgian façades, is a coachman's creation; and although the inns have diminished in number, a tradition of good eating and drinking still survives in the three or four remaining hostelries. Behind the High Street lies the compact little network of streets where the townsfolk live, early Victorian cottages succeeded by mid-Victorian villas, and then a raw row or two of Council houses. Newcomers to the town have tended to build their properties apart, on the undeveloped side where the railway runs.

These newcomers have been the kind of people a small town can afford to welcome—business men from London, or retired couples living on their savings. They have not competed for jobs in the three small factories, or for trade with the 105 shopkeepers. Indeed, in the years between the wars, when one and a quarter million people found homes in the Greater London area, and less than a thousand of them were attracted to Stevenage, the townspeople began to feel that they could afford to welcome many more of the same sort. The local Councillors, in particular, noticed with approval that the rateable value of properties in the district was increasing much more rapidly than its population, and they looked round for ways of encouraging this happy tendency.

In 1937 Stevenage took to town-planning in a light-hearted, optimistic fashion. Mr Culpin, a resident town-planning consultant, was called in by the Urban District Council to draw up a zonal development scheme. His plan caught admirably the Council's mood. Large, attractively coloured patches on an ordnance map indicated where terrace after terrace of owner-occupiers were to inhabit the gentle, well-wooded slopes to the

east and north of the town. A small, striped patch down in the south-west corner betokened a modest industrial zone. The Council inspected the new plan with admiration—and frowned when an awkward Labour councillor wanted to know what the population of the developed Stevenage was to be. The consultant had forgotten to provide the figures, and the committee adjourned for a month so that he could make the necessary calculations. The answer turned out to be 34,000.

In those days local development schemes had to be approved by the Ministry of Health, and Mr Culpin's Stevenage plan took its place in the long queue of similar projects submitted to the Ministry of Health. The war came before approval was granted. Later, an expert with an idle hour on his hands calculated that it would have been possible to house the entire population of England and Wales on the land zoned for development in the Greater London area.

During the war years, Stevenage, like the rest of the country, had little time to spare for town-planning projects. But an influx of war workers and evacuees kept alive the elementary problem of housing. When peace came the Stevenage Council was ready with a building programme for 350 new houses, on a detached estate with its own community centre. Its earlier hankerings for high-class dormitory development found expression in the publication of an official Guide, designed to attract the professional classes.

The *Official Guide and Handbook* is a remarkable tribute to the unclouded innocence of Stevenage worthies at that time. It dwells lovingly on the historical associations of the neighbourhood. It speaks alluringly of the old-established shopkeepers 'who do not overlook in these most difficult modern times the importance of personal attention to their customers'. It describes the many charming walks to be had in the surrounding countryside. The one distinction not mentioned in its pages is that, while the official guide was still being

eighteenth century, it is now a lunch-time car park for passing motorists attracted by its Georgian inns

Photographs by Jan Oplatka

prepared, Stevenage was assigned an important role in the new world by Abercrombie's Greater London Plan.

Yet the oversight is easily understood. First issued in December 1944, in singularly perplexing, uncertain times, the Greater London Plan received only perfunctory attention from the public. The Press summarised it, and unanimously agreed that it was a monumental and inspired contribution to the complex problems of postwar reconstruction. A major recommendation was that eight large satellite towns—each with a self-contained population of 60,000—should be developed in the Outer Country Ring. Ten possible sites were mentioned for the new towns, of which Stevenage was one. Since the alternative was an unplanned sprawl, no one at the time questioned the necessity for such satellite towns.

A few months later Stevenage was given another opportunity to catch up on itself. The Greater London Plan was made available to the public in a handsome illustrated volume; and simultaneously an exhibition based upon it was opened in London by the man whose appointment as Minister for Town and Country Planning in the new Labour Government had been announced only a week before. But again world events were conspiring to distract Stevenage from its own fate. On the same day that Mr Silkin's appointment was announced, the first atomic bomb was dropped on Hiroshima.

So for another eight months conversation in the comfortable lounges of the local hotels ranged with placid variety over matters of secondary importance. Electioneering for a new local Council started, and it was agreed that Stevenage would show the country that here was one town where Labour was kept in its place.

On March 6, 1946, Mr Lewis Silkin made a brief statement on the policy of His Majesty's Government with regard to the planning of London. The conclusions of the Barlow Commission had been accepted. The overall growth of London must be restrained. A planned programme of decentralisation to the areas beyond the green belt must replace the bungaloid scatter of the interwar years. To these ends the Government would work along the lines proposed by Sir Patrick Abercrombie in his Greater London plan.

At last a rustle of rumour spread through the town, and mention of town-planning began to appear in the local election addresses. The Labour party candidates supported the idea of the Stevenage development scheme; the Tories opposed it; neither group had very clear ideas of what was involved. But fresh intimations came daily. The town was mentioned in the deliberations of the Hertfordshire County Council. Government officials visited the Council offices and talked cautiously about water supplies and sewage disposal. On March 12, the local Member of Parliament put a written question to the Minister, and received a reply which began: 'The Government propose that an immediate start should be made with the development of a satellite town at Stevenage'.

Here it was at last, clear and unambiguous. The local electioneering took up the phrase 'satellite town' and made an issue of it. Fearsome word pictures of Dagenham and Becontree were painted by the Tories—and Stevenage, with a shudder, returned only two of the Government supporters. For a moment the townsfolk seemed to feel that they had exorcised the Government devils: a week or so later a local merchant—who afterwards became an outstanding figure in the 'Residents' Protection Association'—purchased (at an outrageously swollen figure) a cottage in the locality, as a wedding present for his son about to be demobilised from the RAF.

The situation had become ticklish. Stevenage was not averse to development—on its own terms. But when it tried to measure these against the Government's terms, a kind of despair seized the newly-elected Urban District Council. The members had been informed that their town was to be the subject of a bold new experiment, that a town of 60,000 people, with industries enough to provide local employment for all, was to be developed within their statutory area. But how the developing was to happen, who was to do it or what the detailed plans were—none of this could they find out. It was to the Council that the people turned for information. The Council could tell them nothing. A deputation of members invited themselves to the Ministry, and were shown some tracing-paper plans but they were unable to take the plans away to study at leisure. Since the Council was predominantly Conservative, it was inevitable that the Ministry's attitude should be construed as a high-handed bureaucratic disregard of local liberties. The real explanation was, of course, almost exactly the reverse. The physical and administrative detail of the New Town Plan was based on the provisions of the New Towns Bill, which was still being drafted. To divulge any part of the contents of this document before it was formally laid on the table of the House would offend a jealously-guarded constitutional right.

While the Ministry continued democratically to hold its tongue, and Stevenage murmured increasingly against this totalitarian silence, the New Towns Committee report was published. Here it was recommended that the new towns should, in general, be developed by independent public corporations, who would hold on lease from the Government all the land required for their purpose and would be empowered to build and supply essential services. On April 17, the New Towns Bill was presented to Parliament, and ordered to be printed. When it reached the hands of Stevenage Councillors a week later, it was clear that the Minister had accepted the Committee's recommendation. Stevenage would be developed by a public corporation.

The language of Parliamentary lawyers does not make easy reading, and while the more industrious Stevenage worthies were scratching their heads over the intricate financial clauses of this Bill, they were subjected to a second, and more deadly, dose of legal verbiage. On the morning of April 24, nearly 200 local householders came down to breakfast to find a letter from the Treasury Solicitor on their doormat. It was headed *Town and Country Planning Act*, 1932 (*Section 35*), went on to speak darkly of powers conferred on the Minister to acquire land either by agreement or compulsorily, invited the freeholder to sell his property at terms 'acceptable to the Minister', and required a reply within 28 days.

The fury aroused by this communication was instant and unbounded. At the railway station that morning commuters clustered in the first and fiercest of the informal conferences which have turned the island platform into a Roman forum. Later the same day the journalists began to arrive in the town. The anti-Government newspapers saw the makings of some excellent political capital in the shape of things at Stevenage. From now on, every small rumour of the Ministry's intentions in Stevenage was to be distended on the sounding-board of the national Press, every hard case was to be magnified into a tragedy, every bar-room grumble to be dignified as an heroic fight for freedom.

All this uproar had clearly taken the Ministry's officials by surprise, and it was nearly a week before they made any response. On May 1, in the window of the local Gas Company showroom, a large coloured masterplan of the New Town was exhibited. The drawing was highly stylised, and sparing in detail. Even the most accomplished reader of town-planning conventions could gather no more than that the layout conformed to the accepted modern principles. But there were anti-Government Pressmen at hand to foster the sense of injury in affected parties. Local shopkeepers had it explained to them that the existing Stevenage formed merely one 'neighbourhood unit' in the plan, and an outlying one at that; so that their secret hopes of multiplying their trade by ten were baseless. Farmers saw their arable land blocked in for building sites, or straddled by an arterial by-pass. Country-lovers found their favourite views despoiled by factories. But most welcome feature of the plan, from the point of view of Opposition journalists, was the projected demolition of Fairview Road to allow the unhampered development of the industrial zone.

Fairview Road, a recent creation of ugly villas on the

continued on page 48

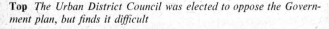

Top *The Urban District Council was elected to oppose the Government plan, but finds it difficult*

Centre *Stevenage tradesmen know nothing of queues, and fear the incalculable effects of new crowds and new competitors*

Bottom *This farmer will have the diverted Great North Road brought to the boundaries of his land. On balance he welcomes the change, but other farmers in the neighbourhood are either less fortunate or less philosophical*

Stevenage: the test case for Town and Country Planning

From the air Stevenage already shows the typical wastefulness of dormitory development. The Great North Road remains the main axis of the town's being, but in building between the wars the railway exercised an increasing counter-attraction. Six thousand inhabitants without a common plan have spread themselves, heedless of the natural amenities of the site. 50,000 Londoners from overcrowded areas will be attracted to the new town. The master plan provides residential areas on the high rolling ground to south and east, and an industrial area on the flat land between the railway and the Great North Road. The old town will remain a distinct entity. Parks in each area make cunning use of valleys and high points. The social and administrative centre, set between works and homes, is a focus for both. Green belts bring the country into the heart of the town, and improved transport services will link the whole area with London.

Map by W. Ritchie

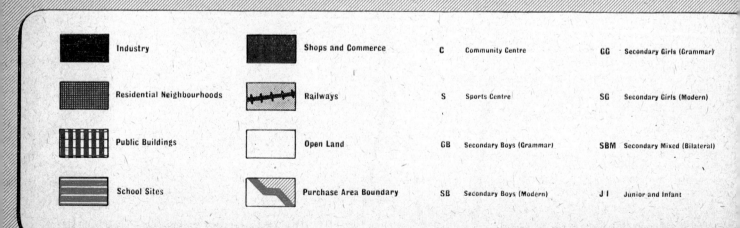

■	Industry	■	Shops and Commerce	C	Community Centre	GG	Secondary Girls (Grammar)
	Residential Neighbourhoods		Railways	S	Sports Centre	SG	Secondary Girls (Modern)
	Public Buildings		Open Land	GB	Secondary Boys (Grammar)	SBM	Secondary Mixed (Bilateral)
	School Sites		Purchase Area Boundary	SB	Secondary Boys (Modern)	J I	Junior and Infant

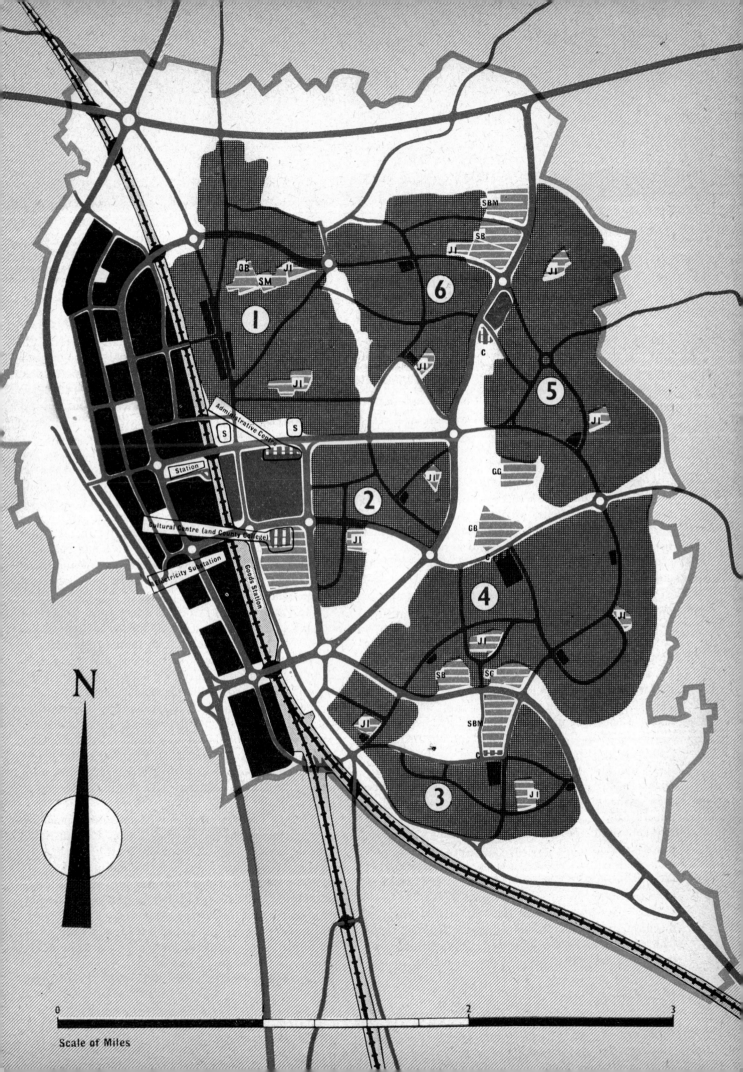

Administrative Centre

S

S

Station

Cultural Centre (and County College)

Electricity Substation

Goods Station

GB

SM

JI

JI

SBM

SB

JI

JI

c

JI

JI

GG

GB

c

JI

JI

SB

SG

SBM

c

JI

JI

1

6

2

5

4

3

N

0   2   3

Scale of Miles

The other face of Stevenage—where scraggy fields meet an untidy conglomeration of backyards. Here there are few amen

'wrong' side of the railway, is inhabited chiefly by respectable people in the lower income groups, many of them retired pensioners. Inevitably some of these houses, purchased through building societies, have not yet been cleared of debt; a few others have been mortgaged at 1945 valuations. In most of them the gardens, after years of loving labour, are just beginning to look their best. There were enough hard cases in Fairview Road to flood the Fleet Street bars with knee-deep tears.

After allowing the people five days to study the plan, the Minister came to Stevenage on May 6, where he was to hold a conference with the Council and address a public meeting. It had been assumed, no doubt, that the five days would have been passed in responsible discussion of the merits and demerits of the plan. Instead the talk was so wild and incendiary that the Town Clerk had to appeal to the County authorities for additional police protection for the Minister. Mr Silkin arrived in the town in the morning, and, amid a wild scramble of Press men and news-reel photographers, paid visits to some of the threatened householders, assuring them that they would not be dispossessed until satisfactory alternative accommodation was provided for them. In the evening, at a meeting so packed that the greater part of his audience had to listen to the proceedings relayed by loudspeakers in the High Street, he gave a reasoned account of Government policy. There were frequent and rowdy interruptions, and for a moment he was stung into undiplomatic language. 'It is no use jibbing,' he said, 'it's going to be done'. The property-owners of Stevenage, who had hitherto suspected him of totalitarian tendencies, were now convinced. The Minister left the meeting to find that gravel had been flung into the engine of his car. Behind him, in the hall, outraged citizens discussed the formation of a Residents' Protection Association, and £40 was collected on the spot towards a fighting fund.

Three days later the new Association held a public meeting of its own. A resolution opposing the New Town plan was passed by the audience of 500 with only two dissident votes. Other bodies lined up for the attack. The parish councils of the two local villages passed resolutions demanding a public inquiry. The Hertfordshire National Farmers' Union passed a resolution in support of the 40 farmers threatened with dispossession. Nor was the Stevenage urban district council idle. The following week it organised a referendum. In a 52 per cent poll, 1,316 votes were cast against the plan, 913 were cast for it, and 282 votes favoured a modified plan.

The organisers of this referendum were surprised and disconcerted by its results. They had overlooked the fact that the other half of Stevenage inhabitants had nothing to lose and everything to gain by living in a larger town. And small as it is, it is easy to overlook the other half in a place like Stevenage. The workers live in their own part of the town, they use different pubs and belong to different organisations. In an exclusive residential town of this kind property-owners tend to be more interested in the wealthier than in the poorer of their neighbours.

The 1,200 votes in favour of a new town seemed on enquiry to have been cast largely for the coming generation. Workers, it is true, look to the new Stevenage to provide a wider choice of occupations. But much more definitely and unanimously they hope for better schooling and a wider social life for their children.

The attitudes which found summary expression in those 1,316 opposition votes warrant closer attention. There is no doubt that it was dominantly a property-owner's vote. And there is no doubt that the major grievances associated with the Stevenage project were against the conditions directly affecting the ownership of local property.

The legal position was clear. Effective town-planning is impossible unless the planning agency has full rights over the area concerned. Therefore the Minister had to exercise his statutory powers to become the sole land-owner in the New Town. The statutory scale of compensation, based on 1939 valuations plus an addition of up to 60 per cent for owner-occupiers, would be applied. Unless the property were scheduled for other purposes, the former owner would be given a 99 year lease in exchange for his freehold, rent to take into account the amount of compensation paid. Where the occupier was

be sacrificed but familiarity with the scene above would make most residents hostile to even the most tactful changes

to be displaced, comparable alternative accommodation was first to be provided elsewhere in the town.

But these legal arrangements take little stock of the deep-seated cultural attitudes which cluster round English country houses. In the literature of no other country will you find so many novels and poems devoted to the subtleties of house-furnishing, the agonies of house-moving, the triumphs of house-inheritance. It was the dumb urge of countless small people to have their own little house in the country which produced the squalid conurbations and ribbon development of the inter-war period. This was only partly a move from urban congestion to rural spaciousness; it was even more definitely a move from leasehold to freehold possession. The 'little freehold property' is one of the most obscurely powerful of our national gods. And among the Stevenage residents are many who have made heavy sacrifices at that strange altar. To them the change of tenure they are asked to accept passively, from freehold back to leasehold, seems like social demotion, a wanton thrusting back to the class from which they have spent their best years in escaping.

Sharper still is the blow to those whose houses are scheduled for demolition at later stages of the plan. The Stevenage they know and like is a small rural town with an 'exclusive' atmosphere. The Stevenage in which they will be offered alternative accommodation will be a large town, inhabited by people from the less salubrious parts of London. Yet to buy another house in another small town would cost double what the Government offers by way of compensation. They resent bitterly the fact that they can only recover their social satisfactions at some considerable financial sacrifice.

And here we catch sight of another strand in the network of attitudes underlying the Stevenage opposition. The declared policy of the Ministry is to build up 'balanced communities' in each neighbourhood unit of the new towns. The intention here is to prevent the physical stratification of income-levels into 'districts'. 'I do not want', said Mr Silkin when introducing his Bill to the House, 'the better-off people to go to the right and the less well-off to go to the left'. But in fact the better-off

people—and there is always somebody better off than somebody else—want to go to the right. The possibility that London slum-dwellers might have gardens adjacent to theirs, that squawling brats with intolerable habits of speech might corrupt the accents of their own offspring, that visiting friends might assume they live in a working-class neighbourhood because they can't afford a better —such considerations outweigh the remoter advantages of balanced communities far more than people will admit.

But in the many speeches made against the Stevenage Plan during the summer months little was said about such feelings and attitudes. Criticism preferred to dress itself in more fashionable colours. The New Town project, it was said, offended against every accepted canon of town-planning. It was situated too near London to be a self-contained town; and the local railway could not be developed to take the traffic of another large dormitory town. The industrial zone was placed where the prevailing wind would blow smoke and fumes across the residential zones. The residential zones were set where the prevailing winds would in winter freeze the inhabitants to death. Excellent agricultural lands were being sterilised by the project. Water supply and sewage disposal would be insuperable problems. A wild bird sanctuary of inestimable value would be destroyed. A number of these arguments cancelled each other out; others had already been taken into account and reluctantly set aside in the Abercrombie Report. And in any case the Minister was too busy at that moment to listen. He was steering his New Towns Bill through Parliament. In the Committee stage he conceded at least one point to the opposition. As first drafted, his Bill made no provision for the holding of a local public inquiry at which private interests could present their case against the designation of a given locality as a New Town. Later he accepted an Opposition amendment on the point.

The announcement that a public inquiry would be held in Stevenage in October provided a focus for the activities of all concerned. A scintillating array of Counsel was briefed on behalf of the local interests, and maps and statistics innumerable prepared for its instruction. But the Inspector hearing the inquiry also caused some confusion by announcing that he could not hear detailed criticism of the published plan, or permit discussion of the rates of compensation, since the published plan was only a guide for the development corporation, who could alter it in the light of local interests if they so wished, while the compensation rates were fixed by Act of Parliament. As a result the most forceful evidence against the project was produced, not by the local residents, but by the representative of the Metropolitan Water Board, who belaboured the Inspector for three hours with hydrodynamic data about the River Lea Catchment area.

Two lighter incidents of the inquiry may be mentioned. The Showman's Guild, taking exception to a recommendation of the New Towns Committee to prevent 'ugliness, rowdiness and squalor in all places of assembly and amusement', urged that, whatever happened, Stevenage should not be deprived of its historic annual Fair. And Mr Culpin, author of Stevenage's earlier development scheme, attacked the Government plan for siting the industrial zone in the very place where he himself had sited it.

The Minister's findings on this inquiry came two months later. He announced that he saw no reason to rescind his Order. The New Town was to proceed as planned. Almost simultaneously he announced the appointment of a Stevenage Development Corporation, consisting of eight members under the reassuring chairmanship of Mr Clough Williams-Ellis, the eminent architect and preserver of rural amenities.

If Stevenage was disappointed by the first announcement, it was enraged by the second. Of the eight people who were to dominate its life for the next twenty years or so, only one, Mr P. T. Ireton, was a local resident—and he was a Labour Councillor. Again the island platform of the railway station hummed with furious debate, and two decisions were arrived at. One, to bring a High Court action against the Minister, contesting the legality of his Order to develop Stevenage, attracted but scant attention in the Press. But the other decision made the whole country ring with sympathetic laughter.

On a snowy December morning the railway station staff came to work to find all the 'Stevenage' name signs carefully removed from the platforms, and replaced by convincing boards, hung in the Moscow manner, bearing the name SILKINGRAD.

This incident was brilliantly staged to gain publicity in the David and Goliath vein. Two months later, Mr Justice Henn Collins, delivering his judgment on the High Court action, rounded it off by providing, as he might well have thought, the traditional happy ending. On the grounds that the Minister had not considered with an unbiased mind the report of his Inspector's public inquiry, he quashed the New Town Order. David, it seemed, had done well to take his stand on the stony slopes of the law.

The action had been hurried by the Ministry, and perhaps the Attorney-General had not had time to prepare his brief well. Building had been scheduled to start in the spring, but now all activities had to be suspended while an attempt was made to secure a reversal of the High Court decision in the Court of Appeal. Urgently—for it was not only Stevenage that was threatened now, but the entire New Towns programme—the law officers were set to work and room was found in the Appeals calendar for the following month. This time David faced a Goliath as well armed with arguments as himself. The Appeal judges reversed the High Court order.

But still the building of new towns could not go ahead, for the Stevenage litigants were given permission to take their case before the House of Lords. At such altitudes, it is well known, the air is too thin to provide rapid acceleration of the machinery of justice. It was the end of July, with the best of the building season over, before the Law Lords delivered the verdict which was finally to decide Stevenage's fate. The decision of the Appeal Court was upheld. Stevenage was to be a new town.

Such is the story of what happened before the first sod could be turned in the building of a new kind of town where the needs of a modern community will be intelligently assessed and provided for. Its primary interest is as a case-study of the Labour Government's lamentable ineptitude in the sphere of public relations.

In a six months' study of local opinion, I soon found that only one side of the Stevenage story had been brought to public notice. Among the smaller townsfolk there has always been a large body of sympathy for the new project. But little attempt has been made to reinforce this sympathy with detailed information, or to encourage its expression. Well-designed exhibitions illustrating the need for, and possibilities of, new towns are familiar enough to those professionally interested; no such exhibition has been taken to Stevenage to be seen by those personally affected. The obvious diplomatic device of linking up the new plan with Stevenage's own development scheme was ignored from the outset. Bald announcements were made in legal jargon, and left untempered to breed anxieties and misconceptions.

These failures have cost a seven months' delay in the building programme of the new Stevenage, as well as thoroughly bedevilling the foundations on which it will be built. That the Corporation is alive to this last danger is indicated by the recent appointment of Mr Charles Madge, poet and sociologist, as its ' Social Development Officer '. No doubt Mr Madge and his colleagues of the Corporation will be able to nurse back this sickly child of the planners to robust health. But it is in the antenatal treatment of the Ministries that the harm is done.

'Oh what a beautiful mornin', Oh what a beautiful day, I got a beautiful feelin', ev'rythin's going my way!'

OKLAHOMA IMPACT

by William Sansom, with illustrations by Leonard Rosoman

Vitality is the one (invisible) import from the dollar area that must *not* be cut. For it is the vital, wholesome gaiety with its implicit message of optimism which accounts, apart from its intrinsic merit, for the stupendous success of *Oklahoma** on London's West End stage. William Sansom and Leonard Rosoman present, in text and illustration, their impression of this sparkling musical comedy, with all its colour and unashamed good spirits

OKLAHOMA is an occasion. It has already been written somewhere that 1947 will be remembered as the year *Oklahoma* came to town. How much the impact of this musical piece from America can compete with the freeze and flood of great conferential disasters, or with the *délices* of great personages paddling at Margate, is difficult at this remove to suppose: but certainly to many London minds the year will bear some of the stamp of *Oklahoma*, in the sense that time may be remembered and relived in a romantic song.

The show has achieved an extraordinary success for these critical times: the ovation seems to be of *Merry Widow* vintage. It has received the almost unexceptional applause of serious critics. It is a box office legend already. In theatrical vernacular *Oklahoma* has become a word. It has crept solidly into popular humour, it appears, well known enough to be unexplained, in contemporary

* Apologies to the author of the play for eliminating the exclamation mark that is properly part of its title, but, repeated, it gets too dizzy.

cartoons—thus a man drawn walking on air through a streetful of devitalised, queue-trodden, rain-soaked London misanthropists becomes 'The man who has just seen *Oklahoma*'. There is more to this than, always most pleasantly, meets the eye.

Two inseparable ingredients make *Oklahoma*'s success. Each is complementary to the other, each indivisible from the perfect whole. First the affirmative, faith-rousing theme; and secondly a most excellent technical production and performance. They are, in fact, those two inalienable artistic friends, content and form, without both of which no work of art is complete. Not even in the minor art form of musical comedy.

The theme is exactly right for the present-day London audience, a mixture of opiate and stimulant in well-calculated quantities; also its flavour is American, which proves an added seduction to many who, though consciously recoiling from what seems here a vulgarity and banality and bathos of the 'American Way' and the 'American Product', secretly envy the state of affairs in

Will Parker, back from the vicious rigours of Kansas City, tells the boys (cow) about it, grasping tight his new telescope, 'The Little Wonder'

that country. Thus the play takes as its vehicle a very simple right-angled triangle between a heroine and a hero and a villain, a tale in skeleton most ordinary. But the flesh on these customary bones is something that England and much of Europe have not tasted for years. It is meat of a fresh, affirmative, unlimited kind almost unremembered by us who have now for so long been rationed of both faith and food. Affirmation, the wholesome restful affirmative, the exact opposite to the *grand écart* of the European mind—this is the essential keynote. The play is set in American farmland, fertile and hopeful at the turn of the last century, in a land where right is positively right and wrong most despicably wrong, where there are no questions to worry the wheat-fed mind, where an Oedipus complex would be misunderstood as a new kind of saddle and politics are something that goes on at Kansas City, where the sun shines all day and people spend most of the time dancing and eating and building right-minded families, where there is space for simple virility and for it every nourishment. It is a bellyful of grapenuts sired by cream out of a strawberry dam. Nonsense, of course, and no dust (except for the villain, who is covered with it)—but nonsense with a kick. To the mind rash with conflicting ideologies, dizzy with broken faiths, the sensation of an hour or two of this return to yesterday's illusion of energetic faith and hope is like falling into some gigantic air-bed thrumming with ambrosial gases, a nectarine place where the head cannot ache. This may be no good in the hard sense, not constructive at all. But it is most certainly the reason why

people leave Drury Lane this year with feet some inches off the ground.

And—why not any old comedy, any old presentation of the simple life, of the simple morality? The answer seems to be technical as well. The curtain rises on a brightly stylised scene, well composed and painted, showing mostly a wide blue sky airy with little white clouds, and beneath it the rich pink, yellow and green Oklahoma farmscape, all framed in pieces of wooden farm-building. Who should be sitting there but an ample arch-matron smilingly churning a tub with a pole in it? And what should happen first but a tall, sunburned, loose- and clean-limbed cowboy in a fresh-coloured suit swings in singing a song whose refrain goes no further than :

> *Oh what a beautiful mornin',*
> *Oh what a beautiful day,*
> *I got a beautiful feelin'*
> *Ev'rythin's goin' my way.*

This is a rolling melodious waltz tune in a major key, the strongest song in the show—and now without more fuss the figure of easy virility sings it right through for some minutes. But in its impact this opening is more than may appear here. It smacks its immediate appeal to the animal senses—it is exactly like opening the window on a very beautiful morning and feeling the weather and the optimistic sun; such weather is difficult to resist, here it is correctly with smiles conveyed. It is like opening the window oneself. One feels that everything is going to be all right. And forthwith most of the more memorable

You're doin' fine, Oklahoma!

Oklahoma, where the wind comes sweepin' down the plain,
And the wavin' wheat can sure smell sweet,
When the wind comes right behind the rain . . .
And when we say Yeow! A-yip-i-o-ee-ay!
We're only sayin',
'You're doin' fine, Oklahoma!
Oklahoma, Okay!'

Backstage at Drury Lane: the Surrey with the fringe on top, two hats, and a haystack

music in the show is handed to you in this first scene, a gift to go with the morning, a frontal injection of melody, and an unusual musical device—for ordinarily some of these songs would be reserved for various climacteric stimulants throughout the play. These songs are sung full-throatedly, no crooning, no tin of jazz. And always behind there is that blue sky, costumes of fresh colour most carefully and effectively composed.

What is the heroine dressed in but white, with a bow in her hair and sensible flat shoes? A charming lady-farmer in her teens, wholesome and twinkling, redolent with youth's lovely dream and, in turn, efficient with woman's disciplinary carpet-beater. Her name? Laurey. His name? Curly. So you know from the start that everything is going to be all right with these two. They cannot even fix a quarrel and keep it seriously. Very different from the snarling protagonists of a Hollywood love dream. They are drowned in the beautiful morning and the cowboy Curly's obvious faith in himself, the future, America. It needs the incidence of a degenerate cowman with a two-day beard and a feeling for dirty pictures to stir up trouble—in fact a flesh-and-blood villain in place of the spiritual villain of misunderstanding that ordinarily prevails.

(In passing, this villain is a strange one to be received cordially in a country obsessed with psychiatry. He is presented as the poor cowman sitting moodily by himself all day in a shack called the smoke-house, friend of nobody, poorest of them all, a melancholic with a mild persecution mania. One would have thought that the humane, civil, brotherly American attitude would have been to attempt some cure for this poor fellow, rather than allow the hero and heroine to bully him without pity. Certainly, he confesses to murder and behaves roughly—but these are subservient to pornographic fixations and beard. In fact, the attitude is so immoral that if poor Jud had only chosen to remain alone in the smoke-

house with his pinned-up nudes—and he is first presented even performing a symbolically onanistic ritual with a revolver barrel—no one out in the golden corn would have worried for one minute. But Jud makes the mistake of not keeping himself so much to himself, he rises to his full unshaven height and says: 'I want a real woman.' This fixes him.)

Of course he goes for Laurey. And he acts in a very surly, boorish way about it. And of course *Oklahoma* wanted a real villain. It is odd, though, that they did not choose a healthier, more predatory tough—instead of an ill maniac. But then perhaps this was calculated the better to portray evil against things affirmative? Or it may be a subtle tactic to invite sympathy with your villain? Or both? But in any case the character feels overdrawn—not by the actor, but in its conception.

However, whether this smoke-house Ahriman is not quite correct for *Oklahoma*'s tall Ormuzd is not exactly the point. The point is that the battle between good and evil is on, and good wins hands down all the time—a particular luxury for us. Evil makes little sallies, but instantly suffers sharp defeats—so that there may be a constant resurge of optimism and the gay colloquy of dancing, singing, colour. Only once does Ahriman get the girl, and that is in a dream scene which comes in the form of a mime-ballet—that is, on the plane of dream and ballet, something fascinating yet unbelievable, and certainly not of the wheaten spheres on dry land outside.

The ballet is a good moment to remember the element of form in the piece. For it is all immensely well produced, technical, efficient, smooth and not slick, virile and bright and cut to a sharp T. This must be emphasised to assert the validity of the theme which, described here in words, with none of the crisp dancing and full-throated singing and lively colour, must sound too much like saccharin to our sugar-starved spirits. But it is not saccharin. The colour-tone, the vigour of performance drown this.

54

Dialogue is cut to its minimum. Most often the audience is watching acutely staged dancing, or hears singing that is rich and disciplined. The actors stamp about the stage, stamping like sailors sure of a ship's deck; the women trip with certainty. They all work at speed and hard, harder and less fussily than seems ever seen in London—and, of course, this is transmitted to the audience. One feels they have been fed on beefsteak and raw eggs for years (which quite probably they have not). And, above all, the stylisation of the piece—with its spotted-shirt cowboys, its witty Edwardian dresses of the women, its finely sketched sets—combines a sharpness of colour and line that lifts each scene out of the possible mustiness of the era depicted, injects a judicious modern comment, serves up fresh and live.

Straightforward production, free of whims and slow fancy, distinguishes the speed. A case of this is the transition from action to ballet, from life to dream. The girl Laurey is sitting in a grove on her farm, it is evening, she is about to dream. What veils of cheesecloth, what flutterings and purplings of light, what distortions of music and wavings of arms and wailings of hidden choirs, what Pepper's Ghosts such a transition would normally invoke! But here the substitute dancers step on to the stage quite obviously, stand behind Laurey and Curly, wave to each other, wait for a black backdrop swiftly to descend, allow Curly and Laurey to walk off. Lights, up with the black backcloth, and with a click you're dreaming.

The ballet, and several other features—notably a charming *conversazione* of lady-farmers early on, and a picnic-ball held in the second act—form sequences that perforate the main wheaten atmosphere with vision, irony

and wit that, though never spoiling the background of faith and hope, correctly acidulate what otherwise might resolve into too soft a treacle. Subsidiary characters liven the plot with counter-plot and various fun—notably a tall girl called Much Ado Annie, with a piercing voice and what must be one of the finest figures this side of two wars, who has ceaseless trouble with the boys. Lyrics, too, are better composed, purer than usual; there is a pleasing jingle sung by the hero to invite the heroine into his 'Surrey', an elegant black buggy with a bright yellow fringe on top:

> *The wheels are yeller, the upholstery's brown,*
> *The dash-board's genuine leather,*
> *With isinglass curtains y' can roll right down,*
> *In case there's a change in the weather.*

But here is no place to put into words a show that is all movement and colour, and not much concerned with thought. It is the essential energy, the vigour and the American new-world hope that most concerns us, the audience of this weary old world. None of the New York cacophony here, no Hollywood bad temper. This is fresh. Yet . . . apart from its technical production and some special flavourings, this show need not really have been American. These cowboys in their many colours, with their swashbuckling dances and their yells, could easily have been Hungarian bowler hats from the Puszta, or Ukrainians, or any other body of horsy picturesque men with good soil under them, a sense of freedom, respect for each other, and an affirmative attitude towards life. It may be all a dream, but it is a good one, making a nice rest from a splitting headache, a split mind, a split Continent.

JINNAH

first gentleman of Islam

The surgical solution of 'partition' is now a popular device for solving conflicting racial or diplomatic claims. Whether it is India, Palestine—or Germany—it is the nineteen-forties' practical substitute for the Wilsonian drafts of minority safeguards of the nineteen-twenties. Nowhere is partition put to a more fateful test than in Pakistan, and nowhere is the responsibility for partition more clearly vested in one person: Jinnah, who as ruler of seventy million Moslems finds himself, after thirty years' struggle, the most important power of Islam

CONGRESS were not the first to find that H.E. Mahomed Ali Jinnah, Governor-General of Pakistan, was a tough nut to crack. Thirty years ago Edwin Montagu, one of the ablest of all Secretaries of State, toured India to devise a scheme of constitutional reform. At the start of his travels he met a deputation of the leaders of Congress and the allied Home Rule League: Mrs Besant, the colourful Theosophist; the great Tilak, lately released from seven years' penal servitude for incitement to murder; Gandhi, already dressed like a coolie. After the meeting he ruefully recorded in his diary:

'They were followed by Jinnah, young, perfectly mannered, impressive-looking, armed to the teeth with dialectics, and insistent upon the whole of his scheme. All its shortcomings, all its drawbacks, the elected members of the Executive Council, the power of the minority to hold up legislation, the complete control of the Executive in all matters of finance—all these were defended as the best makeshifts they could devise short of responsible Government. Nothing else would satisfy them. They would rather have nothing if they could not get the whole lot. I was rather tired and I funked him. Chelmsford [the Viceroy] tried to argue with him, and was tied up into knots. Jinnah is a very clever man, and it is, of course, an outrage that such a man should have no chance of running the affairs of his own country.'

Now Jinnah is no longer young but in all other respects there is no difference, although he is not so good at dialectics. In those days he was still a passionate Nationalist, observing no distinction between Hindus and

Muslims. But signs of a break were on the horizon. Jinnah believed in reforms obtained by peaceful and persuasive means. Gandhi and his adherents were talking of civil disobedience. Jinnah was ambitious for leadership and so was the future Mahatma. The same organisation could not support them both for long. Gandhi, with Tilak dead and the troublesome Mrs Besant manoeuvred out of the way, grew in influence while Jinnah declined. Neglected, and disgusted by the increasing turbulence of Congress politics, he said goodbye to his co-workers for Indian freedom and turned his energies to the tottering, unimportant Muslim League. There, he knew, he would have no rivals of the same calibre to frustrate him. A little more tact and consideration at that moment towards the proud young Muslim on the part of the Hindus in Congress might have been sufficient to have ruled out the possibility of Pakistan altogether.

The Muslim League, founded in 1906 by the initiative of a few Muslim landlords anxious to safeguard their property and their status in the face of Hindu encroachment, was in a bad way when Jinnah came to it. No Muslim took it seriously as a full-scale political movement. Initially the task of reconciling the conflicting elements under his control and making the party of national consequence was almost too much for him. At one period he nearly gave it up altogether and retired to London where he practised as a lawyer and unsuccessfully attempted to enter British politics.

Doubtless it was this stay in England that confirmed his admiration for the British; an admiration still reflected in the glass of whisky in the evening, taken only when no other Muslim is present because alcohol for Mahomedans is against the rules; reflected in the English clothes which emphasise the sparseness of his tall figure and provide a setting for his sharp, handsome face with just a trace of weakness in it; in his English-style house in Delhi, built by the same architect who designed the Viceroy's house. But since he could not be an Englishman in England he returned to India in search of all-India fame and power.

From 1934 he has been yearly re-elected President of the Muslim League without opposition, and has made its policy without a dissentient voice. Jinnah saw the problem of the Muslims in India from a minority angle. Bred in Bombay where Muslims are outnumbered by Hindus by ten to one, he realised that the impetus towards Muslim unity must come from the areas where Muslims smarted under their numerical inferiority to Hindus. For years no Muslim in the Punjab, in Western Bengal, in Sind or in the North West Frontier Province, where Muslims are securely established by weight of population, paid any attention to him. The support came from Bombay or the United Provinces or Madras—anywhere but from the future Pakistan.

But Jinnah was not discouraged. The minority Muslims had genuine grievances and fears to be worked on and extended to their fellow religionists elsewhere in India. The Hindus were better educated and smarter at business deals. Their money-lending and their industries expanded rapidly while Muslims remained virtually unable to cope with commerce. The Hindus were quicker-witted and made rings round the slower-moving Muslims in local politics. They used their superior numbers to obtrude their religion on Muslims by ostentatiously withdrawing from them in public places and conveyances, regarding them as another brand of the Untouchables. As greater provincial autonomy approached, the Muslim apprehensions of Hindu persecution were multiplied, particularly as Hindus spoke more and more of divorcing themselves entirely from the British connection. Muslims became scared at the prospect of becoming subordinates controlled by Hindus in a land where they had been the masters until the British came.

Jinnah based his campaign on two negatives: hatred of Congress and terror of Hindu domination. The genuine fear was that of economic domination. Jinnah converted it into a religious one. Before long he was addressing mammoth meetings of fifty and a hundred thousand all over India. Order was kept by green-shirted Muslim League youths, and for the vast concourse it was a parade as much as it was a political meeting. Jinnah himself spoke slowly, as though a little uncertain of any other language but English. But understanding was always complete.

Gradually that body of Muslims hitherto unaffected by League propaganda began to get irritated; began to think, in the towns and the villages, that there was something in what Jinnah said, and Jinnah was not slow to prompt them to it. When the Congress governments finally resigned on the outbreak of war, they had committed no concrete wrong against the minorities, only a psychological one. Even their opponents were sorry to see representative Indian Governments go. But Jinnah ordered a day of rejoicing and release from the Congress Governments, and issued at the same time stories of atrocities which everyone knew to be untrue in so far as they referred to his own area, but that might easily be correct for some other area. Islam was in danger. All who were true Mahomedans must rally to the ranks of the Muslim League and fight the pernicious Hindu and his traitor Muslim friends who still worked with him in Congress.

In the meanwhile Jinnah was widening his objectives. Each time he had stepped up his demands he had added recruits to his organisation. He could see that offers to co-operate with Congress in running a federal constitution for the country or joint Governments for provinces only weakened his position. He advanced whenever he called blood and thunder down on the heads of the Hindus. Only the promise of a fight stirred his followers and he could not move them by suggestions of compromise with the infidels he accused of aiming to destroy the true religion. He began to drop the purely passive reactions of hostility to everything proposed or done by Congress and to formulate positive proposals of his own. From seeking safeguards for a minority he advanced to the theory that a democracy which automatically produced one party, and consequently one community, to rule over another was, in fact, an autocracy. Parliamentary government was not the system for India if it was to be applied to the country as a whole. From there it was an easy transition to the claim for a complete division of the sub-continent into two states. Hindu Raj must be defeated by the creation of Pakistan as a homeland for the Muslims.

At Lahore in 1940 the All-India Muslim League Council obeyed its master's voice and passed the resolution which opened a new phase in Indian politics— the demand for absolute Muslim independence. Jinnah was once again insistent upon the whole of his scheme. . . 'They would rather have nothing if they could not get the whole lot'.

The immediate response from Muslims was enthusiastic. Here was a leader to bring back the glories of the Mogul Empire. It was no concern of theirs how it was to be done. Congress were shocked but not alarmed. They were convinced that the movement was too fanciful to catch on.

As the war years continued, Jinnah reiterated his claim to represent the entire Muslim community. He tried to talk to Congress on that basis and he dealt with the British on the same assumption. When Cripps arrived in India at the beginning of 1942, Jinnah turned up at the conference to insist on the rights of Muslim provinces to secede from any Union of India. In order not to prejudice the negotiations, the Congress leaders reluctantly accepted his terms, although the standing of the League did not yet justify the vehemence of its leader. But it was at the end of the year that Jinnah's opportunity really came. The August risings inspired by Congress failed miserably, and the entire Working Committee found itself in jail for the duration of the war. Congress was banned because of its opposition to the war. The League sat more delicately on the fence and neither supported nor opposed it, escaping the dangers of arrest and obtaining the advantages of political propaganda without competition.

The offer by Cripps of Dominion status after the war was over was a shock to the Muslims. It seemed evident that 'Quit India' might become a reality and so might Hindu domination. Jinnah clarified his demands. Pakistan was not merely the areas where Muslims were in a majority. It was all the provinces where they formed the highest single element, even though by a bare majority, and for strategical reasons Assam (30 per cent Muslim) was added. Pakistan must be a workable state, albeit if thirty or forty million unwilling Hindus had to be included in it. Vigorously, religious fires were fanned and the fuel of economics was added. To the peasant in West Bengal, Pakistan somehow came to mean that one day he would own the village corner shop and not a Hindu. The League was now solid, except for the North West Frontier Province and a few cracks in the Punjab. By the time the Congress leaders were released in 1945, it was prepared to do battle with far greater chances of success than in 1937.

Wealthy Muslims and ambitious Muslim politicians have always been notorious for their corruptibility. At one time the market price of a substantial fringe of the Muslim members of the Legislative Assemblies in the Punjab and Bengal was well known to all parties. For that reason, Jinnah trusted no one in his own organisation apart from a few with outstanding integrity—an integrity not compensated for by brains. All the planning, all the details, were kept in his head. Nobody knew whether Pakistan represented his minimum demands or whether he could be made to climb down. He was aloof, the absolute dictator of the Muslim League. His Working Committee existed to ratify his proposals; unlike their Congress counterpart, they never suggested a new course or had full discussions. Jinnah was the Quaid-E-Azam, the Great Leader.

An audience with him, with his forbidding sister, the mistress of his house, in the background, is a nerve-wracking affair. All his conversations are conducted with complete lack of humour, and rapidly adopt the form of the culprit-victim sitting on the edge of his chair, listening to yet another playing of the old, old record grinding out the Muslim demands.

For advice on technical matters, in which he was hardly interested, he relied on one or two of the more able Muslim Civil Servants sympathetic to his cause. When a newspaper correspondent, or another politician, asked him what the economic structure of Pakistan would be, he would answer: 'Leave it to me and you will see'. This answer was put down to his arrogance, but it should have been attributed to his ignorance. He just did not know. Nor did he know the extent of his boundaries, the resources of the country he was demanding, nor how its administration would be conducted or its Army raised and financed. He refused to be side-tracked into discussions with anyone, least of all with Congress. If further definition was required of him he would reply: 'Admit the principle of Pakistan and we can talk business afterwards'. The outside limit of his bargain was set as the only condition for negotiations. Gandhi tried to deal with him and, with his tortuous darting mind, to trap him. But the Great Leader did not budge. The only thing that resulted from the Gandhi-Jinnah conversations was a half admission from Gandhi that no unwilling units would be compelled by Congress to remain within the Union of India. Jinnah still clamoured for the principle of Pakistan.

Of Hindu descent and not particularly versed in Muslim culture, religion or literature, Jinnah nevertheless understood the Muslim mind. His unbending, determination to win an impossible objective was their rallying point. Basically, Jinnah is not a brave man. He has been badly rattled on more than one occasion but his followers have never realised it. To them he stands out as the embodiment of courage and inflexibility. He is the king whom no courtier dare approach without deference and trembling. On political and economic matters which are the bread and butter of European politicians, he is a child. For him everything would come right if the Muslims could have their own state.

Another vital factor that he seized on was the need to impress India with his importance. In India, if two great men meet, the winner in public estimation is the one at whose house the meeting takes place. If Gandhi wanted to talk to him, then Gandhi must come to see Jinnah at Bombay. When the Cabinet Mission last year arranged to hold a conference between Congress and the League at Simla, everyone was agreed that the talks should begin on Saturday morning. Mr Jinnah, however, regretted that unfortunately he had several important engagements to fulfil in Delhi and could not be present to begin the discussions until Monday. The three Cabinet Ministers who had flown four thousand miles, and the Viceroy, humbly waited his pleasure and Mr Jinnah won again.

His enmity was always directed at Congress, but particularly at 'that Gandhi fellow who sits behind the scenes and pulls the strings and never comes out in the open'. His ambition was to be treated by the authorities as his equal. If Mr Gandhi could be provided with a special train to take him half across India, Mr Jinnah must have something equivalent and he usually got it.

At the back of his mind, his chief hope for Pakistan was always the British. Only the British could give it to him and only the British could make it secure for him. In his reading he had discovered that the British never did anything until there were some broken heads about. If the British wanted broken heads, he was quite willing to supply them. His nuisance value he maintained at high pressure, thumping it in that no settlement could be reached without submission to Muslim demands. If the British wished to get out quickly, although he thought that it was unnecessary for them to go, they would have to give in. Allied with this threat was the suggestion that it would pay the British handsomely. Pakistan would stay in the Empire. Pakistan would have a Governor-General appointed by the King. Pakistan wanted a British Commander-in-Chief. Pakistan needed consumer goods from Britain. The Hindu capitalists were twisters and would sabotage British influence. The Muslims were honest, respected the British, and would work with them.

All his life Jinnah has admired the British and their administration in India. It has seemed to him to be exactly right for the situation. He has never run counter to it and never failed to observe its forms. Sometimes he would hint that the British could stay in India indefinitely if they would only co-operate with the Muslim League. Together they could crush the Hindus.

As the British administration deteriorated and the need for a definite arrangement of some sort in India became of paramount necessity for the British, the possibility of Pakistan grew stronger. In this last passage of arms with the British and with Congress, Jinnah's nerve held. No compromise, no federal structure, no weak centre— nothing but Pakistan would do. Congress was sick of it all and it was no affair of the British. The Muslim League stood steady and Congress collapsed. Then it was publicly revealed that the boundaries set by Mr Jinnah to Pakistan were not a minimum demand but a maximum. He accepted the diminution of Pakistan by vast tracts of territory in the Punjab and Bengal, and decided, after all, that such a Pakistan would be workable, despite the fact that it had nothing more than the Muslim majority areas at its disposal.

One final triumph he could not deny himself. Until a few days before the presentation of the Indian Independence Bill in the British Parliament, it was understood that both the new Dominions would ask for Lord Mountbatten to stay on as their joint Governor-General. With the Bill in print, Mr Jinnah suddenly announced that his nomination for the Governor-General would be Mr Jinnah. All the dreams of his life have come true. He will owe allegiance only to His Majesty the King, and ex-Emperor. He will be a British Governor-General with British Governors under his control, while his rival Gandhi across the border fades into aged retirement.

The new Governor-General will stick to Britain for defence and for commerce. Echoing the British Raj, he will not tamper with the States and he will have a strong objection to Communists. He will be no constitutional monarch but will remain the aloof, the remote figure, and the details will be worked out by someone else.

2 DANIEL LAFORTUNE *Cock, Hen and Chicks*

Painters of Haiti

by F. D. Klingender

The rate of social and artistic change during the past ten years has nowhere been more marked than in some of the more undeveloped areas of the world. This was apparent at a recent UNESCO exhibition in Paris which showed the astonishing range of young painters from China, India, Africa and Latin America, and how much they had in common: for instance, a vigorous use of colour and the choice of social and human subjects. The selection of modern painting from Haiti, reproduced in the following pages, is typical of this new spirit and of this new and exciting school of indigenous art

NICHOLAS DAMBALAH, VOODOO DIVINITY is the surprising title of the picture reproduced on the opposite page (1). It is the work of Hector Hyppolite, who earns his livelihood as a house painter and decorator on the island of Haiti. *The Prostitute* in her gaily decorated bower (3) and the brilliant *Pot of Flowers* (5) are further examples of this artist's work. All are painted in Sapolin on cardboard panels, about 24 inches by 30 inches large, their vivid colours accentuated by a glossy finish.

Meeting Hyppolite, one would never suspect him to be capable of producing such gay and exciting work. He seems depressed and even melancholy in his bearing, as if haunted by the memory of the wrongs his

1 HECTOR HYPPOLITE *Nicholas Dambalah, Voodoo Divinity*

3 HECTOR HYPPOLITE *The Prostitute*

4 RIGAUD BENOIT *Rural Market*

5 HECTOR HYPPOLITE *Pot of Flowers*

6 LOUVERTURE POISSON *Flower Piece*

people have suffered ever since they were torn from their native Africa and shipped west as slaves. At 54, Hyppolite, too, has known many hardships. But this air of submissive resignation—a heritage from the days of slavery—is merely the deceptive outer husk below which the passion and love of beauty, so eloquently expressed in his work, are concealed. It is the pride of the disinherited which is the source of his power and which fills him with a deep regard for the half-forgotten traditions of his people. In his eagerness to recapture those traditions he has even visited Africa himself. Such are the roots of Hyppolite's sincere and original art which has long been admired both in his native country and in Washington and New York, where it is regularly exhibited.

Hyppolite is only the most gifted of a whole school of Haitian painters, the very existence of which was all but unknown in Europe until the recent international exhibition organised by UNESCO in Paris. At that show the Haitian section was one of the major surprises, in spite of the fact that it arrived too late to be included at the opening. Even its size was astonishing, for who would have suspected so small a country of being able to muster 52 works by 28 original and interesting artists for a show of that kind?

About half the Haitian artists whose work was sent to Paris by the Centre d'Art, Port-au-Prince, are self-taught 'Sunday painters', like Hyppolite. But each of them works in a personal idiom. Their individuality is particularly marked if they are grouped according to their age. Philome Obin, for example, was born at Cap-Haitien in 1892 and is thus of the same age as Hector Hyppolite. But as his *School Sports of* 18 *May* 1945 shows (10), his work is as neat and precise as Hyppolite's is fantastic. His sense of pattern and the careful arrangement of his figures, in which a desire for map-like clarity is more important than a regard for the laws of perspective, produce an effect that is strikingly similar to that of the battle scenes illustrated by the mediaeval miniaturists. Both in its composition and in its bright colouring, Obin's picture, in fact, closely resembles the watercolour drawings, now in the Royal Library at Windsor and recently shown at the exhibition of Greek Art at Burlington House, in which a 'naive' Greek artist working in the Byzantine tradition recorded the various campaigns of his country's liberation struggle in the 1820's. Although Obin was taught drawing at the Lycée and although he obviously takes the greatest pains with his details, he too remains a 'naive' painter in the best sense of the word, unselfconsciously recording whatever interests him in contemporary life. His one ambition is to find a job as an art teacher or in some capacity that would enable him to earn his living while continuing to paint.

63

Two other painters of the 'self-taught' group, who are in their early thirties, are similarly contrasted in temperament and style. Rigaud Benoit has worked as a taxi-driver, shoe-maker and jack-of-all-trades. He now supervises the section of popular painting and decorating at the Centre d'Art. His *Rural Market* (4) has the same 'primitive' quality as Obin's work, but Benoit seems more concerned with vividly observed details and with movements than the older artist. He is a great story-teller: another of his pictures shown at the UNESCO Exhibition bears the intriguing title *The Imprudent Wife and the Musician*.

Quite different, indeed, the very opposite of primitive in its emotional intensity and accomplished form, is the small *Flower Piece* painted in oils by Louverture Poisson (6). Poisson, who was born in 1914, is a sergeant in the Haitian Air Force. He has drawn and painted since childhood, covering odd scraps of cardboard or any other suitable material he could get hold of with his designs. Most of his subjects are imaginative, but occasionally he fixes on some external object that has struck his eye, as this bunch of flowers has done, to express his feelings.

The next three artists (represented by 2, 7, 8 and 9) are still in their teens. Daniel Lafortune, the painter of the splendidly drawn and characteristic *Cock, Hen and Chicks* (2), is, in fact, still a schoolboy. Wilson Bigaud is fifteen years old and only began to paint at the Centre d'Art in May, 1946. He had previously, however, learnt to draw in a village school. The subject of a *Political Demonstration* which he has so vividly depicted (9) is a favourite one among Haitian painters; it occurs more than once among the works sent to Paris. Another painter who chooses his subjects from the ordinary life around him is Louis Agenor, one of several young artists who live at Cap-Haitien, in the north of the island. His *Small Farm* (8) differs from the other works reproduced in that it is almost monochrome. It is painted almost entirely in brown watercolour washes, a sober medium perhaps better suited than the gay and glossy Sapolin to depict the squalid poverty of a small peasant holding in the tropics.

Although the style of the sophisticated Haitian artists differs essentially from that of these popular painters, there is no fundamental opposition between them, for the spirit of their work and the sources of its inspiration are in both cases similar. The sophisticated group includes not only professional painters in the strict sense of the term, but also a lawyer, a businessman, a young architect recently appointed Social Affairs Officer to UNO, and a Catholic Priest who paint in their spare time. There are also several women artists. Their work, not un-naturally, shows more or less pronounced traces of modern European influence which

7 GEORGES REMPONEAU *Attitude haitienne*

8 LOUIS AGENOR *Small Farm*

9 WILSON BIGAUD *Political Demonstration*

seems to have been transmitted to them through such American representatives of the 'modern movement' as Feininger, but it is far more profoundly indebted to contemporary Mexican art. Mexican painting, with its profoundly social meaning based on the national liberation struggle of a semi-colonial people, is indeed the true counterpole of the School of Paris in the international world of art today. Its influence is profound throughout the colonial and semi-colonial world, wherever similar political conditions prevail; it played an active part in the brief artistic renaissance during the heroic struggle of Republican Spain, and it greatly influenced North American painting during the New Deal period. The character of the movement, as expressed in Haiti, is well illustrated by the sombre oil painting *Attitude haitienne* by Geo Remponeau (7). Remponeau, too, has drawn since childhood (when, curiously enough, he always insisted in making his drawings up-side-down). Today, at thirty, he is a successful professional painter, whose work is well known in the United States, where he has also spent some time studying industrial design.

Inside Bata

by Ernest Davies MP

*Three officers of the Bata Workers'
Council and a deputy Director at one
of their regular conferences. The
author (facing camera, centre) sits in*

Each Bata worker is a part of the Czechoslovak Two Year Plan. The management fixes a daily target for output, pays by results

Halfway between the Western and Eastern ideas of 'Democracy', the Czechs have worked out for themselves an ingenious compromise. 'National Enterprise' is the theme of the Two Year Plan of industrial reconstruction. With 80 per cent of its industry now publicly owned and operated, the programme is complete. The Czech system has produced an administrative form which combines managerial responsibility at the factory level with workers' participation through Workers' Councils. Mr Ernest Davies MP recently revisited the world-famous Bata factory town at Zlin, in Moravia, for the second time since the war to assess the credits and debits of this enterprise of Czechoslovak nationalisation

PLANTED in a wooded valley in the Moravian hills is Zlin, American manufacturing town in miniature: an incongruous cluster of rectangular brick and concrete factory blocks surrounded by square red-bricked workers' homes which spread themselves up the tree-lined slopes. A modern department store, hotel and cinema, all Bata-owned, and all constructed in the same functional and unimaginative American skyscraper style complete this Hollywood technicoloured set of red-brick buildings, and green slopes and woodlands. Little remains of the old rural town, and its agricultural community, which was invaded by the former shoe-peddler Thomas Bata with his Henry Ford ideas of mass production and company owned towns, on his return from America a few years prior to World War I. That conflict made Bata.

Now a second revolution has come to Zlin, and its citizens are no longer owned body and soul by Bata; nationalisation has come to Zlin and Bata is a *narodny podnik*, a national enterprise. But the ghost of the late Thomas Bata still haunts the town, for the memory of this benevolent but hard-driving patriach is still green among the older workers. But his sons have deserted the ancestral factory: Jan, last heard of in South America, has been sentenced *in absentia* to a term of imprisonment for alleged collaboration with the enemy; Thomas, ex-Canadian RAF, prefers to run the segregrated foreign branches under private enterprise.

Before the war Bata prospered. Its mass produced shoes sold at low prices in Bata-owned shops throughout the Republic; and the peasant of Czechoslovakia was better shod than any in Europe. Bata factories spawned over the Continent; their goods were exported throughout the world. The range of products grew from boots and shoes to stockings and socks, to motor tyres and other rubber goods, to gloves and leather goods. Bata did its own building and constructed its own machines. Not only was the Bata enterprise a self-contained unit but so was the community that served it. To Zlin were brought men and women , boys and girls, from the towns and villages of Bohemia and Moravia, Silesia and Slovakia. The youths were apprenticed in schools, lived in dormitories; they grew up to sit or stand beside the ever-moving assembly belts, to work at high pressure to earn the just adequate wages fixed on the speed of the faster worker. Assigned a daily quota that had to be produced to attain the basic wage, more often than not overtime was necessary to fulfil it, and overtime brought no extra reward. A deficit on set production meant less than the basic, an excess, more wages. And the basic wage was so fixed as to ensure maximum speed.

Finished at the bench, the workers returned to their modern, low-rented Bata homes to lead lives in conformity with Thomas Bata's strict moral code; to pass their leisure in approved fashion and, above all, to eschew politics and trade unionism. For those who liked an ordered life, when Bata was in full production, life in Zlin was pleasant enough. A greater range of cultural interest was provided than in towns of comparable size; there was a community life. But those who would be free to lead lives unrestricted in thought and action were unhappy, and for them there was even less security of employment than for the rest. For none was there complete security; in times of depression this town of one enterprise exclusively owned was a truly distressed area.

The war, revolution and liberation have changed all this. Today the assembly belts travel at a slower speed, wages are higher, annual holidays are paid for, and there is security of employment. Bata is fully unionised and politics pervades the enterprise from the MP Managing Director down to the politically representative Workers' Council. Lives are no longer supervised and leisure is passed at will. But the good that Bata brought to Zlin is preserved; the workers' homes are still let at low rents and more modern flats and houses are under construction. Teams of office and factory workers give their labour to assist, while colleagues make up their time in the factory. The excellent apprentice scheme continues as do the cultural activities. Zlin is still a unique community to which peasants and workers come to work at Bata from all over the Republic. 27,000 work there, 51,000 more in other Bata nationalised enterprises in Moravia and Bohemia, 8,000 in Slovakia.

Change came this way. During the war Bata was working for the Germans. Most of its output went to the Reich, but tyres for vehicles of war were the only essential war material produced at Zlin. Following D-day in 1944, Allied war planes flew frequently over Zlin at a great height. They caused no alarm and few sought shelter when the sirens sounded. Then one day some American planes dropped a handful of small bombs, returning as usual from their morning raid, doing no material harm. This was taken as warning of raids to come, and when in November 1944 the air raid sirens sounded, the people of Zlin flocked to the shelters and scattered themselves over the countryside. It was 12.45 pm and lunchtime. Few were in the factory when bombs poured down and great destruction was done in the space of but a few minutes. Sixty per cent of the buildings were destroyed. Casualties were fortunately few. From then until the end of the war Bata was practically out of action; slowly it succeeded in bringing a few shops into production again.

In the spring of 1945 the Red Army came to Zlin and for a while Bata worked for the Russians. Meanwhile, with the revolution there were set up National Councils for all towns and provinces and they took over the factories seized by the workers. A Bata worker, Dr Holy, had been appointed by the National Council of Zlin to the National Council of Moravia and became Chairman of its Industrial Section, responsible for all factories seized in Moravia. The Moravian Council appointed Dr Holy head of Bata. Confirmed in office since, through the due legal process provided in the October 1945 Presidential decrees legalising nationalisation, he is today Managing Director of the Bata Enterprises in Moravia and Bohemia. The Slovakian enterprises were segregrated. For this he gets 20,000 crowns a month, that is, £1,200 a year, a car and certain expenses.

Dr Holy is a Communist. He was neither active politically nor otherwise outstanding before his appointment. In 1945 he was returned to Parliament as Member for Zlin. In his early thirties, he has been given great responsibility ; he was a member of the strongest political party at an opportune time and was thrust forward in the disorganised days following revolution. Graduate of Brno University with a Doctorate of Law, he left that city in 1939 for what he calls 'political reasons', and came to Zlin where he was first employed in the Bata library and worked for its publishing house TASK. In 1941 he transferred to the export and buying section, 'Kotva', where he worked till the end of the war. Somewhat on the defensive against criticism of his appointment through alleged influence, he volunteers that his job gave him a working knowledge of all the Bata enterprises since he was concerned with the distribution of all its output. He will tell you he was closely associated with 36 sections of the enterprise. More important, 'coming up from below', he says, 'I understand the workers' point of view' And that, of course, is essential to the success of all Czechoslovak nationalised industry in which the worker is given responsibility by right.

In the days following liberation, Dr Holy's job of getting bomb-damaged Bata going again was difficult. The morale of the workers was low. Food was short, and there had been years of working without enthusiasm for the enemy. The factory had no stocks, and materials could not be obtained. The Zlin National Council solved the food problem and the Russians provided some materials. 'The first help was given by the Russian army', Dr Holy points out. 'We worked for them. There was no connection with the West'. Later, of course, UNRRA helped with, among other materials, rubber and, of all things, soot, essential to tyre manufacture. The second difficulty was the sixty per cent destruction by bombing. This was overcome by doubling up the assembly belts on the floors of the usable shops. Two assembly belts now operate on floors formerly occupied by one. Workers sit side by side and back to back, crowding upon each other and the noise is appalling. Only thus can an economic output be achieved. Already new buildings are going up and the congestion will be substantially relieved before the year's end. Today Bata is said to be making profits.

The third problem that confronted Dr Holy was the attitude of some of the older and key workers. Trained in the old Bata tradition, they disliked change and introduction of new methods. The right way had to be found to win them over and to re-educate them. Dr Holy proudly claims success inasmuch as out of 3,000 concerned only 250 were changed for 'social reasons'.

Assisting Dr Holy is the Administrative Council consisting of his three deputies, Rudolf Ferebauer, Liboslav Masner and Karel Sykora, all three former Bata men. Holy was confirmed in his job by the Central Management for the leather and rubber industries, which itself was appointed by a committee covering all nationalised industry and made up of economists, professors, financial experts and the trade unions. This central board for the whole industry appoints the managing director only. The three other members are nominated after consultation between the Works Council, the Trades Unions, the National Council of Moravia and the political parties. Little wonder that there was much bargaining before three were agreed upon, and that each of the two

Socialist political parties other than the Communists—already represented by Holy—were included. Ferebauer is a Social Democrat and Masner a Czech National Socialist; Sykora is a no-party man. Between the Board duties are functionally divided. Dr Holy has responsibility for finance, and complete direction. He enjoys a right of veto over the Board but, on exercising it, he must report the reason to the Central Management; the Chairman of this in his turn has a veto over his Board, and he must report its use to the Minister of Industry.

Sykora, formerly Manager of Bata's Slovak shoe works, supervises the shoe, rubber and tyre sections. Masner, who was manager of the Bata Research Institute, is responsible for research, construction and the ancillary departments such as chemicals, paper and textiles. Ferebauer takes care of the commercial section which includes Bata's 1,500 retail stores, and the import and export sections; he is also responsible for the personnel and welfare sections. Ferebauer, now 41, joined Bata's as a technical chemist in 1928 and has worked for it both at home and abroad mainly in the tannery department. From 1935 to 1938 he was engaged in Holland founding tanneries, and during the war he was deputy manager of Bata's ancillary departments—tanning, paper, textiles, chemical manufacture, etc. His salary, and that of the other directors, is 18,000 crowns a month—£1,080 a year. He lives with his wife and two children in a Bata five-roomed house and likes to spend what leisure he has on amateur photography or reading, or, if occasion offers, game hunting or travelling. These directors have security of their jobs only until the Two Year Plan is completed. Reconsideration is then due.

Ferebauer is a Marxist Socialist of the old Social Democratic school. He has been a member of the party since a youth though never previously active politically. Now he wears the Social Democratic badge. He says he has watched Czechoslovakia travelling the road from liberalism to State Socialism by way of German totalitarianism. He regards the difficulties inherent in the tortuous journey philosophically and, placing nationalisation against this background, regards it comprehensively, not in the narrower terms of Bata enterprises only. He sees Bata's problems, and those of Czechoslovakian nationalisation, arising from the difficulties of shaking off the controls imposed by German centralised and supervised economics. The methods have seeped into businessmen and that makes it harder. 'The problem', he says, with feeling, 'is to shed the control organs; to get out of them. It's a hard job to find the way and no one has the guts to order them away'. He regrets the increase in central control and the subsequent increase in paper work. 'We know that Socialism brings bureaucracy and we don't yet know how to control it in the proper manner'. But Ferebauer is no faint heart; he sees Socialism in Czechoslovakia in its early stages and has faith in its evolution. Dr Holy too shares this view, and

The main block of the Bata works built by Thomas Bata between the two world wars

Workers' tenement flats—clean, spacious and functional. More flats are going up: teams of voluntary workers assist

All Zlin shops at the well-stocked Bata-owned departmental store

69

believes that 'experimentation will find a way and, if necessary, there must be changes'.

Central control is exercised both by the Central Management and Government departments—Ministries of Industry and Finance and the Central Planning Board. Each has the right to send inspectors to the nationalised factories. These flying squads descend without warning and report. The Ministry of Industry can audit the accounts and review the organisation and administration. The Ministry of Finance has the right of financial inspection. The Central Planning Board has recently instituted an inspectorate to ensure standards of quality, the necessity for which arises from export trade disappointments. These external checks may entail overlapping and extra administrative labour, but they provide a desirable check over the operation of nationalised industry which is not subject to such direct Parliamentary control as in Britain.

To the Central Management the Bata Board must send a weekly report covering finance, output, stocks, capital expenditure, etc. Here paper work enters in. Holy and the Chairman of the Central Management of the Rubber and Leather Industry admit that relations between the nationalised factory and the centre are difficult to adjust. Differences do arise, but, according to Dr Holy, they are mainly over different interpretations, differing viewpoints, and can generally be satisfactorily resolved. In the last resort the Central Management has mandatory powers, and if they are used for commercial reasons no friction arises. Should, however, there be interference with the existing scheme of things, they would be unacceptable to Dr Holy who could be relied upon to defend his ideological practices with true Communist fervour. He is backed in this attitude by a belief that the relationship between the national enterprise and the centre depends upon the strength of the leaders in the factories.

Holy has faith in the workers. 'We have the fantasy of revolution. We are working for ourselves. We like it. And even without piece rates', he adds, realistically, 'we would have the incentive to produce for the Republic'. In the factory one finds a combination of the two. All welcome nationalisation, and work for what they can earn. Here in the main shoe production shops with conveyor belts circulating, some so slowly that movement is hardly perceptible, others more quickly, the whole completing shoe production from the cutting of the leather to the lacing of the finished product, men and women sit or stand beside the belt, others work at machines beside it. Question them and they reply while going on working—disliking to lose time, as to do so might upset the whole plan.

Among the bareheaded girls dressed in light frocks is one with a shawl around her head, an obvious newcomer, not yet wooed from her peasant convention by the modern environment. She has come from a Slovak peasant home and has been here only six weeks. She lives in a dormitory; earns already 700 crowns a week and says she likes the work. It took her but three weeks' training to do the stitching machine job at which she works. At the end of the belt the foreman inspects the finished shoes as he removes them from their belt. One order is completed and he places a metal flag on the belt to indicate the commencement of a fresh run. The women work well, he says. And the men? Better than before nationalisation. What is the incentive? There is a daily target which the workers are informed of each morning and that is in conformity with the Two Year Plan. Main incentive to fulfilment of the target, he admits, is to earn as much as possible. There are now goods in the shops and with crowns they can be bought.

At a shoe-stitching machine, an elderly shoemaker is skilfully and rapidly stitching the soles of ladies' shoes for export. Asked his preference as between the old days and nationalisation, he is so surprised at being so questioned that he remains dumb for a while, and when pressed echoed Dr Holy's phrase: 'We're working for ourselves now!' Asked what benefits nationalisation brought, he adds: 'We get paid for our holidays and can go to the spas'. He had not been to a spa but the fact that he could go pleased him. Further down the belt, a more politically conscious worker, a member of the Social Democratic party, summarises the advantages. First, security: a worker could no longer be wrongfully dismissed, he could not be victimised if his way of life was disapproved. Second, there was fair treatment as regards wages and working conditions. The changed system of wages which was agreed with the workers themselves was a basic wage plus piece work, and payment for overtime, no deduction for deficiencies. The pressure was much less and the workers worked far better since nationalisation, though the pace was intentionally slowed down due to the previously excessive speed of the belt. He pointed out, however, that provision was made for the varying speeds of workers; the belts on different floors operating at different speeds so the faster workers could transfer if they wished. A third worker is questioned and he volunteers that better work is done now than formerly because there is pride in the job. But he points out that before the war the type of shoe on which he is working was produced at the rate of 1,100 by two people in a day; now it takes two people in a day to produce only 650. He indicates other machines and says on those two people used to produce 1,100, now it takes three to produce the same number in the same time. This is not criticism but justification for nationalisation. He confirms that the pressure was too great before, the earnings less, and security absent.

The story is the same in all the numerous workshops at Zlin where some 27,000 men and women are employed. They come by bus and train, cycle and on foot from miles round, work for the most part 48 hours a week. At 6.30 Zlin is awakened by the first long warning siren, and at 7 the workers stream through the gates, clocking in as the second whistle blows, defying anyone to lie late abed in Zlin. Shift workers toil till 3 pm with no midday break, but all have a 15 minute rest at 9 am. The remainder work from Monday to Friday from 7am to noon, and from 1.45 pm to 6 pm, and on alternate Saturdays for a half day only. The long lunch interval enables most workers to go home to the midday meal; for the others there is a canteen where lunch costs a shilling. During the lunch interval an hour and a half cinema show is given free in the Bata cinema; feature films are shown in two parts on successive days. Wages average around 1,200 crowns or £6 a week. A foreman's wage packet disclosed 1,550 less 250 tax, his wife's 800 less 100 tax. They were childless and occupied a three room flat with a weekly rent of 157 crowns or 15 shillings and sixpence. An ordinary but elderly worker, 20 years with Bata, earned 1,000 crowns a week and with a non-working wife as dependant, paid 170 crowns tax. Their Bata house cost five shillings a week. PAYE has been found a deterent to overtime working and a new law exempts overtime from tax, and gives incentive reliefs on a production basis.

The Chairman of the Workers' Council explained the workers' attitude to nationalisation. Duhajsky, shoemaker and typical Communist, with intense inner conviction and dogmatic utterance, says: 'Nationalisation has had a deep morale effect. The workers now look after their materials. They are aware the factory is their property and they help one another to achieve the desired result. They don't waste leather any more, and they are trying to improve their work. It is improving, too, and they now make better products with the same

amount of material'. A worker at a sewing machine in the factory confirmed this. He showed the overlapping leather of the uppers overlapping its stitching to the soles, and volunteered that in the old days of Bata they had to cut it much finer; but even so because of the greater care taken they use no more material.

The Workers' Council, a legal requirement of all factories, plays an important role at Bata, as in all Czechoslovak nationalised industry, but it has not the complete support of all workers,. Asked if he participated in the Workers' Council an old worker returned a blunt 'No'. Pressed, he added simply: 'I've no use for that. It's politics'. And to some extent it is. The law demanded that the proposed membership list, drawn up by the Trade Unions and submitted to the workers, required 80 per cent of the eligible votes for election. Failure entails a fresh election. If the requisite 80 per cent of votes is not forthcoming at the second attempt, the Trade Unions nominate the Council. This happened at Bata where twice only 65 per cent of the workers voted for the list. The inadequate vote was because the nominated list was not proportionately in keeping with the political party's strength. There were more Communists than members of other parties considered justified by their strength in the factory. Of the 46 workers on the Bata Council, five are elected by the Council to serve full-time. They receive the same wages as before appointment and must be neither better nor worse off than previously, or for a year afterwards.

Functions of the Council are evidenced by the six committees into which it is divided: economic, social, women, the Two Year Plan, financial and wages. On all

Every year young men and women leave their peasant homes in Bohemia, Moravia and Slovakia to work at Bata's. After a time the girls discard their conventional peasant costumes for modern functional frocks. Newcomers live in dormitories, soon realise the advantages of nationalisation: security, fair treatment, less work pressure, good wages and holidays, excellent and cheap canteens, sensible hours

these matters the Workers' Council consults with the Administration. The Administrative Council consists of the Chairman, Dr Holy, and the three deputy directors. The Chairman of the Workers' Council sits on the Administrative Council and must attend its meetings. He can speak but not vote. In the earlier days of nationalisation there was considerable dispute as to the relative rights and functions of each. It has now been formalised and at Bata all denied there was any confusion or friction. Each inclined, however, to define the responsibilities of the bodies on which he served and the rights of the other somewhat differently.

Thus, Duhajsky claims the Workers' Council is the organ of control. It controlled the administration and the workers. This was so, he argued, because the administration had to show everything to the Workers' Council. That is true enough, the Council having the right to see the accounts and to be kept informed of output. Once monthly the Administrative Council meets with representatives of the Workers' Council for this purpose, and once every six months the whole Administrative Council gives a full report to the Workers' Council. Not Ferebauer. He admits it can demand all information from the management and it has access to the books, but he also stressed that it can only make recommendations to it: it cannot direct. Management consults and responds to inquiries, no more. Ferebauer further claims the power of the Works Council has been reduced; it can no longer name heads of departments. And here friction had arisen at Bata's.

Together, the Chairman of the Workers' Council, Duhajsky, the Deputy Chairman, Hribal, a Social Democrat, a clerk, and Alexa, another full-time member and a Communist machinist, discussed the subject. Says Duhajsky, the Communist: 'Before the war, the worker was against the owner. Since nationalisation, it is our duty to work and co-ordinate the function of the administration with the needs of the workers. It must never be forgotten', says the Communist, 'that after liberation the workers had an influence on nationalisation itself.'

'But we always respect the resolutions of the administration,' interjects Hribal, the Social Democrat, 'we admit the administration is better informed. Up to now there have been no major differences. Often it is enough for the Administration to explain'.

Pressed for an instance of disagreement, Alexa intervened to describe the appointment of the director of a chemical factory to replace one sent to Slovakia. The Administration did not accept the nominee of the Workers' Council and the Workers' Council objected to the nominee of the Administration. 'There was a very lively debate,' says Alexa, and the others with reminiscent laughter chip in. Four members of the Workers' Council met with Dr Holy and the rival candidates appeared before them. The candidates told each other their faults to the amusement of both sides, and a third compromise candidate was selected.

'The main thing', concludes the philosophic Social Democrat, 'is that in the end agreement is always reached'. Maybe, but agreement by compromise may mean the rejection of the superior and the choice of the mediocre.

Wages, adjustment of piece rates within the agreements, is the main job of the Council, but more often than not it is over welfare matters that differences arise. The provision of accommodation, for instance, where the administration desires to provide vacated houses to those urgently required at the factory, while the workers wish them to go to those whose living conditions are the worst.

All insisted such decisions were not influenced by politics. The Social Democratic idealist said: 'We don't want to have political arguments in Council. But the most important problem is to get people to have a healthy sense of politics . . .'

Above the Workers' Council stand the Trade Unions. To them the Council takes any irreconcilable differences that arise with the Administration. The freedom to strike is maintained, but as yet there has only been a brief demonstration strike at Bata since nationalisation. The Trade Unions can give orders to the Workers' Council but they need not be carried through because the Council is appointed by law, the Trade Unions not. But in the last resort the Trade Unions can dismiss the Workers' Council, even though elected, and nominate a fresh one. Generally speaking, though, the Trade Unions act much as in Britain. They remain the main body for collective bargaining on wages agreements. And at branch meetings, resolutions are passed demanding better train services to bring the workers to Zlin.

At Bata nationalisation has succeeded. On the credit side, production mounts, quality improves. The morale of the workers is excellent. On the debit side, costs are high, and exports increase but slowly, and are a mere fraction of prewar days. Paper work involves an excess of time of the administration. Relations with the centre are none too happy. Above all, politics have too big an influence.

One lesson Bata has to teach all nationalised industry. Its workers have learnt the benefits of nationalisation and have a sense of responsibility. They know they work for themselves, and work well and hard. They discipline each other and impose fines for absenteeism which is no problem. They are colleagues in executive positions and know the way to promotion is open to all. Explanation of the workers' high morale is both psychological and material. Payment by results is an essential incentive to production. But political education, combined with improved working conditions and better social services, has brought benefits of nationalisation to the homes of the workers. Finally, and of prime importance, consultation and co-operation between workers and management, and workers' participation through the workers' council, create a sense of worker responsibility without which public ownership cannot succeed.

THE CAUSES OF WAR

by Harold Nicolson

War, like cancer, has no certain origin and no certain cure. Is war endemic or epidemic? This essay attempts to unravel the tangled motives that have driven men to war, from Helen of Troy to Hitler, and draws distinct conclusions about the material and psychological factors which combine and produce the phenomenon of war

FOR the last two thousand years men have asked themselves what are the causes or conditions of war. No answer—no approximate answer even—can be given to such a question, since the causes are multiple and the conditions vary in every generation. The most we can hope to do is to analyse and define some of the causes and conditions which have led to wars in the past. Nor is such an analysis wholly otiose.

War is always a resort to force; but resorts to force are not always war. When, for instance, an attack is launched by a powerful State against another State which is comparatively incapable of resistance, the ensuing operations are not always described as 'a war' but are often given some different name. Thus we do not speak of the 'Ashanti War'; we speak of 'the Ashanti Expedition'. We do not refer to the 'German-Danish War'; we refer to 'the German occupation of Denmark'. There exist also certain means of physical pressure (economic sanctions, pacific blockade, naval demonstrations and so on) which, although acts of force, are not acts of war. Moreover, when the resort to force occurs internally, special conditions have to exist before it can qualify for the title of 'Civil War'.

Thus a resort to force, whether it be external or internal, is only called a 'war' when each party to the conflict possesses sufficient strength to fight, controls an important area of territory, and can establish a reasonable degree of civil or military administration. I shall not, therefore, be discussing piracy, free-booting, infiltrations, rebellions, forceful pressure, or those colonial wars which come under the heading of 'punitive expeditions'.

Is it, in the first place, possible to distinguish between different types of wars and to contend that, whereas some wars are natural and permissible, others are not? We should not today assert with Sully and the Abbé de St Pierre that wars between members of the same type of civilisation are wrong, whereas wars between members of different types of civilisation are justified. Often, however, we do make a distinction between wars of aggression and wars of self-defence. We must admit that in every war each of the combatants seeks to represent its opponent as the aggressor. Sometimes this accusation is justified by the historical facts; but in general the arguments as to who started the war are not convincing or scientific arguments.

Wars do not arise from clear-cut or simple causes, but from multiple causes and mixed motives; they are provoked when a certain combination of circumstances reacts upon certain accumulated states of mind. Thus I do not propose to base my argument upon any definable difference between aggressive and defensive wars: the dividing line between them is in general too blurred to furnish any valid distinction.

THE MEANING OF THE WORD 'CAUSES'

My use of the word 'causes' also needs some definition. It has long been recognised that the 'occasions', or the 'pretexts' which provoke war are seldom its essential causes. Thucydides was the first to point out that the cause of the Trojan War was not, as many had supposed, the infidelity of the wife of Menelaus, but the desire of the inhabitants of the Greek mainland and islands to obtain the richer grazing grounds of Anatolia. The cause of the Crimean War was not a dispute regarding the precedence of the Orthodox clergy in the Church of the Nativity, but the fear that Russia might extend her influence over the Ottoman Empire and the Middle East. The cause of the First German War was not the mad act of Gavrel Prinzip on that June day in 1914 but the accumulated and dual rivalry between Russia and Austria in the East, and Germany, France and Britain in the West. The cause of the Second German War was not so much the aggression against Poland, as the accumulated conviction that the Nazi system could not be controlled or limited except by force. It frequently occurs, moreover—and especially in democratic countries—that the actual occasion or pretext of a war is forgotten once war becomes inevitable or that some other pretext is substituted in its place. Thus, although the cause of the First German War was what one might roughly call the maintenance of the Balance of Power, the pretext presented to the British people in those early days of August 1914 was, not the assassination of an Austrian Arch-Duke, but the German violation of Belgium. Governments always tend, when embarking upon a war, to provide public opinion with some pretext which will appeal to sentiment or imagination; they always discover some Jenkins's ear. Although this search for sentimental pretexts, although this frequent substitution of false pretexts, and although this constant confusion between pretexts and causes, have done much to confuse public opinion, they do not, of course, account for the inability of historians to agree upon any definition of the causes of war.

It is not only their complexity and variety which have blurred any agreed diagnosis; it is also that the cumulative emotional affect of provocation has not been sufficiently recognised. In our own memories we have an almost perfect instance of the determinant influence exercised by this process of cumulation. Public opinion in this country came to regard war with Nazi Germany as inevitable, not because they had any particular views, or even emotions, regarding the Polish question, but because the accumulation of provocation on the part of Hitler created a general feeling that negotiation with such a man had become impossible. Viewed from this angle of cumulative provocation, one would thus identify as one of the major causes of the 1939 war Hitler's occupation of Prague on the Ides of March, 1939. Why is that date so important? Until that date, the ordinary man and woman in this country had sought to persuade themselves that there was something to be said for Hitler's desire to liberate Germans living outside his frontier, and that once he had achieved this ambition he would become a reasonable member of the society of nations. After that date, it became apparent to many millions in England that the ordinary processes of negotiation and contract no longer applied to this daemonic personality; and that since force was his only standard, it was only by force that he could be restrained. If taken as an isolated incident in Hitler's power politics, the occupation of Prague was no more violent than his previous actions in seizing the Rhineland and Austria; but taken as an accumulative provocation, it becomes of immense importance as a cause of the 1939 war. I sometimes feel that the historians of the past have not paid sufficient attention to these 'last straws' that break the camel's back.

With these reservations and suggestions, I now propose to analyse in schematic form what historians and philosophers have defined as the causes of war.

PSYCHOLOGICAL CAUSES

The first to be considered is that school of thought which contends that wars arise as a simple result of human nature. There are those, for instance, who suggest that wars would never occur were it not for the instinct of pugnacity or combativeness which is implanted in the human temperament. In primitive societies this may well have been true. One has only to recall the frequency with which Homer uses such expression as 'well versed in the lust of battle' or 'rejoicing in in his own prowess' to admit that in the heroic age battle was, in fact, as Aristotle said, 'a species of hunting'. It is obvious, moreover, that if everybody, everywhere, always, was too frightened to fight, wars would not arise. Yet it would be an exaggeration to find in this pugnacious instinct a major cause of modern wars. War today has become so highly organised that heroism itself is rendered communal and the opportunities for personal prowess or pugnacity have much diminished. Thus the combative instinct, even if we admit its existence, is fused today among a multitude of attendant motives and emotions.

There are those, again, who contend that wars are caused by states of fear. 'In this age', writes Kantorowicz, 'of government by the people and of warfare by the people, the decisive, and almost the only, cause of war is fear of war.' Certainly, when considering the cumulation of effects, which I have already referred to, we must attribute a major role to the cumulation of uncertainty and anxiety. There may come a stage when the sense of insecurity, the despair of reaching any valid or stable agreement, causes widespread desperation. People increasingly say to themselves: 'Anything, even war, would be preferable to this constant and prolonged uncertainty.' But is it really fear of war, as Kantorowicz says, that produces war? Is it not rather fear of something else; of loss of power, of freedom, of honour, of independence? Is it not, in other words, the element of self-preservation? And can fear be defined as the motive for a purely aggressive war, for a war, that is, which is undertaken for purposes of gain and which becomes, therefore, in Aristotle's words, 'a means of acquisition'?

Obviously some wars in the past have arisen from a sense of fear; but not all wars; and thus while we must accept fear and pugnacity as frequent components of the states of mind which produce wars we cannot define either of them as actual causes. Let me suggest a further argument. If fear were, in fact, the main cause of war, then preventive wars would be much more frequent than they are. The United States, for instance, would wish to provoke war with Russia in order to destroy her before she can herself develop the atomic bomb. Yet, in fact, preventive wars pure and simple (that is, wars delivered against a potential enemy without provocation and solely in order to prevent that enemy from gaining strength) are comparatively rare. They usually occur when one State is engaged in war with other States and desires to prevent a surprise attack by a third State. Napoleon's Spanish campaign and Hitler's attacks on Greece and Russia were in this sense preventive wars. Preventive actions, as distinct from preventive wars, are less uncommon. We have the example of Nelson's action at Copenhagen and,

rtrait of Harold Nicolson by Derek Adkins

in more recent and tragic memory, the attack upon the French fleet at Mersa-el-Kebir.

In discussing the psychological causes of war, there are two other emotions which must briefly be mentioned. The first is revenge for previous defeat, which is unquestionably a most powerful incentive. It operated upon French opinion between 1870 and 1914, and on German opinion between 1918 and 1939. The second is a sense of grievance. The effect upon German feeling from 1870 onwards, and on Italian feeling from 1918 onwards, of an imagined denial of opportunity was a most pernicious effect. The Germans felt that they had been ill-used by history in that they had achieved unity and power only when the spoils of the world had been distributed to others. The Italians felt that their services in the 1914 war had not been duly rewarded. This sense of grievance, of injustice, is a further psychological factor which we must bear in mind.

WAR AS AN 'INSTITUTION'

A further theory which is sometimes advanced is that war is not an occurrence but an institution—that it is one of the regular and settled modes of human action, for which provision is made in the ordering of life in our great political communities. It is certainly true that some degree of preparation for war is common to all modern States. It is also true that war only becomes war when organised military institutions exist. Thus a revolution only becomes a civil war when each side has some institutional apparatus; without that it rests at the stage of a revolt. Moreover, raiding expeditions, such as the Viking descents upon this island, or the European occupation of Polynesia, were not exactly wars since no organisation existed on the other side. To say this, however, is not to say that trained armies and navies, or the existence of a munitions industry, are the causes of war. You cannot have wars without them; they may in certain conditions develop into aggressive militarism; but it is to my mind a mistake to say that the existence of trained forces and an armament industry is an institutional cause of war. One might as well contend that railway accidents are caused by trains.

Let me now pass from these theoretical causes, from these institutions and states of mind, to a consideration of the more practical causes of war.

PRACTICAL CAUSES

(1) *Dynastic Causes:* It was the fashion after the 1914-1919 war to contend that the old dynastic causes of war were no longer operative. This illusion arose, I suggest, from a too narrow interpretation of the word 'dynastic'. It is true, I suppose, that a situation is unlikely to arise in which the King of England would seek by force of arms to establish his brother on the throne of Hanover.

But dynastic wars were not undertaken solely for purposes of family aggrandisement. The dynasty in the old days represented a highly centralised authority operating by dictatorial methods. Any authoritarian system is bound to be extremely sensitive to prestige. In a democratic State, the electorate is not so prestige-conscious, since, if things go wrong, they can always blame it on the Government and, if necessary, replace that Government by another. But any authoritarian, dictatorial, or single party system is bound to be sensitive to prestige. As history has taught us again and again, such a system is not only obliged by its own dynamics to be increasingly successful, but it cannot (in that it possesses no alternative to itself) discover any alternative to success: it cannot survive either failure or loss of face. Had it not been for the potency of this 'dynastic' motive, Napoleon could have secured a reasonable peace at the Chatillon Conference.

We have seen this dynastic, or single party, danger operating before our eyes in the history of Fascist Italy and Nazi Germany. We see it operating today in the case of Soviet Russia. The main argument, to my mind, against any totalitarian system is that it includes no alternative to its own success. In this, as in other respects, it is infinitely less elastic than a democratic system; it possesses no buffers or cushions to act as shock-absorbers. Thus if you extend the meaning of the term 'dynastic' to embrace all systems in which a minority holds power by force, and in which that minority is obliged by its very nature either to succeed or perish, then we must admit that the 'dynastic' causes of war are as operative and as menacing today as they were in the sixteenth and seventeenth centuries.

(2) *Religious Causes:* It was believed again in 1920 that, with the spread of universal toleration, there was no longer any danger of religious wars destroying the peace of mankind. This also was an illusion, based upon too narrow an interpretation being given to the word 'religious'. Since, even if we isolate the causes of the Wars of Religion from the dynastic and acquisitive elements which they contained, there remains a hard core of dogma which was certainly a cause of war. A given State came to believe that its own form of dogma or revelation was so infinitely superior to that possessed by, or revealed to, other States, that it was morally justified in imposing its own theory upon others by force of arms. When to this moral purpose were added (as they always were added) intentions of expansion, security, domination and gain, a powerful combination of motives was created which constituted an incentive to war. It is of little use, when such situations arise, for the menaced States to assert that they much dislike war and have little care for dogma. The proselytising State wishes to convert the heretics and to bend them to its will; it is little use, as the Incas and the Zoroastrians discovered, for the heretics to argue that they have no wish to be converted.

One cannot counter fanaticism merely by sweet reasonableness.

Nor is this all. All rigid dogmas are based upon certain axioms, beliefs, certitudes and hallucinations. This is especially true of those dogmatic systems which are founded, not upon spiritual concepts, but upon dialectic materialism. The logic of the Soviet dogma, for instance, forces them to believe that the capitalist world will be unable to break the cycle of booms and slumps and will thus in the end be obliged to resort to dictatorial systems which can only end in war. It may be that if we can preserve world peace for fifteen years, and if, in the interval, the United States and ourselves can prove in practice that we can avoid slumps and inflation without destroying liberty, it may be that, if we can achieve this difficult task, the Soviet fanatics will be convinced that the Marxist dialectic was incorrect. But until that can be proved, there will be many influential members of the Russian governing class who will regard it as part of their dogma that a war between the Western and Eastern worlds is sooner or later inevitable. Of all the causes of war, the most potent is the belief that war is inevitable. And thus, so far from having emerged from the stage of Wars of Religion, we are about to re-enter that stage under new and disturbing conditions.

(3) *Economic Causes:* The third, and to many minds the most operative, cause of war is the economic cause. It would assuredly be the most compelling cause of all, were it not that no State can in modern conditions impose unendurable economic pressure upon another State without causing damage to itself. Thus, whereas high tariff walls can be erected (and can cause much resentment, and even suffering, in other countries) there comes a point at which excessive tariffs work to the detriment of those living inside the wall. Serious friction may also be caused by attempts on the part of a Government to deflect the normal flow of trade, such as the various subterfuges of state trading, dumping, bulk purchase, credit and the endless currency and exchange devices which Herr Schacht and others practised with such acumen. All these must certainly be recognised as causes which, in certain combinations of circumstances, can provoke wars. To define them, however, as the sole, or even the major causes of wars is, to my mind, to underestimate the interaction of advantage which is inherent in all economic relations.

More serious perhaps than these purely economic causes is the pressure of population. We all know that many of the wars of the past, even in pre-history, have been caused by this pressure and by the migration of peoples seeking subsistence. In more modern times this pressure was relieved by mass immigration to the new world or to Australia. With the introduction of immigration restrictions, such as the American Immigration Restrictions Act of 1924, this safety valve was clogged. In Japan, for instance, this population pressure became almost unendurable; they sought to solve it, partly by industrialising themselves in order to feed their people by exports to food-producing countries and partly by physical and forceful expansion. To a perhaps lesser extent, a similar population pressure explains Italy's wars with Turkey and Abyssinia. And Hitler was not merely using a phrase when he exploited the slogan 'Volk ohne Raum'. This demographic problem has been a frequent cause of wars in the past: it may also be a cause of wars in the future.

The problem of war materials or the blocking of transit and transport are also problems which may, in coming generations, constitute a major cause of war. Hitherto raw materials have been either fairly equably distributed or have been comparatively available to the countries having need of them. Now that certain raw materials, such as oil and uranium, have acquired such enormous importance, we cannot be certain that the old easy-going methods will continue. And we must face the fact that if conditions arose which denied to a powerful country raw materials essential to its industry or its defence, or blocked its natural inlets and outlets, a situation would be created which might induce that country to secure these raw materials and outlets by force. Thus, while it would be an exaggeration to state that all wars are in the final analysis caused by economic needs, it would be true to say that some wars have been so caused, and that the denial of such needs in future may create a situation of the utmost danger.

(4) *Political Causes:* Karl von Clausewitz, as we know, defined war as 'the continuation of policy by other means'. This is often regarded as a monstrous statement to have enunciated. It does not seem to me a monstrous statement; it seems a precise and sensible statement. In a world organised into separate sovereign States, recognising no authority more ultimate than their own national sovereignty, it is evident that powerful countries will, if they are unable to obtain their desires by consent, endeavour to obtain their desires by compulsion. It is also obvious that other powerful countries, when exposed to such compulsion, will resist. This seems to me a truism.

It is obvious also that occasions may arise when countries suffering from a totalitarian system, possessed of great physical power and a dominant aggressive class, and faced with other States whom they believe to be weak, but who may in reality be merely pacific, are apt deliberately to provoke wars for purposes of national or dynastic aggrandisement. The Napoleonic wars were so provoked; even as Hitler's wars were so provoked. If, on the other hand, the other States are too weak to resist this imposition, then you have the dominance of a single Power, as you had under the Roman Empire, or as you might have had under Hitler, had it not been for the resistance manifested by Russia, the United States and ourselves.

The danger to international peace represented by a

strong State which desires to dominate other States is too obvious for discussion. More interesting is the effect upon States, who believe themselves to be immune from aggressive tendencies, of the need for security or self-preservation. We are familiar with the process by which, in order to secure the frontier of territory A, territory B is occupied or protected, whereas territories C, D and E are thereafter drawn into the zone of security, and before one quite realises what has happened vast Empires, or areas of influence, have been marked out. In modern conditions, where naval and air bases are far distant from each other and dispersed, this search for points of security or defence may have unexpected developments. The political or strategic purposes of non-aggressive Powers may thus acquire a scope and magnitude which differentiates their expansion but slightly from that of Powers who are avowedly and unashamedly aggressive. The uncontrolled search for ever widening zones of security may thus be just as much a cause of war as the purely predatory ambitions of an aggressive State.

CONCLUSION

My contention is that wars arise when certain conditions combine to affect certain states of mind. If the conditions are present and the states of mind absent, then war may be avoided: if the states of mind are present and the conditions absent, then war may also be avoided; but if both the conditions and the states of mind are present together, then you have a situation which is very likely to produce war.

It is not my intention to consider the prevention of wars. That would require a separate analysis, under the possible title of 'Causes of Peace'. I would suggest only that the principles to be followed when disorder threatens either internally or externally are constant principles. They are, first, the maintenance of law; secondly, the redress of grievances. The first must be a prior and immediate policy; the second must be a long-term policy.

The only condition which will deter an aggressor from provoking war is the certainty that he will lose it. In domestic affairs that certainty can be provided by the overwhelming power of the forces of law and order; in international affairs there are no comparable forces of law and order, and other devices have to be adopted. There is the Balance of Power, under which the forces of order, so to speak, are at least equal to the forces of disorder; but the Balance of Power is a precarious, unconvincing and often dangerous expedient. The old conception of the Balance of Power, or the Just Equilibrium, has therefore been succeeded by the newer conception of some universal institution, such as the League of Nations or the United Nations Organisation, designed expressly for the prevention of war. But owing to the existence of national sovereignties, with their attendant reservations regarding 'vital interests' and 'national honour', mankind has as yet been unable to create any institution of international law and order which can compare in certainty of function, or immediacy of effect, with the institutions which exist within civilised and ordered States. The short-term policy should be, therefore, to create an institution which, if not universal, shall at least place the preponderance of physical power in the possession of those States which desire peace more than they desire war. And, finally, such an institution should aim, as a long-term policy, at the redress of grievances. One has only to state such a policy to realise how difficult it will be to attain and how invidious it may prove in its application.

One thing alone is certain: one cannot avoid war merely by proclaiming that one much dislikes it, any more than one can avoid cancer by signing a pledge never to have it. One can only hope to avoid it by remaining vigilant, strong, united and patient to a degree. And lest it seems that my conclusion is too inconclusive, I can say that I do believe profoundly in the passage of time. A war postponed may often (as in 1875 and 1878) be a war averted.

WEEKEND AT WILTON PARK

by Patrick Gordon-Walker MP

Wilton Park, a Georgian mansion near Beaconsfield, houses an interesting experiment—a German educational centre on British soil. Selected prisoners of war and some German civilians live here and take part in study groups and discussions aimed at reawakening their interest in a democratic way of life. The author reports on a recent visit: the result is a picture of the types and attitudes which are bound to influence the new Germany

A GOOD way of telling the national character of a people is by their attitude towards the education of the prisoners of war in their hands. Some countries will take the hard-boiled view that it is not worth doing at all; others will erect a great instrument of indoctrination; others will make a lot of ballyhoo about what they are doing. How do the British set about it?

Wilton Park, near Beaconsfield, is the central institution for prisoner education in England—the apex of a system that spreads itself in the form of libraries, classes, newspapers and publications into camps all over the country.

As you enter Wilton Park, it is difficult to realise that you are in a prisoner-of-war camp at all. You have to get quite close to the door of a fine four-square Georgian country house before you can read the neat notice on the front-door: 'Officers' Mess'. Even that does not get you very far; you may only be in another of the War Office's requisitioned properties, with rather less barbed wire about than usual. The first sign that you are in the most successful educational centre for German prisoners of war in the world is when you suddenly realise that the few figures casually strolling about the fine grounds, some of them with books under their arms, have diamond patches in the seats of their trousers or round blobs in the middle of the backs of their jackets.

That was about all I had had time to notice when I encountered the two guides who were to show us round. The guides were two tutors, one English, one German.

'Where do the prisoners live and work?'

'Over there, through those trees. Can you make out a Nissen hut and what used to be the stables?'

As we strolled across the park, past a field of wild and fading daffodils, towards a bank of elms, chestnuts and Scotch firs that hid the former stables, I asked: 'How many students do you have altogether?'

'A little over 300 on each course. It lasts six weeks, and we are now a week or two into our ninth course.'

'Are some of them German civilians?'

'About 50 on this course. That's the most we've had yet. We have about 250 prisoners from camps all over the country and about a dozen "veterans", as we call them.

They are the prisoner students who are kept over from earlier courses. The veterans make it easier to run the whole thing and they save a lot of time.'

'Do you have any serious problems of discipline?'

'No, we haven't had a single serious case. No one has ever dreamed of trying to escape, though they have the run of the whole park and visit English families in the neighbourhood. They're all dead keen. One of our problems is to get them to spend any time at all away from their work and take exercise. Well, here are the classrooms. They used to be cells and interrogation rooms when high-ranking German officers were brought here during the war.'

We were in a long corridor running the whole length of the building with rooms opening off on either side. In the corridor were bilingual notices: 'Silence please'—'*Bitte Ruhe*'; 'Library'—'*Bibliothek*'; 'Unauthorised students not admitted'—'*Unbefugten Studenten Zutritt verboten*'.

In the entrance hall giving into the corridor was the best laid out wall-newspaper I have seen. Neatly typed columns of letterpress with cross-headings in colour, drawings and cartoons. A crowd of about a dozen students was reading it.

'It has only just been put up; it's a new edition. To-morrow there will be a milling crowd around it.'

I elbowed my way in and read a brisk descriptive article about the experiences of a batch of prisoners in course of repatriation. It had been sent by a recent ex-student from Germany. They had smiled, he wrote, when, marching to the docks at five in the morning, they had found the Commandant standing stiffly at attention and received from him probably the last military order of their lives: 'Eyes left'. As each section marched past him, he saluted them punctiliously. We smiled. But, added the writer, it was fundamentally a decent act on the Commandant's part, an act of courtesy. What German Commandant would have got up at three a.m. to do the same?

As we moved away, my eye was caught by an extremely well designed poster announcing that I was to speak in German that evening in the hall on the Development of Labour's Programme. On the opposite wall was a poster that caught my notice because its style was so much below the others. It was a duplicated diagram giving exact details of how boots, mess-cans, bed-clothes and so forth had to set out by prisoners of war for the Saturday inspection—an oddly anomalous note of militaristic discipline.

In the Press class half a dozen German prisoners and a couple of civilians were busy working at different tables. They all rose politely as we entered. Most of them wished to be journalists when they returned to Germany; very few had been journalists before, being too young to be anything before they were called up.

Another production for the camp is a daily bulletin recommending articles and news stories in the British daily Press. I looked at the list of headings under which the references were grouped. The overwhelming majority came under 'Political', a few under 'Economic'. There were none under 'Sport' or 'Arts'.

'Isn't that rather dull for the readers?'

'Oh, no. That is what they want. You see the ones who can read English are pretty serious-minded.'

'Do you get English papers in the camp?'

'Yes, the papers are available in fair numbers in the library and are closely read. Papers from Germany arrive irregularly. It is quite impossible to follow out the general line of these papers, so they are of little value for the students in the Press class.'

'That ought to be easy to remedy, at least for papers from our own Zone.'

'You would have thought so. . . . Come over here a moment and I'll show you our chief pride.'

The Press class tutor showed me a huge bound volume containing eight issues of *Die Bruecke*, the camp-magazine produced for each course. German prisoners of war the world over seem to be under an irresistible occupational urge to use the title *Die Bruecke—The Bridge*.

Each student gets a copy of *Die Bruecke* at the end of the course—treasured by many as a sort of old school tie. The standard maintained since the beginning is extremely creditable.

The old school tie aspect of Wilton Park has caused some problems. Dr Koeppler, Principal of the School, was an undergraduate at Oxford, to which he came after his education in Germany. He himself has experienced the impact of British education upon a German. So successful has he been in awakening the loyalty of his students to the continuing standards and traditions of this most recent of boarding-schools that some resentment has been caused by the return of the Old Wilton Park Boys to their camps around the country. These prisoners know they have been to the best school in the prisoner-of-war world. Wilton Park Clubs have also spontaneously sprung up in Germany.

The authorities have sought to check these developments by banning the use of the name Wilton Park. It would be easier to break the public school tradition by rechristening Eton 'Windsor Multilateral School'.

Classes were in full blast on either side of the long corridor, as we left the Press class. As these rooms had once been cells and investigation-rooms, you could look in through peep-holes in the doors. From such a clandestine scrutiny the students came off better than the teachers. Or so it seemed to me who, having once been a teacher myself, have always been conscious of the ludicrous aspect of a teacher's performance before a class.

The teachers' justification was the students. Scribbling in a wild attempt to keep up with the lecturer, scratching head with fingers, chin in hand and eye intent on the teacher, some scowling, some serene—through peep-hole after peep-hole they made a classic picture of attention.

'Where do you get these pictures on the walls from?'

'The British Council sends them. They are regularly changed. We get exhibitions and photographs too.'

Above: *Generals, Gefreiters, civilian administrators queue for plates of stew in their university-prison camp*

Right: *While Patrick Gordon-Walker lectured, Walter Goetz sketched this impression of his attentive audience*

Below: *The prisoners produce their own newspaper. Many of them are ex-journalists or journalists-to-be in their own country*

Right at the end of the corridor, across a little patch of ground where a few flowers had been planted, were two Nissen huts that housed rather special classes—the Music class and the Culture class. The students here have to spend a great deal of time together, having not only to study themselves but also to provide the main entertainment for the rest of the school. All their leisure time is taken up with practising.

We knocked on the door of the Culture class and came into a little entrance hall that served as a common room. Off it opened the offices where the different sides of the class's work were carried on. Plates of stew were being set on the table in the entrance hall.

Pinned up on the walls of the Culture class are the programmes of pieces produced in the eight courses since Wilton Park began—plays ancient and modern, German and English. As usual, make-up and layout were professional.

One section of the class was rehearsing a puppet show due to be produced in a few weeks' time. The puppets are handed down from course to course and added to by each generation of students. With great pride one of the students—a veteran of several months' standing—showed us the puppets, highly-coloured caricatures made of papier maché and dressed in ingenious rags and scraps.

'This is our Principal, Mr Koeppler. . . . And here we

have to bring in the fraternisation theme: this is the English Maiden.' (She was a horror with protruding teeth, highly coloured visage, and of a stature exceeding the male puppets.) 'We're rather pleased with this one, he is always a great success at the shows; the PID man (Political Intelligence Division, which is responsible for prisoner-education). He has only one line, but he says it very often: "I'll see what I can do".'

A few yards away is an identical Nissen hut where the Music class works and lives. Three of them were just beginning to rehearse a Trio-Sonata of Handel under the instruction of a prisoner who is a professional pianist.

'They're very high-brow. It's the same on every course, and it's the same in the Culture class. The rest of the students prefer it on the whole. Whatever the reason, there's very little tendency towards light escapism. The fiddle is a Bavarian who wants to be a pharmacist. The clarinet is said to be a clerk in civil life.'

Both these were prisoners. The 'cello, a civilian, was dressed in plus-fours. He was a high school teacher.

Back into the long corridor to keep an appointment with some students with whom I had arranged to talk.

The first man has been in the camp since October, that is about eight months. He works in the Press class and wants to be a journalist. He had been a parachutist.

While I was waiting for the next man to come in, I could hear the lecture going on next door. '*Vorteil ist. . . ,*' said a calm and pleasant English voice, and then went on patiently to explain the advantage of something or other; but I never discovered what, as I had to start talking with my next visitor, a civilian. He explained at once that he was a Social Democrat, President of the Works Council at the Siemens Works in Berlin. He asked me to give his regards to Morgan Phillips, Secretary of the Labour Party.

The man who came in with him was in the Educational Office at Solingen in the Rhineland. He was concerned with the training of teachers and was visiting the Ministry of Education in London in a few days. There were, he said, practically no schools in Solingen and Düsseldorf.

'What's the most important immediate job in German education?'

'Political education. By that I mean' (and he searched for the word and then brought it out in English) 'citizenship. We've got to learn to be able to run ourselves and think of the whole community. I wish the British Administration in Germany were better at distributing news. It's important for us to know what is actually going on in Britain. But it's hard to find out.'

'What do you think of Wilton Park? Ought it to be continued after the prisoners have been repatriated?'

'Unquestionably.'

Supper in the Officers' Mess, where we learned what a good German cook can do with ordinary army rations. Then back across the park to the school buildings.

The tutor who was to preside at my lecture took an Oxford BA gown from a peg in the corridor and slipped it on. 'We always wear gowns on the more formal occasions.'

As we went into the Hall, the whole audience stood up. These evening lectures are entirely voluntary; but practically the entire school comes to them.

After I finished, the questions began. Intelligent questions about strikes under a Labour Government, about a wages policy, about liberty for the Opposition. The prisoners who had been a good while in Britain performed much better than the civilians. They asked brief and precise questions; the civilians tended to make miniature speeches and used a much more involved and cumbersome German. The prisoners, too, were more relevant. They asked questions about Britain, about which I had been talking. The civilians asked about Germany.

Late that evening I sat talking with the tutors, a dozen in all. All were young and extremely keen on their work, like the brisker masters in a public school. Most of the ten British tutors had been recently demobilised, many had been engaged in Intelligence work. One, the chairman at my lecture, had been a prisoner of war in Germany for five years; another had been interned as a British civilian in Germany throughout the war. The two German tutors got on with perfect ease and unconcern with their British colleagues. Besides the resident tutors, who hold small seminars and see all the students individually, there are some thirty visiting lecturers, most of them German.

'What sort of things do you teach them in these classes?'

'Academic subjects likely to be of use to them. A good deal of modern German history; Bismarck and the Weimar Republic, you know. Economics, British institutions, Church and State.'

'How is the experiment with civilians working out?'

'Not too good at first, but it is getting much better. The proportion of civilians in each course is being increased. If it is decided to maintain Wilton Park as a lasting institution, it will in due course become a school solely for volunteers from Germany.'

'How many courses have civilians attended?'

'This is the third. At first there was a good deal of suspicion, and the civilians tended to behave with great lack of tact. They treated the prisoners as if they were ignorant backwoodsmen. But relations have got steadily better and on this course the admixture is proving very successful. Don't you think so?'

All the other tutors nodded agreement. One of them went on to point out that an important point of contact between civilians and prisoners was their common acute concern with politics.

'Do you find that the politics of the prisoners is about the same as in Germany?'

'No; there's a constant and very interesting difference between the political balance at these courses here and the political balance in present-day Germany. In each course we hold mock elections. They arouse a lot of interest and are keenly participated in. The Social Democrats always prove the stronger party.'

'Due perhaps to the protective colouring of prisoners in a country with a Labour Government?'

'Perhaps a little; but only a little. The Catholics consistently do less well than in Germany; the Liberals much better than in Germany. The Communists do badly, about the same as in the British Zone. In the last mock election the Communists got 35 votes to 180 for the Social Democrats.'

'How are the civilians selected for the school? Is it done on a political basis?'

'That's how it largely works out in practice. Various organisations in the British Zone are invited to nominate students: parties, trade unions, societies of one sort and another. But the whole thing tends to be rather political. You can't avoid that in Germany today.'

'Has the school had much effect on the views of Communists?'

'In the main they go back with the same ideas that they came with. A few have been visibly impressed by what they have seen. How long the impression lasts after their return I don't know.'

'How do the prisoners who pass through Wilton Park get on when they return to Germany?'

'On the whole, they are rather disliked by the German Administration, that is, by the Germans in charge of firms, offices and departments. Many of these Germans were executives under the Nazis, and in any case they tend to treat the returned prisoners as intruders who know nothing of Germany today. On the other hand, some Wilton Park men have done very well and hold important jobs. The introduction of civilians is helping here. One of the men you were talking with this afternoon, the editor of an important paper, has found three men on this course to whom he has offered jobs in Germany.'

Ex-members of Wilton Park write masses of letters to their old tutors. They pulled several out of their pockets and showed them to me. Many were like the letters of a good public school boy who is beginning to be disillusioned by the real world. 'Some of the old members of Wilton Park who were there with me have become very cynical. . . . The British out here do not always behave as we had learned to expect at Wilton Park.' And so on.

'How many of you would like to stay on in this job permanently if Wilton Park is continued for civilians?'

Everyone with one exception wanted to go on with this job as his life-work.

*   *   *

As I lay in the bed in which Kesselring had once slept, I thought over this curious experiment, a typically English experiment, costing a good deal of money and run by a man who has become completely English without ceasing to be a German.

The tutors work extremely hard, but without any doctrinal objectives to guide or inspire them. Amongst them, all political views were represented. If asked, they would probably say that they wanted to help each of the students to develop to the best of his ability, to think things out for himself and to be tolerant. This would be more important in the long run than training them for specific jobs.

Underneath it all, of course, was the quiet and unquestioned assurance that if the English way of doing things is allowed to appear quietly in practice, without any preaching, it will do the trick of re-education. With some it will not work; but they are then *ex hypothesi* ineducable.

Prisoners guy themselves and their guards in their puppet theatre. Left to right: The prisoner; the Nazi General; the British PID man, who has only one line: 'I'll see what I can do'

THE SOCIAL BALANCE OF POWER

by David Mitrany

Professor Mitrany: a portrait by Bunyard

When Britain's Foreign Secretary recently declared himself in favour of a 'functionalist' solution of the world's great reconstruction problems, he endorsed the view of David Mitrany, whose original and essentially constructive thesis of 'functionalism' is now rapidly gaining ground among thinking people all over the world. Here he applies his practical ideas of functionalism to the immediate issue of the Western Powers' relations with the Soviet Union

PEACE has its strategy no less than war; to the Western powers it sets a revolutionary problem. For a century and a half Britain helped the peace by upholding a political balance of power in Europe. More than thirty years ago a Foreign Office memorandum urged that 'if a European power gobbles up small states as an hors d'oeuvre, England is likely to be the next course'. That still expresses England's political instinct. But the old balance of power no longer is a possible policy because the elements for a political balance have ceased to exist. No counterweight could be found in Europe now to the sheer power of the Soviet Union; and those who would make up such a counterweight by means of a Western union or some such grouping forget that the material aspect is not the most significant part of the change. The power of the Soviet Union rests as much on the influence she has on social groups and trends beyond her borders as on the strength she has built up for herself within.

That new social factor is as unsettling for the states of Europe as was the national idea for the old empires after the Napoleonic wars. This is the social century. Just as the strategy of war has to be thought out afresh in the face of guided missiles and atomic power, so has the strategy of peace to be reconstructed in the light of social ideologies and national planning. The general problem can be stated quite simply. During the century of nationalism strife was kept in check through a balance of power between states. But now the new unsettling force which . adds so much to Soviet power, playing the part played by alliances in the past, is active *within* those states. At a party rally at Nuremberg, in 1936, Hitler said that 'wars and defeats have a less disastrous significance in the lives of nations than the internal crises of their social structure';

and he was speaking as a politician who had risen on an internal social crisis to be dictator of Germany and, almost, of Europe. In so far, then, as the aim of international policy is to keep Europe on an even keel, a strategy of peace must now be worked out which shall achieve not a political but a social balance of power.

Yet a single fact which marks the change sharply also brings out how stiff and complex will be the task. For three-quarters of a century the Socialist movement has been the spearhead of internationalism, both in theory and in practice. Now Socialist parties arrived to power are applying the most nationalist economic policy since the mercantilist era. Marxism had taught confidently that the state would melt away in the redeeming fire of the proletarian revolution. Now the first experiment in Marxism is building up an iron-bound state which, even in details, reveals itself as startlingly akin to the corrugated nationalist vision of Fichte's 'closed economic state'.

What is the meaning of this contemporary paradox? Again in simple terms the issue is plain enough. The victorious Socialist parties are pledged to bring about a social transformation which by nature and tempo cannot be well carried out except through public action; and the only public instrument ready at their hands is the national state. Hence the older slogan 'Socialism in our Time' now has to run in double harness with 'Socialism in our Country'. There is nothing in the nature of these aspirations that could not be advanced more happily by international means. But so far there are no established international means that could be used for those social ends.

The consequence is the strange and ubiquitous wave of social nationalism—which, but for the fact that the name has been unpleasantly pre-empted, would be more appropriately described as national-socialism. To give two illustrations from different parts of the world—striking because they are so blunt: last March the Mexican Confederation of Labour decided to change its Marxist slogan 'For a Classless Society' into the nationalist 'For the Emancipation of Mexico'. And the Labour Party's new handbook for party workers issued last spring, far from being apologetic for the failure to revive the Socialist international, rather denounced the idea as making sense no longer. 'An international with a fixed constitution', it said, 'a permanent bureaucracy, and the authority to compel its members to carry out decisions can function only if all the Socialist parties recognise that they have at all times an overriding community of interest. But when a party becomes a Government, it becomes responsible no longer simply to its own members but to the country as a whole; it cannot then remain subject to the decisions of a foreign and sectional body.' Indeed, in east-central Europe, the more Socialistic the new regime, the more nationalistic is its temper. The only strategy of peace possible is therefore one which would restore some social balance in a progressive way in line with the new popular aspirations.

Painters often get a truer impression of the general effect of a picture by looking at it upside down. Our picture may gain in sharpness if we look for a moment at its obverse, as seen through Russian eyes. Since the end of the war, Soviet Russia has pursued a peace strategy of her own, one which could perhaps not be unfairly described as a policy of unsettlement. Two general traits of Soviet policy deny any hope that Russian and Western aims are at present compatible. Whatever the past sins of Western 'power politics', there is certainly a new outlook developing among us. At no time since the Christian society of the Middle Ages has there been so live a sense of community among the peoples of the Western world. With brave leadership there is hardly a limit to what might be achieved in the way of international government. Unfortunately, the Soviets, so recently come to strength and influence, seem to prefer just that system of spheres of power and interest which the peoples of the West are trying to outgrow. Whether the Soviets do so out of suspicion or fear matters little. What matters tragically is that two incompatible conceptions seem again to be thwarting the chances of the greatest of all historical advances in political evolution.

Soviet policy has split Europe into two zones which are becoming increasingly estranged from each other. For Russia has coupled with her exclusive form of policy an ideological trait, the open encouragement of social revolt, just as Napoleon in his imperial adventure helped his search for power with incitement to national revolt. Even if one discounts some of the rumours about her use of Communist groups in various parts of the world, the link between Russian foreign policy and local social policy in the countries within her sphere of influence is quite open. The evidence is equally unmistakable in her attitude in the United Nations. The issues raised by Russia and her friends—such as the conflicts in Greece, in Indonesia, etc—were not issues as between two sovereign states, the kind of issue in which an international organisation is supposed to take a pacifying hand, but always between two factions in a particular state. The Western powers, with their complicated economic organisation, are naturally anxious to get ordinary life going again and are apt to encourage compromise wherever they carry any influence. Soviet Russia, economically self-contained, seems cheerfully indifferent to these anxieties; in so far as she is suspicious of the Western powers she may even see some advantage in their being politically tangled up in the Middle East, in south-eastern Europe and elsewhere. In brief, the Western powers need and crave stability; Soviet Russia, if anything, finds some advantage in restlessness abroad.

But to assume that the Soviets are responsible for all the restlessness in the world is too flattering to them—and much too easy for us. The part of Communism in that state of things is relatively insignificant; were Communists to disappear from Europe and China and India, there would be some difference in the streets, but little difference in the homes. The Soviets have not the power to bring about such universal instability; nor, paradoxically, can they do much to assuage it. They can only exploit it. And with the present tendency to social nationalism among Western Socialist and Labour governments, the effect, in practice, is to leave Communism and the USSR as the only relevant factors in the philosophy and movement of internationalism.

The lesson is, therefore, as clear as the problem. The only alternative strategy of peace is one which through positive economic and social action would remove the opportunities now left open to revolutionary imperialism, and open up the prospects of a true international community of interest and life. To be effective, such a peace strategy must take account of two points which are of the very nature of the new trend. First, its sectional and ideological factor: there are no clear-cut geographical divisions in social nationalism, as there were in political nationalism. In the earlier phase the several parts of the people stood together in pursuit of a common national ideal; now in most nations the parts are deeply divided in their view of the social ideal. To build a new strategy upon some geographical grouping would be to start with an intractable cleavage within that group; and the economic division between the two groups would soon degenerate into political conflict. 'Such seems the disposition of man', said Dr Johnson, 'that whatever makes a distinction produces rivalry.'

A second and still more crucial point is the social nature of the present trend. To champion merely the forms of constitutional democracy, as the Western governments have done hitherto, is futile and irrelevant in a revolutionary situation. To put it rudely, what the masses want is not a voice, but a mouthful. The revolutionary elements of a century ago treated with contumely the legitimist claims of dynasties and the privileges of aristocracy; now the masses are as scornful of the legitimism of constitutions and the privileges of property. The democracy they want is one of social action.

The two essential conditions for such practical democratic action are, therefore, that it should not be organised on exclusive geographical or ideological lines, which would in effect confirm the division we deplore so greatly in Soviet policy; and that it should meet the social needs and further the aspirations of the masses in Europe and elsewhere, without invading unduly their political individuality. The only approach which can satisfy both these positive and negative conditions is a functional one, which would enable those activities which should be run jointly to be organised on a technical non-political basis. More specifically, the criteria for selecting the fields of action are, first, that we should deal with those interests which, like oil, aviation, etc, carry with them a risk of political friction; and, secondly, with those which stand foremost in the effort to attain a better life for all. Obviously the latter are now the more urgent group. With a danger of collapse in European life, the provision of food and clothing, transport and, above all, coal, could be organised satisfactorily only by joint practical action.

The war has already given us many examples of new organs of international co-operation on practical, technical levels. There are equally urgent needs now which could be handled on the technical level by joint expert agencies, with the national governments retaining only a general power of supervision, but which might get hopelessly muddled if dealt with by the old methods of national bargaining and competition. We also gained in the war much experience of regional action that might be usefully applied now to Western Europe. It was tried with great success, for instance, for linking together production and other activities in our West African colonies. In the words of the *Economist*, 'the Resident Minister's Office has all along been functional in its organisation. Machinery has been created to tackle specific problems of supply, intercolonial collaboration and development. It has remained an elastic instrument of policy, and has allowed the logic of events to formulate each extension of its activities.' Again, the Middle East Supply Centre achieved a remarkable degree of functional co-operation between the habitually isolated peoples of that region; among other things making it possible for the first time since the Biblical era to deal effectively with the locust plague. The Ruhr problem will never be dealt with satisfactorily except under some such functional regional authority. For to achieve the best results for all it ought to be linked up economically with the neighbouring coal and iron regions; and only under this type of authority could it be made to give practical service to all while being politically neutralised.

Peace cannot be restored to Europe unless we find means to reduce economic chaos without rousing political fears. That is something which the Western Powers could do supremely well. They have no need to invade the political life of others, while they have resources, skill and experience far beyond anything which Russia could muster for a long time to come. If they pulled together they could restore conditions of life which would leave the Russian zone far behind. The very fact of showing so clear and practical a common purpose would do more than anything else to remove that sense of frustration which at present provides the soil for the short-sighted Russian encouragement of social unrest. The remedy is not counter-intervention by Britain and the United States, but a strictly practical line of action for the good of our several peoples. If Russia were unwilling to join in, it would be action without her, but not against her; if the countries in the Russian zone have to stay out, that would be a limitation in space, not a failure in kind. The most fanatical Communist in our midst could not denounce this as anti-Russian policy as long as this is of her own choosing, and as long as the door with the West is left open for her all the time.

But that door can be left open only if our own actions are of a non-political and practical kind for popular needs, and are not allowed to swell into a settled division from her whole Empire by exclusive blocs of our own. What is happening in India might serve as an additional illustration of this point. With India divided into two or more new states, the only prospect of unity will be through the joint performance of much-needed common but specific activities; whereas any premature ideas for a political link-up would cause even proposals for practical collaboration to be suspect. Russian policy is obsolete and cannot be effective unless tied to social friction elsewhere. By a generous pragmatic approach the West could prove its statesmanship and achieve its aspirations while still leaving open the road to a fuller international unity. Such a neutralisation of the political factor is especially vital for England in her delicate position between America and Russia, half-way between their two social ideologies. Any policy of division would mean for England no longer a balance of power, but subservience to power. Any policy which, through practical co-operation, leads to a revival of international life would bring not only economic relief, but also the opportunity for England to put her political genius in the service of a wider and more peaceful commonwealth.

PROPHET OF CHANGE

Reflections on H. G. Wells

by Peter Quennell

A portrait of H. G. Wells taken shortly before his death

IN mid-August 1946 died H. G. Wells, 'peacefully', at his London house, one of a majestic terrace overlooking Regent's Park. Little had been heard of him during the last few months; but old friends who occasionally crossed his threshold spoke of the veteran world-planner as growing tired and fretful—'tired as a sick child' was Desmond McCarthy's phrase—oppressed by the realisation of all his worst forebodings and dejected by the apparent bankruptcy of the innumerable hopes and schemes that he had spun from his own spiritual viscera for more than half a century. Now his optimism had reached its limit; and the twilight of the prophet's existence was gloomy and unrelieved. His contribution had long ago been made; nothing he had recently added seemed likely to increase its value; but the obituary notices, when they appeared—tributes which ranged from the dignified insipidity of a *Times* editorial to a paragraph of measured depreciation published in the *Tablet*—agreed that in H. G. Wells we had lost one of the most representative literary figures to emerge since 1890.

Otherwise, whether friendly or hostile, the writers of these notices were not very successful in their attempts to supply a balanced portrait. They spoke of the diversity of his achievement, and of the continuity of his purpose; of the vigour of his mind, of his obvious limitations. They wrote with warm appreciation of the early novels and of the scientific fantasies; they could not explain the transition from books they admired to books they found less admirable, or the gradual diffusion of his literary gifts that characterised the later periods of his gigantic life-work. The task was evidently beyond them. Indeed, one would require Wells's own knack of compression, and perhaps something more than Wells's imaginative insight, to chart the astonishing course on which his mind had travelled, or to summarise the temperamental gear and the intellectual bag-and-baggage the traveller carried with

him. Himself he was often impatient of the past, and intolerant of the burdens that tradition lays upon us; yet it is impossible to understand Wells unless we understand his background. And his background was complex and curious, being made up of two contrasted but inter-related pictures, drawn from different aspects of modern English history.

On the one hand, we see a mean shop and a perspective of shabby streets; on the other, an English country house, independent, aloof, tranquil, still girt around with all the apparatus of semi-feudal splendour: Uppark had romantic links with the life of an earlier century; for Sir Henry Fetherstonhaugh, who inherited the house and estate as a gay and rakish young man in 1774, kept among his early mistresses a girl called Emma Hart (afterwards notorious as Nelson's Lady Hamilton), and cut an extravagant dash at the court of George IV. In his old age, he married and settled down, his choice falling on a country girl—by some accounts a dairymaid—whom he had previously had educated in all the proper social elegances; and the sister of this Lady Fetherstonhaugh was still living at Uppark, among Sir Henry's fine eighteenth-century furniture, in the year 1880, when Sarah Wells, the wife of an unsuccessful and improvident tradesman, was promoted to the rank of housekeeper, to rule over footmen and maidservants in satin and lace cap. The scale of life at Uppark was generous and patriarchal. Mrs Wells's children often visited her, spending months at a time about the house and gardens. The most promising was 'Bert', a fragile, sandy-haired little boy with a long enquiring upper lip. He rummaged among Sir Henry's books and examined the stars through an old telescope that he had found and reassembled.

There can be no doubt of the decisive influence of these childish 'below-stairs' associations on H. G. Wells's development. It was not an influence that he himself denied, and in *Experiment in Autobiography* he went so far as to acknowledge the debt that English civilisation owed to the life of its country houses, whose owners had been a bulwark of taste and a focus of liberal thought. One is bound to add, nevertheless, that behind any gratitude he may have felt was a tinge of mistrust and an undercurrent of resentment. It is interesting, for example, that, although Uppark is one of the most beautiful houses of its kind that still exist in England, the beauty of his surroundings should have left him totally unimpressed, and that he dismissed them in his autobiography with a brief and chilly phrase, observing that the mansion was 'a handsome great house looking southward, with beech woods and bracken thickets to shelter the dappled fallow deer of its wide undulating downland park'. In *Tono Bungay*, which deals at length with this phase of his evolution, he is scarcely more expansive; and it is hard to resist the conclusion that life in the great house—and its associations, if not with the sense of servitude, at least with the idea of social inferiority and economic helplessness—bred in him a psychological opposition to certain forms of beauty, that it hardened and exaggerated the strain of philistinism which is always to be detected running through his life-work. He loved beauty when it was alive and sensuous: he feared and distrusted the beauty that is static, the grace that tradition has crystallised, on which time has laid a hand.

For always, looming large over his imagination, was the other aspect of his boyhood. Bromley, where his mother and father had brought up their children and, as incompetent shopkeepers, had struggled, floundered, worried, was already, at the end of the nineteenth century, being engulfed by London suburban squalor. Fields and woods were 'developed'; streams were piped underground or dwindled to rusty rivulets; private enterprise flung out to right and left long, monotonous, yellowish streets of badly-built, inconvenient, unattractive houses. It struck Wells, early in his career as a thoughtful human being, that development of this kind was both essentially uneconomic and utterly unscrupulous, and that there was a connection between these manifestations of modern commercial enterprise and the conditions of his parents' life, their pathetic struggle to exist and their endless hopeless preoccupation with halfpennies, sixpences and shillings. Beneath the shop at Bromley was an underground kitchen, also used as a living-room; and there the family ate its meals, by the dim light that filtered from above through a grating in the pavement. He looked up at the pavement-grating and watched the boot-soles of passers-by, as they hurried down Bromley High Street. From his privileged position, he was able to observe that they were generally worn through.

Back to Uppark Park again, where the dappled fallow deer grazed on the turf, and Sarah Wells, in the white-panelled housekeeper's room, a small defeated figure, rigidly respectable and timidly inefficient, took refuge from harsh reality in a world of pious platitudes. What was the connection between Uppark and Bromley? The great house continued to stand firm, but the social system that it symbolised was rapidly decaying. Round these oases of calm and dignity, a new universe of squalor and confusion was being fast created, a universe dominated not by aristocrats of the traditional stamp—the men who had built Uppark and stocked its library shelves—but by adventurers of a strange and alarming type, possessed of titanic energy but entirely innocent either of an inherited sense of social responsibility or of the revolutionary ability to look and plan ahead. They were changing England, and they were changing Europe. The consequences of the change, the implications of the upheaval they had created, were subjects that did not concern them: the future might take care of itself.

Here one must make an exceedingly important point. A conviction of social injustice, in the narrowest, most abstract sense, cannot be included among Wells's ruling motives. His aspirations were completely practical. First came a passionate desire for personal emancipation, a longing to escape himself from the deadening pressure of his economic circumstances. He escaped with the help of education, and the education he acquired was primarily scientific. Had it been classical or historical, the evolution of his mind might have proceeded very differently, and what he lost in impetus he might have gained in breadth of vision. But the message of science, at the time when Wells absorbed it from the lectures of J. H. Huxley, was still positive and cocksure. In those days there were no mystical physicists, no philosophical astronomers, to confound us with a hint that science itself had definite limitations. Science supplied the assurance that the young man was in search of; and from science he graduated to Socialism and, having lost patience with Socialism of the cultivated Fabian school, Wells began to concoct a brand of Socialist teaching that would suit his own requirements. Confronted by the muddled landscape of late-Victorian England, where Uppark co-existed with Bromley, and blind tradition lived cheek by jowl with the blind, undirected forces of private commercial enterprise, he dreamed of the master-plan that was destined to replace them both, of a world reorganised by science through the agency of men who, like himself, had received the supreme benefit of a scientific training.

Yet Wells did not conform in his youth, nor would he ever conform, to the conventional pattern of the revolutionary Socialist. Lenin, when they met in the Kremlin, described him in conversation afterwards as a typical *petit bourgeois;* and Wells all his life remained persistently —even bitterly—critical of the orthodox Marxist creed. He deplored the worst excesses of individualism; but he was still an individualist, a practical thinker who, having solved his own economic problem, was now anxious to help in the clearing up of some of the preposterous muddles, private and public, he watched proliferating all around him. He was tidy in his mind and methods, whereas the methods of the militant revolutionary are lavish and extravagant. He abhorred waste; and no revolution can be made without a reckless expenditure of human lives and happiness. To that extent, he was *bourgeois*. He lacked, moreover, the cold mystical fire of the revolutionary agent; and it was not anger against society that inspired him year after year to prophesy, preach and proselytise, so much as the sheer impatience he felt at the sight of human inefficiency. The remedy was clear—so brilliantly clear—if the confused reader would have the goodness for a moment to borrow H. G. Wells's spectacles!

His impatience increased as time went on. And, as it increased, the role of the artist in his literary life grew more and more subsidiary. The artist, he suspected, must get in the planner's way. He would repudiate art. Yet it is an odd fact that his career from one point of view may be interpreted as a justification of aestheticism, since it demonstrates that for a writer to think aloud in print, however clearly and consistently, is seldom quite enough: that a whisper may be as influential as a loud emphatic statement: that there are more things in heaven and earth than were ever dreamed of at Huxley's feet in the class-rooms of South Kensington. The situation would be simpler if Wells had been simply a bad artist, or a journalist to whom questions of art were totally irrelevant. Indeed, he had uncommon artistic aptitude; the gift of selecting and placing words; an unusual faculty of description, and a fancy at once precise and sweeping; together with a sympathetic appreciation of his fellow human creatures.

No one who was not a magnificent story-teller could have carried to success the long and memorable series of scientific fantasies, in which his early technical training, at work on the imagination of a receptive literary artist, caused him to anticipate some of the most startling developments of the years 1914 to 1945. The scientific romances brought fame and security; and there followed a period when he experienced (he admitted himself) 'a craving to figure as a novelist pure and simple', and wrote *Love and Mr Lewisham, Kipps, Tono Bungay, Ann Veronica* and *The History of Mr Polly*. There the artist was given his chance, but somehow failed to take it. At least, he failed to get the complete grasp of his material that makes a literary masterpiece; with the result that each of these books had many admirable passages, but none of them can be enjoyed as a finished aesthetic whole. They have vitality, but the life that animates them is diffuse and shapeless. Perhaps Wells despised perfection. It may be (as I have already suggested) that symmetry of form and beauty of detail were associated in his mind with the vision of Uppark, its graceful proportions, its harmonious setting. And what he denied himself, he tended to distrust in others.

Towards those contemporary writers most interested in literary form, Wells maintained an attitude of mocking incomprehension; and, while Henry James ventured in a friendly fashion to deplore Wells's tragic misuse of splendid natural faculties, Wells—equally friendly but somewhat more unguarded—made exuberant fun of Henry James in his agonised pursuit of the inevitable expressive word. For, if it is true that he came within measurable distance of being a great story-teller, it is also true that H. G. Wells was nearly a great satirist; and there are few funnier essays in literary caricature than his imaginary account in *Boon* of a protracted conversation between Henry James and George Moore, the two accomplished stylists entirely at cross-purposes but each continuing to unfold his fine euphonious monologue; so that, while James is 'labouring through the long cadences of his companion as an indefatigable steam-tug might labour endlessly against a rolling sea', piling parenthesis on parenthesis, and qualification on qualification, George Moore is engaged in describing, 'with an extraordinary and loving mastery of detail . . . a glowing little experience that had been almost forced upon him at Nismes by a pretty little woman from Nebraska, and the peculiar effect it had had, and particularly the peculiar effect that the coincidence that both Nebraska and Nismes begin with an "N" and end so very differently, had had upon his imagination': till they are suddenly interrupted by the uncouth apparition of the Editor of the *New Age*.

No account of Wells could pretend to completeness that did not include some reference to the youthful sense of fun, half affectionate, half malicious, which still thrust its way to the surface and threw up bubbling geysers, even in the products of his last decade, when his hopes for humanity as a whole seemed to be steadily declining. Thus he had the vehemence of a prophet but none of the solemnity; ever and again he would turn round on himself with an engagingly candid smile, as who should say: 'You are all muddlers—incurable muddlers—but at least when it comes to personal problems, I am as muddle-headed as the worst of you, and quite as impulsive and emotional and hopelessly undirected!' In his concern for the future of humanity, he never lost his warm and abounding interest in humanity's present pains and pleasures, with especial reference to the manifold difficulties that surround the relations of the sexes. This sympathy is the keynote of the group of novels published between 1896 and 1914. None is, strictly speaking, auto-biographical; yet each encloses large fragments of personal experience; for, just as his Socialism began at home, so did his understanding of human desires and emotions. When rereading these books, it is advisable to keep open at one's side the two volumes entitled *Experiment in Autobiography*, and check the adventures of his imaginary personages by the adventures of his own youth, from Bromley High Street onwards. His reflections on Uppark, and the place occupied by such relics of the past in the existing social structure, are expanded at considerable length in the pages of *Tono Bungay*, and the early effects of his scientific training are analysed with immense care in the brilliantly amusing story of *Love and Mr Lewisham*. But no less important is the experience supplied by his first and second marriages. The emotional restlessness that always characterised him, his own dependence on women and vague persistent aspiration towards the perfect human relationship that he somehow never quite achieved, also characterise Mr Lewisham and the heroes of *Tono Bungay* and *The New Machiavelli*. At the moment it would be neither permissible nor discreet to enquire into the autobiographical foundation of *The New Machiavelli* and *Ann Veronica*; but these books, it is pretty clear, possess a common basis, and there is little to choose between the elopement of Ann Veronica and her enamoured scientist and that of the heroine of *The New Machiavelli* and her love-lorn politician. Each book has a 'happy ending' that strangely fails to ring true.

Tono Bungay he once described as, in the field of novel-writing, probably his most ambitious effort. It is certainly the most delightful of the half-dozen important books published in that period; and its shortcomings—for it has many—are typical of the literary imperfections to be found in all the others. But let us begin upon the credit side. The central theme is brilliantly worked out, and interwoven with that theme are two memorable, sympathetic and closely detailed portraits—Edward Ponderevo, promoter and financier, and his wife, the narrator's aunt, who follows Ponderevo with quizzical devotion through his meteoric progress.

In describing the adventurer himself, Wells would appear to have derived his inspiration from several different sources. There was the tragedy of Whittaker Wright, a fraudulent financier who killed himself behind the scenes at a London court of justice; and at the opposite end of the scale there was the astonishing career of Alfred Harmsworth, who invented modern popular journalism and concluded his career, rich and honoured, as a member of the House of Lords. Individually, they are not to be compared; but both exemplified the dazzling opportunities offered during the period of Wells's early manhood to men of ruthless drive and energy. Wells liked and admired Harmsworth; he recognised in him at last 'a certain admirable greatness' and admitted that he had 'travelled far from the mere headlong vulgarity of his first drive into prosperity'. But he was alarmed by the almost unlimited power that, in the conditions of modern society, such an individual wielded, and by the contrast between 'the real vastness of the opportunities and challenges that crowded upon him . . . and the blank inadequacy of his education' for other than competitive aims. Harmsworth's success, according to Wells, had caught him unaware and blown him sky high. In Edward Ponderevo, he drew the portrait of a small man boosted up to the heavens by tremendous accidental opportunities, who flames there like an exploding rocket, then hurtles down to earth again as a charred and extinguished stick. Ponderevo, the product of the new world, is balanced by a portrayal of stately anachronistic Bladesover. Both are depicted with skill and gusto; but in

neither instance does he spoil the proportions of his narrative by ramming home a theory. Ponderevo is never a type; and 'my aunt', who nags and loves, and laughs at him and humours him, remains one of the more memorable creations of the twentieth century novel.

The weaknesses of *Tono Bungay*, on the other hand, are startling and obvious. What perverse spirit induced the novelist to attach to his main theme, first an irrelevant adventure story—the account of how the narrator attempts to retrieve his uncle's fortunes by stealing from a desert island a hoard of some mysterious radio-active substance: second, a love story as clumsy and unconvincing as it is emotionally banal? Strange that H. G. Wells, the critic of Bladesover, should let Bladesover beguile his imagination with the vision of an aristocratic siren called 'The Honourable Beatrice Normandy': and that, having thoroughly explored the same theme some years earlier in *Love and Mr Lewisham*, he should hark back to the disillusionments of an early ill-adjusted marriage! Yet so it is: the general effect of *Tono Bungay* is over-loaded and top-heavy, and remains an irritating mixture of the best and the worst in Wells. Faults of taste, errors of construction, appear in all our greatest novelists. Wells's mistakes, on the other hand, are not merely superficial, but are related both to his view of life and to his conception of the novelist's art. Thus, he wrote endlessly of love: but, owing to some failure of comprehension or lack of emotional delicacy—it was not sympathy he lacked or the desire to understand—his handling of the subject was often trite and vulgar. *Ann Veronica*, for example, is an absorbing but, in the last resort, eminently unsatisfactory volume. Today, it has a vivid historical interest; the battle which it concerns had been won by 1918, and Ann Veronica's struggle with her father for the right to 'lead her own life' seems now almost as remote as the struggle for parliamentary reform in the early nineteenth century. But, apart from its value as an historical document and the satirical glimpses of Fabian reformers and militant suffragettes, *Ann Veronica* has begun to show its age, while the idyllic episode with which it terminates has a saccharine vulgarity that sets the teeth on edge. Wells's lavish employment of three dots is nowhere more exasperating.

Kipps and *Mr Polly*, on the other hand, are made of solider stuff than the runaway science student, since they crystallise an important aspect of the novelist's own character—his cocksureness and his humility, his persistent hopeful strivings towards a good and happy life, his refusal to conform or to be shoved by circumstances into the Procrustean bed of any established social category. He has been called the prophet of the Common Man; but one must add that it was the uncommonness of the Common Man that always most attracted him. He saw the ordinary man as a creature of soaring aspirations —usually stifled at birth—and of vast potentialities, which in ninety-nine cases out of a hundred were never fully realised. Perhaps he erred on the side of optimism. But then a tendency towards radical simplification was at once the weakness and the strength of Wells's intellectual methods. His literary imagination was bright but shadowless. It lacked a place for the finer and softer shades; it disdained, for example, the qualifications and reservations that lend so much to the beauty and variety of Henry James's life-work.

Moreover, Wells despised humility. Brought up by his mother to be humble, to accept the dispensations of an all-wise Providence which had ordained Uppark and its housekeeper's room upon the one hand, Bromley High Street and its subterranean kitchen-living-room upon the other, he faced the world with perky self-assurance, stared it straight between the eyes and declined to take off his hat. Thus the religious emotions, though in the middle life he produced an unfortunate book named *God the Invisible King*, were almost completely beyond the range of his sympathy and understanding. His greatest limitation, both as a novelist and a prophet, was a refusal to admit that his view might possibly be limited; for the essence of his gospel was a conviction that every problem could be solved—and solved immediately and permanently—if good will and a trained scientific intelligence were only brought to bear upon it. In the early, even in the middle books, there is still, vaguely apparent here and there, a lingering sense of mystery; but after a certain period, the universe he surveyed contracted rather than expanded, and his belief in his own prophetic infallibility grew more and more insistent. He dismissed the experts, as he had dismissed the aesthetes, and in the *Outline of History* sought to reduce the whole recorded human past to the intellectual level of Kipps and Mr Polly.

Yet there can be no doubt of the incalculable debt his contemporaries and successors owe him. If the modern Ann Veronica now enjoys, for what it is worth, her 'freedom', if the Kipps of today is a person less class-conscious and mentally circumscribed than his late-Victorian prototype, they should think with gratitude of H. G. Wells, whose function it was to tear open many fast-sealed windows and let a gust of fresh air into the stifling, insanitary, middle-class basement in which he spent his childhood. 'No writer' (said Desmond McCarthy in an obituary broadcast) 'contributed more than Wells to the moral and intellectual make-up of the average man and woman in the first half of the twentieth century.' 'Wherever a young man, from the Arctic to the Tropics' (wrote J. B. Priestley) 'was determined to free himself from mental squalor, fear, and ignorance, there was Wells at his side, eager to instruct, denounce, startle and inspire.'

Perhaps 'eager' is the most revelatory word. About him, even during old age, there was a disarming air of eagerness, reflected in the brisk movements of his small, neat, grey-clad person and echoed in his high electrical squeak of a voice when he grew interested or excited. His was an exceedingly mercurial mind. 'Although he would not have enjoyed being told so,' (continues Priestley's article) 'he had the temperament of an artist and not that of a scientist or a philosopher.' His mental processes were essentially intuitive; and, just as his prophetic preoccupations always tended to hamper his progress as an artist, so his artistic temperament made him a disseminator of ideas, a populariser of theories, rather than an original philosophic or scientific thinker. In his composition the conflict between the artist and the journalist-propagandist was never really settled. After two decades of increasingly tendentious work, during which the artist seemed to have sunk low indeed behind the literary horizon, he suddenly burst out, at the age of seventy-two, with that astonishing and disconcerting production, *Apropos of Dolores*, a novel without propagandist taint, in which the writer, angry as a boy at his first disappointed love affair, rails against the possessiveness of womanhood, its greed and its stupidity, through episode on ludicrous episode, and page on envenomed page.

Among unexpected products in an entirely different field, one must also mention the thesis he submitted towards the end of his life for a doctorate at an English university. Entitled *A Thesis on the Quality of Illusion in the Continuity of the Individual Life in the Higher Metazoa, with particular reference to the species Homo Sapiens*, this rare pamphlet seems calculated to undermine a great deal of Wells's previous teaching. If 'there is not and never has been such an original mental unity' as is implied in the conception of self-hood, and if all 'consolidations' of our personality are largely artificial, the idea of human perfectibility seems destined to go by the board, at least till the human organisation has reached a further stage in its development. But, when this thesis was submitted, the shadows were already deepening. In one of his last published essays, Wells acknowledged a suspicion that the human race, having failed to adapt itself to its circumstances and surroundings, was an experiment that had failed and that, like other natural experiments, it would one day be superseded: that there was no issue from chaos: that no generation of *Men Like Gods* would ever arise on earth to justify his hopes and dreams: indeed, that only his nightmares, and not his dreams, were destined for realisation. The first atom bomb descended a year before his death; but during the twelve months that remained he had little taste for prophesying. He had helped to build a new world on the ruins of the nineteenth century, to open up new prospects—perhaps deceptive— of order, toleration, progress. He saw the insecurity of its hopeful foundations, and died, as in the midst of an earthquake, with the stable and civilised universe rocking all round him.

How to tell the People

A DISCUSSION ON THE BRITISH GOVERNMENT'S PUBLIC RELATIONS

between

ROBERT FRASER

Director-General of the Central Office of Information

and

FRANK OWEN

Editor of The Daily Mail

Chairman:

KINGSLEY MARTIN

Editor of The New Statesman

Photos:
W. St. John Glenn

Robert Fraser and Kingsley Martin

Kingsley Martin and Frank Owen

Kingsley Martin: *The first thing in discussing public relations is to get a clear definition. Some people think that there is too much 'Government propaganda', others that there is not enough information about what the Government are doing, or, in their view, should be doing. Some people want more news in order better to combat the Conservative Opposition's whispering campaign: others are furious at the idea of the Labour Government being able to use the official machinery of publicity to send out news which may counteract that whispering campaign. Now, Fraser, how do you in your job differentiate between the requirements of these two schools?*

Robert Fraser: I agree that these different criticisms are heard. But I can perhaps best begin my rather neutral contribution to this discussion by saying that they are all based on an approach to the problem which has little or nothing in common with the one we make ourselves. There is, it seems to me, extreme confusion about the nature and purpose of Government Public Relations. Doubtless this is in part due to the novelty of the official

Information Services themselves. Adapted from the wartime propaganda organisation, they were incorporated into the permanent machinery of the State only in April of last year (1946). When people use the term 'Government Public Relations', they may be referring to four quite separate things. Firstly, they may mean the technical publicity service of Transport House and its Press Department. The Labour Party is a political organisation believing in a certain number of things in which other people don't believe, and maintaining, like other Parties, its own propaganda organisation which is financed from Party and not public funds. Secondly, there are the Government's own relations with the public—the quality of the personal links with the people which the Ministers of any Government must have, and the goodness or badness of which will be determined by the flair, personalities and the programme of the men who form the Administration. Government Public Relations in this sense existed long before anyone had ever thought of Directors of Public Relations or Official Information Services. If you had said to Disraeli or Gladstone or Joseph Chamberlain: 'You are faced with an acute problem of public relations', they would not have understood what you were talking about. They conducted their own relations with the public and expected to do so as part of their political leadership.

Kingsley Martin: *Some of our Ministers have always understood the value of close contact with the problem and some have not. I think the curious thing about the present Prime Minister is that he has the same kind of delicacy as Lord Salisbury: he thinks it is wrong for a Prime Minister deliberately to heed what the public is thinking about him, and then deliberately to play up to the public. A long series of Prime Ministers had a quite different attitude.*

Robert Fraser: You are giving an illustration upon which I could not properly comment one way or the other. Let me rather pass on to the third thing people may mean when they talk of Government Public Relations. This is the purely Departmental aspect of Public Relations. Like Imperial Chemical Industries or the United States Steel Corporation, a large Government Department must attend to the quality of its relations with those with whom it deals. The purpose of Public Relations in this sense is just to create real understanding between the organisation and the public. There remains the fourth: the Official and publicly financed Information Services themselves. As I have said, these Services did not exist before the war. We had really not evolved beyond the conception of Departmental Public Relations in the sense that I have just defined them. Thus the Post Office had developed a vigorous Public Relations policy. The Service Departments had done the same, largely because they had a serious recruiting problem on their hands.

Kingsley Martin: *Because they wanted to get more money out of the Treasury than Parliament was willing to give them!*

Robert Fraser: I wouldn't know. With the war came the establishment of the Government's propaganda and publicity services. I think the significance of the decision not to dissolve and disband them lay in the fact that for the first time the Government was consciously accepting some measure of responsibility for seeing that a fully enfranchised people, confronted with manifold and difficult problems, received all the information they needed in order to enable them to make up their minds about the answers, and generally to act as intelligent citizens. The first of my four kinds of Public Relations arises from the needs of the Labour Party. The second arises from the needs of the Government. The third arises from the needs of the Departments, the fourth from the needs of a self-governing people. Unless one makes these distinctions quite clearly, there inevitably follows a dreadful muddle in which people fail to separate, on the one side, the duties of political and of Party leadership, and, on the other, the duties of the official Information Services. I emphasise again that the Information Services are neutral. They deal not in opinions but in facts and explanations. Indeed, the vigorous operation of the Information Services could conceivably injure a Government by executing their real task of public enlightenment.

Kingsley Martin: *I want more explanation about your last point. I cannot readily draw the boundary myself between propaganda for the Government and information about the things it is doing. I would have thought the frontiers were indefinable.*

Robert Fraser: In practice I don't find this so. And I think that most people in the Central Office or in the Information Divisions of the Departments will tell you that they do not experience practical difficulties; and I also think I can draw the distinction in principle. Broadly speaking, the official Information Services are not seeking to persuade anyone that any contestable proposition is true. It is no business of theirs to convert all opinion into Government opinion. That is someone else's job. They are seeking to ensure that the public receives the facts and explanations it needs in order to form its own opinions. Let us take a simple case. It is part of the work of the Information Services to distribute, analyse and answer questions about the unemployment figures. Supposing that the unemployment figures were rising, rising, and rising, as indeed happened in the crisis of 1931. It might well be that the more effectively the Information Services did their work—that is to say, the larger the number of people who came to understand that the unemployment total was getting higher and higher—the worse the Government might seem to the public to be doing. If the issues were controversial, the official Information Services would have to stand outside the debate. They could give facts but not enter controversial argument. This still leaves a true and important function for them to perform. When the fuel crisis began on that grim weekend last winter, the Ministry of Fuel and Power asked me and one or two others to go down to work out with them what sort of information arrangements we should institute. In fact, the most important things the Ministry decided to do were very simple: firstly, to have a daily Press conference with a chairman of authority; and secondly, at that Press conference, to throw all the statistical cards face upwards on the table. We were simply organising a big flow of accurate information, and we did not find it necessary to touch at all upon the highly controversial issues which might be held to underlie the fuel crisis. Yet the Press conferences were a great success, as I think everybody felt. The point I am making is that quite outside the field of political controversy the Information Services have a big and real job to do. The test I apply is this. I think it wrong to spend public money on advancing a controversial proposition by the Government if the Opposition denies its accuracy.

Kingsley Martin: *Well, that's an interesting suggestion; do you agree with it, Owen?*

Frank Owen: You've got to make up your mind what you're trying to do in this field and, decidedly, it is not easy to define. With a dictatorship it *is* easy—there can

Home Requests come
from Government Departments. The Central Office is not a first source of information or policy but the place where information and policy are 'processed' into films, exhibitions, posters, magazines, and other media, and the distribution of these things is controlled. COI does not deal with the Press, except that it runs the distributing machinery for Government news, through its News Distribution Unit

Overseas Requests
come from the Foreign, Colonial, and Commonwealth Relations Offices and their information posts abroad. COI is not responsible for British publicity policy overseas, nor for its local execution. It produces the material and advises technically on distribution. Of COI's London staff of about 1,300, well over half work for overseas. (COI also employs about 300 people in its regional offices in England and Wales)

Campaigns Division runs the Government's Press
and poster advertising campaigns. Industrial and Service recruiting, production and exports, fuel economy, health, road safety are current subjects. It also arranges factory and other talks through COI's extensive regional organisation

Social Survey Divison is the Government's social
research organisation. Using modern sampling techniques, it collects and analyses data not otherwise available about, for example, mining, recruiting, the incidence of sickness, shop closing hours, and the effect of COI's own publicity

Films Division produces all Government films for
theatrical and non-theatrical showing at home and overseas. COI has its own film production organisation, Crown Film Unit, and its own non-theatrical organisation, the latter run from COI's regional offices

Exhibitions Division arranges exhibitions and
displays at home on industry, the Commonwealth, social services, health, and science. It also produces touring exhibitions for overseas, such as 'Britain Rebuilds' and 'Britain Goes Ahead'

Photographs Division works for overseas, pro-
viding regular services of general photographs, feature sets, mats and ebonoids, printed photographic display sets, and film strips. Subjects are predominantly social and industrial. It also supplies the photographic needs of COI's other divisions

Publications Division produces all the COI
magazines for overseas; also *Coal*, the COI's one home magazine. It supplies all the material for Foreign Office publications produced overseas, edits and designs books for official publication in this country

Production Services Division is the COI's
internal common service technical division. It runs the studio, the printing section, and despatches all material. It promotes the sale of COI's overseas magazines, and assists the overseas distribution of British newspapers and periodicals

Reference Division is COI's factual storehouse. It
keeps overseas posts supplied with all the information needed for their work in the form of reference papers, handbooks, and regular reviews of home and foreign affairs. It also supplies COI's other Divisions with their factual information

Overseas Press Services Division edits and
transmits a daily world-wide wireless-morse service of special news, features, comment, background information, and factual elaboration for posts overseas. It supplements this service with half a dozen regional services

be no argument about it. What the Government says is always right, and if you don't like it, things will be just too bad for you.

Here in this country, however, we are still trying, with some pains, to make a really democratic State in which one Party is 'in' and another is 'out'. The party which is 'out' criticises the party which is 'in'; but they do it with the sobering reflection that the next week they may have to undertake the responsibility of government themselves. Therefore, I agree with Robert Fraser that if we fail to draw a clear line between 'Government' Public Relations and 'Party' Public Relations, we shall run headlong into trouble. For example, you could not expect any self-respecting Civil Servant to switch his entire approach to any national issue in a few hours. Therefore, you must fix firmly in advance at what point Government propaganda must end and at what point Party propaganda may begin.

Let me offer two practical examples of what I mean. Our most thoroughly nationalised services are the Armed Forces of the Crown. These Forces have both the advantages and disadvantages of nationalisation. All parties are agreed in trying to operate them on a non-party basis. Thus, we carry out our national recruiting campaigns, our campaigns to improve the lot of officers and men and so on—all in a non-party spirit. These excellent campaigns succeed largely for the reason that they are recognised by all as being valuable. When you come to deal with things like the coal mines, which have been nationalised, well, the public has now accepted the fact that the mines are the property of the State and that the miner has a status in society which he never had before. During the war, we drew a picture of the soldier or the sailor or airman doing a hard and heroic job; to-day the Government are rightly going out and telling the story of the miner.

Kingsley Martin: *On that basis, if we nationalised all industries, official publicity might fairly be used to dramatise all kinds of workers.*

Frank Owen: No, I do not say that. For one thing they do not live the same dangerous life as the miner. Nor is there the same general agreement about the control of other industries. The moment you begin to move away from the accepted things on to the controversial things, then you get on to the dubious ground which Government propaganda should avoid. That the mines should be nationalised is agreed.

But don't gallop away with the idea that a miner is wonderful because he works in a nationalised industry. You don't say the airman is a fine chap because he works in a nationalised service, you say it because he flies, an occupation which still has considerable hazards.

Kingsley Martin: *What then are your main criticisms of the Government's publicity?*

Frank Owen: I do not join the Government's Fleet Street critics in charging them with abusing their publicity machine; indeed, I consider that the Government are

using it with commendable restraint. What is more, I recognise and approve in principle the use of publicity by the Government. But I am pointing out certain dangers inherent in it. Go back to your mines again. It is proper to stress that the miner is doing a hard job well. But if you were to claim that the miner is doing his stuff simply *because* he is nationalised you would be entering the field of party controversy, and at that point the Opposition would properly object.

Kingsley Martin: *Does that mean you are satisfied with the Government's publicity in general?*

Frank Owen: No, I consider that Government publicity in general is poor. But let's begin with a few bouquets! I think the finest publicity job done in this country for years was that carried on by the department of which my friend here, Robert Fraser, was head during the war. They ran the most exciting, stimulating pamphlets, such as the grand story of the Battle of Britain, of Fighter Command, Bomber Command, the Atlantic Bridge, etc, all beautifully produced. I have heard that Fraser is now going to produce one on the coal crisis called *How We Got Through*. I look forward to that story.

Kingsley Martin: *You would not object to it in any way?*

Frank Owen: I would not. But I want on the front page of that pamphlet the portrait of the miner, the Man who Cut the Coal. When Fraser paid the 14th Army the honour, after the war, of publishing their story and telling the world what they did in Burma, he did a particularly good job. On the cover of the book he put the picture of a soldier—not of Mountbatten, then Supreme Allied Commander, who is a very photogenic being; not even of Sir 'Bill' Slim, the Army Commander, who isn't quite so photogenic—but of an unknown Tommy, slogging his way through the muck of a jungle. That soldier was 'Private Everybody'. It made every soldier who had served there proud to think he had been part of that great crusade.

Robert Fraser: I wonder if I could get Owen's criticism into focus by telling him the various heads under which the Information Services try to work (I am not now talking about political leadership), and then ask him under which of these heads he thinks they do the least well. Firstly, there is just the simple business of getting out of the complicated machinery of Government the facts which people must have and yet which exist alone somewhere inside the boundaries of administration: facts which no one else but the Government knows. Some very simple illustrations are the facts and figures about manpower, production, exports, housing and so on. These facts and figures must be provided to the Press and the BBC and perhaps be presented in other ways. All that is just the plainest and most straightforward provision of information. Secondly, the Information Services have a job to do in the field of instruction. The people in this country have duties and rights conferred upon them by legislation. It may be a duty to refrain from burning gas or electric fires in the winter, it may be

95

a right to draw certain benefits under National Insurance, it may be some change in the value of points or the value of clothing coupons. That· sort of utilitarian personal instruction must be provided, and provided as simply and clearly as possible. Thirdly, the Information Services have a legitimate job to do in the field of persuasion. They are at the moment heavily engaged in a number of persuasive publicity campaigns designed to make people do something that, in the absence of publicity, they would not do, or do well, or do in such numbers—such as joining the mining industry or the Armed Forces as regulars, or getting home safely, or immunising children against diphtheria. These are certainly persuasive campaigns, opinionated campaigns if you like, but each one of them is directed towards a non-controversial end. Fourthly and lastly—this is the point which Owen was developing, and it's a subtler and more difficult point—I think the Information Services have upon them the responsibility of trying to deepen the national consciousness by giving people a clear picture of the nation to which they belong, a deeper awareness of its methods of going about its business, of its problems and difficulties, and of its objectives. We did a lot of work in this field during the war. And we did not exhort, we did not say: 'Be brave; do be good; please endure.' We proceeded on the principle that if we could project sufficiently vividly before people's minds a true picture of the national war effort at its best, we could leave it to the powerful psychological forces of emulation and team spirit to do the rest. That is why the unknown soldier is on the cover of *The Campaign in Burma*. He makes people feel: 'I can be like that and I will be like that.'

Kingsley Martin: *In the early days the Ministry of Information made exactly the mistake you have been trying to correct. There was the famous poster: 'Your courage, your cheerfulness, your resolution will bring us victory', which was much laughed at. You altered it by making it: 'Our courage', etc, to identify people with the nation.*

Robert Fraser: And that kind of morale-building publicity intensifies the group spirit of the nation.

Kingsley Martin: *Only there is great danger, don't you think, Owen, in that?*

Frank Owen: No, I do not think so. I consider the efficiency and stability of any organisation depend largely on the extent to which people serving in it can identify themselves with a common purpose.

Kingsley Martin: *I think Hitler could have said that in exactly the same words. I'm not criticising you, but I am saying that there is a real danger. You are going to use the resources of the State to increase the morale of the people in the same way as the National Socialists did.*

Robert Fraser: I suppose it has to be admitted that the psychological factors underlying group feeling are, broadly speaking, the same, however the group is organised. It all depends on the kind of picture of the character of the national group which you are projecting. You could project the kind of picture that would make

Magazine
for Miners

Edited and designed by COI and published by the Stationery Office, Coal is a 32-page photogravure monthly. Sales: about 115,000. Readers: miners and their families. Sponsors: Coal Board

Magazine
for Germans

Blick *sells 500,000 copies a month in the British zone in Germany. COI edits and designs for the Control Commission. Printed in gravure in Hamburg from film sent from London; 64 pages*

Poster
for the bad lands

This anti-VD poster, with its grinning death's head under the over-alluring hat, was used as a war-time shocker in areas where infection was rampant

Advertisement
for the Millions

This prophetic Press advertisement was one of an 'economic ABC' series run nationally by COI during the summer. Press advertising is largest single item in COI's budget

people dogmatic and cruel or the kind of picture that will make people, as I hope we tried to do during the war, kind, tolerant and freely united. There is certainly a strong political element in this. But then I think the fundamental principles expressed in our picture are, in political terms, the principles of parliamentary government; and I hope we won't regard those as controversial in our country.

Kingsley Martin: *I think you probably agree with that, Owen. But what are your criticisms of what the Government have actually done?*

Frank Owen: I am extremely critical of what they have *not* done. I think that in the matter of informing the nation of the perils which surround it, the Government have failed very badly. They neglected to warn us about the economic crisis. When the crisis came they put out the most uninspiring and even depressing slogans: 'We're up against it' and 'We work or want', which is a wretched workhouse threat. That's rotten propaganda. It will never get the British people up on their feet— they are not a people who react to menaces. The right way would be for the Ministers to concentrate their efforts upon the physical task of refashioning this country, avoiding as far as possible political arguments, which tend to divide us. For example, we are all agreed that we need more machines and more workers, even if it means importing foreign labour: it's absurd to say we don't. Well, the job is to get the vital idea across—and to the whole nation—in a way calculated to produce solid results. They haven't done it.

Kingsley Martin: *Surely you are confusing criticism of Government publicity with criticism of the Government's actual handling of the economic crisis recently. You are attacking them for incompetence.*

Frank Owen: The Government attempt to popularise their own economic White Paper is an example of crass incompetence. First, they bring out a White Paper in a language which is largely not understood by the people— Tom Harrisson's Mass-Observation report has shown that. Next, they put a pretty coloured picture on the cover, with exactly the same indigestible stuff inside, and sell it on the bookstalls as a 'popular version'.

Here is another example of incompetence. One day in the *Daily Mail* office we learnt that the Prime Minister was going to deliver a speech on the radio, not as the leader of the nation, but as the leader of the Labour Party. Nevertheless, we thought we would allot him the utmost space we possibly could, to give the fullest expression of his views to the public. This was at 12 o'clock on Monday morning. For 27 hours I tried my hardest to get through to the Public Relations Adviser to the Prime Minister, and at 3 o'clock on Tuesday I succeeded in piercing the defences. I pointed out that the next day the big popular penny newspapers would have only four pages, and that if the Prime Minister did not go on the air that night until after 9 o'clock it would be quite impossible for any of those newspapers to give him adequate

coverage, especially in their earlier editions. Therefore, if we could have the copy of his speech by 6 o'clock that evening we could strip our leader page and fit the Prime Minister's discourse in there. I said I was not asking this on account of Fleet Street (I had no right to do so) or even to benefit the *Daily Mail* alone; but if the speech could be put out in advance via the Press Association, every newspaper in the kingdom could carry it. This was done, with the result that the *Daily Mail* was able to give it 36½ inches while the *Daily Herald* gave 24. It's not good public relations when a national newspaper has to fight for a day and a night to get through to the Prime Minister's Public Relations Department.

Kingsley Martin: *Now, Fraser, it's your turn to comment on publicity during the fuel crisis.*

Robert Fraser: The fuel crisis is an extremely interesting story and it will serve well to illustrate the difference I have been trying to draw between the Government's relations with the public on the one hand and the activities of the Information Services on the other. Until the weekend of the crisis came, the fuel problem was a problem for the Government. The assessment of the situation, the decision about the measures that might avert the crisis, the plan for dealing with it when it came—these were questions with which only the Government could properly deal. I won't go into the debate about whether warnings of the impending crisis were or were not given or should have been given. That, of course, is not my business. It belongs to Ministers. I will only say the warning could not come properly and authoritatively from the Information Services as such. On the other hand, when on 'Black Friday' the country knew that large sections of its industry were to be dead silent on the Monday, the problem certainly became one in which the Information Services had a plain and important duty to perform. I may be wrong, but a lot of newspapermen have told me that I am not, in thinking that the daily Press conferences at the Ministry of Fuel and Power, supported so fully as they were by the newspapers and the BBC, did a great deal to keep public opinion steady and to secure an astonishing degree of public co-operation in pulling through.

Now let me go back a bit and settle the point which Owen raised about the circulation of the Economic Survey White Paper. I am afraid I still regard the White Paper and the bookstall edition as a remarkable publicity triumph. About 120,000 copies of the White Paper itself were sold and about 170,000 copies of the bookstall edition. I say with some confidence that no one who has had direct experience of selling pamphlets or books about the kind of subjects with which the White Paper deals could hold these sale figures to be anything other than remarkable. You see, the economic situation of their country is not the most passionate of the interests of the British public, and anyone trying to sell a textual or illustrated pamphlet presenting a serious account of some range of economic facts is engaged in strenuous uphill work. Half a dozen allegedly incomprehensible sentences in the White Paper have been widely quoted in criticism, though none of them is incomprehensible in its context. The White Paper is written in language perfectly intelligible to that section of the population willing to buy something between two covers that contains a serious description of the nation's situation.

Kingsley Martin: *I don't agree.*

Frank Owen: I am not going to suggest that you didn't sell all the copies you claim of the White Paper, but I greatly doubt if all your customers read it. You claim the only way to sell a book is to have it talked about—but once you had got rid of this thing—your first edition I mean—why, the sale was dead. I suggest that you got away with murder in an initial blaze of publicity.

Robert Fraser: How can you suggest that? We put out the bookstall edition 14 days afterwards.

Frank Owen: Yes, but nobody knew they were buying the same thing until they had bought it and read it!

Kingsley Martin: *You make a perfectly good point, Owen. Do you not agree, Fraser, that it would have been possible to reach a larger public if it had been entirely rewritten and put in much simpler language?*

Robert Fraser: Not significantly larger, and perhaps smaller. If I had poured all the technical competence I may have as an editor into a pamphlet of that kind, I don't believe the sales achieved would have exceeded 50,000 copies. During the war we sold many millions of pamphlets and booklets, but the sale of those dealing seriously with non-military home affairs was very small. Manpower during the war was a wonderful story and no one could have written it better than Priestley did in his brilliant little text for the official booklet *Manpower*. Yet the sales were not more that two or three per cent of those of *The Battle of Britain*. The publishing fallacy lies here. There just isn't a mass market for that kind of pamphlet, and I think that those who choose a pamphlet on this range of subjects as a means of communication to very large numbers of people are just making the first of all technical errors in the technique of publicity—they are choosing the wrong medium for the job. The right means of communication for this sort of subject are broadcasting, the news columns of the newspapers and, to a lesser extent, posters and Press advertising.

Frank Owen: Ah, that brings me to another criticism I want to make. The Government have neglected two more of the greatest media of publicity—films and radio. What a difference if, at the time of the coal crisis, Mr Attlee had gone on the air and spoken to the people in their homes that evening! If he had said: 'Please turn out the light, if it is still on—and listen to me', then told the grim story and ended by saying: 'Ladies and gentlemen, there is an end to this story—and it can still be a happy one if we all do our part. Now you can turn on the light—and by the way, by listening in the dark you have saved so many thousand tons of coal.' Showmanship? Of course. It is a large part of leadership.

I recall another crisis, the day that the Russians came into the war. I was staying with Lord Beaverbrook in the country. As soon as he heard the early morning news he drove off to see the Prime Minister. I believe he got Churchill to go to the microphone the same night and say that now that these people were marching against our enemy we must march with them—that we were all in it together at last. If Mr Attlee had said on his own Black Friday: 'We are all in it, and we have all to get out of it', he would have evoked the spirit which always gets us out.

Kingsley Martin: *As a matter of historic interest, are you asserting that Churchill wouldn't have made his speech if Beaverbrook hadn't gone to see him?*

Frank Owen: All I know is that at six o'clock in the morning the news of Hitler's invasion of Russia came through. Beaverbrook heard it first. He said to me: 'The Germans have invaded Russia, and we have won the war.' He then called for his car and went at once to see Winston, returning about 8 o'clock that night. He told me that Winston was writing his speech, and that he was going to say that we would carry on the war as the comrades of the Russians.*

Frank Owen: The point I make is that *somebody* had the wit to use the radio at once in the crisis of 1941 and nobody did in the crisis of 1947.

Kingsley Martin: *We are coming to the crux of this argument. Owen, you have said that the Government haven't used the* BBC *properly; do you mean that they should have used it for controversial purposes, or taken it over as an emergency measure?*

Frank Owen: I hold that the risks here should have been accepted, and that the spokesman of the Government should have gone on the air on the night of Black Friday and said: 'Here is the trouble, and this is why it has occurred. Coal stocks in the factories have run down, the roads from the coalfields are frozen and we can't get the stuff away. Even the pithead gear is snowed up—this is the crisis.' The Government spokesman should have so phrased his information and appeal that the ordinary person, while being resentful of the fact that the crisis had broken suddenly upon him, and being inclined to be critical, wouldn't have condemned it as a party speech. He would have said: 'OK. This is crisis for all of us.'

*At this point, Mr. Noel Newsome, war-time Director of the BBC's European Service, who was present at the discussion, interpolated: 'At 5am I was rung up at home by the Night Editor of the European Service and told that the German Army had invaded the Soviet Union. I went straight to the office and dictated a news story which began: "Britain today has a great new Ally." This story led all bulletins from 5.30 onwards, starting in German, and went out dozens of times in various languages during the following few hours. At about noon I received a visit from a Foreign Office official who told me that a grave blunder had been committed by the reference to 'a great new Ally', and that it was by no means certain we should regard the Soviet Union as an Ally; the Prime Minister was unapproachable and busy on a speech he was to deliver after the 9 o'clock news, and that until he had spoken no one would know what the attitude of the British Government would be—and so on. The rest you know.'

Robert Fraser: Surely the difference is that, when there is a crisis, you may go on the air and explain both the facts of the situation and what is being done. But you cannot present a controversial account of the origins of the crisis unless you are willing that an alternative account should be presented by those who do not accept yours.

Frank Owen: Fair enough.

Kingsley Martin: *Now, Fraser, will you say something about films?*

Robert Fraser: Well, one thing first: for good or ill, the cinema of this country is primarily, like the theatre, a form of entertainment. The screen is not as flexible and comprehensive a medium as the Press and the radio. It can't bend to this purpose and to that as they can, and it is no good trying to cut too much across the grain.

Frank Owen: I don't entirely accept that.

Robert Fraser: Well, isn't it just an obvious fact? The information film occupies a tiny place on the screens of British cinemas. I'm not discussing what should be or might be, but only what is.

Kingsley Martin: *Well, documentaries do exist.*

Robert Fraser: I know. The Central Office is much the biggest source of documentaries in this country. We are proud of them and believe in them. But how do the numbers of those who see them compare with the numbers of those who are reached daily through the newspapers and the BBC?

Frank Owen: Might I come in on this for a moment? During the war—in the early part of the war—we tried to get a film made. The idea began with a memory of that astonishing old agitator, Jim Larkin, getting up many years ago in Dublin, and saying to a great mass meeting: 'Who built this great, fair city? *We* built this city!' Well, we wanted to do a picture which started with a man on Westminster Bridge saying: 'Who built this city?' We wanted to show the men building the bridges, making the concrete which makes the bridge, cutting the coal which makes the concrete; we wanted to show a fire or a flood in the pit, and brave men jostling each other to go down into that terrible place and get their pals out. We took this to the Ministry of Fuel, but some genius there told us that if we did this we should frighten the people out of the pit. Good God! Don't the miners know these perils for themselves? It was the rest of the country that needed telling. They need telling about lots of things. They should know the wonderful story of the fisherfolk who man the lifeboats round our coasts—how they go out in seas where all hell is raging, to save the lives of men they've never even seen before. The film is the medium for that—and for much else in our daily lives

that the Government take an interest in. Now, the Government have no film apparatus of their own—yet. But they'll find the film industry willing enough to co-operate with them for national purposes.

Robert Fraser: I don't disagree with you. I think we can make both more energetic and more considered efforts to put up ideas to commercial film producers, which is what you have, I think, in mind. Of course the Government is a big film-maker, and the Cinematograph Exhibitors' Association gives us practical help in securing distribution.

Frank Owen: Since the Government publicity organisation has been under fire all evening, may I add one word about newspapers, which do so much of the firing? The less *they* 'propagand', the better, too. I know I prefer to get my own news without being told in every other paragraph what I should be thinking of it. I like to see any newspaper speak its own mind—but only in one place— its leader column. Every other column belongs not to itself but to the public. I believe you have tonight made it abundantly clear that you agree a similar demarcation must exist in the Government Information Services.

Kingsley Martin: *Owen's criticism is that there is a distinction to be drawn between party propaganda and Government propaganda, because he thinks it is possible to draw the line between giving factual information which is recognised by everybody as non-controversial (even though it may contain elements which are morale-building) and information on matters about which the country is really not certain. That distinction Fraser broadly accepts. It isn't the duty of the Information Services to spend Treasury money on that which is controversial, and the truth of which can be denied by the Opposition.*

But that, in Fraser's view, is not a complete answer, because there is a side of publicity that inevitably goes beyond 'information', which increases the public consciousness of social issues, and which is, therefore, morale-building. A definition cannot easily be laid down. Owen makes the further criticism that, within the limits imposed by this distinction between information and propaganda, the Government doesn't make the fullest use it can of the Press, of the wireless and of the films. The Information Services could initiate more ambitious projects, and as far as that criticism goes, Fraser agrees, but says that it is due to the fact that the Information Services, like most other services, are very overworked and undermanned. As for the general failure of the Government's publicity, that is the failure of Ministers rather than of technicians. On the technical matters which have been criticised, Fraser defends himself, with, I think, considerable ability.

IN SEARCH OF A FOREIGN POLICY

Anthony Nutting   *R. H. S. Crossman*

An exchange of letters, written during the summer of 1947, before the Parliamentary recess,

between R. H. S. Crossman, leader of the group of Socialist MP's who oppose Mr. Bevin's

foreign policy, and Anthony Nutting, a Vice-chairman of the Conservative Party, chairman

of the Young Conservatives and a specialist on foreign affairs

MY DEAR CROSSMAN,

I have just been rereading the section of *Keep Left* which deals with foreign affairs and I should be glad if you would explain a few points which I find rather puzzling.

As I see it, your main thesis is that we should aim at an independent foreign policy—that is to say, a policy independent of both America and Russia. You claim that as a result of Russian tactics in Persia and other fields we have been thrown into the arms of the USA and, by co-operating too closely with America, have aroused Soviet suspicions and driven the Russians into hostile isolation.

As your solution to this situation, you advance the idea that we should strive all we can to prevent the world becoming divided into two rival blocs by, in effect, creating a third bloc, presumably of ourselves, France and the rest of Western Europe.

The trouble about these theories is that they ignore not only present world conditions but past practice as well. Now let us take your independent foreign policy. Ever since we ceased to follow a policy of isolation from the affairs of the European continent, we have surely based our foreign policy on an alliance with some other power. At one time it was Prussia; at another, France. Now surely it is both right and proper that it should be the ally with whom we worked so closely during the war

and whose capacity to help us today is so immense. Indeed, if we are to criticise our foreign policy since 1945, we should surely say that we have sat on the fence between East and West far too long, in order not to arouse Russian suspicions and hostility.

Where else can our desperate needs of raw materials, capital equipment and food be satisfied but in the Western Hemisphere? Russia is in no position to supply them. Indeed, she is in every bit as desperate straits as we ourselves. In fact, all Europe is in the 'Have Not' category. Surely, therefore, we have no alternative but to work with the Americans who are not only able but also willing to help Europe to its feet.

If the Soviet Union were to join with us, we should, of course, welcome her with more than ordinary warmth. But so far she has held out and the signs for the future are not encouraging. We cannot, therefore, blind ourselves to the fact that the world is already divided into two rival blocs. We cannot prevent this happening. It is an accomplished fact. And to suggest either as a preventative or as a cure that we should get together with Western Europe and be a third bloc between America and Russia is a policy which would truly bring us, as it has brought us to date, the worst of both worlds.

Yours sincerely,

ANTHONY NUTTING

My Dear Nutting,

I have been meaning to answer your letter for several days. But I decided to postpone it till after the Foreign Affairs debate. I must admit the debate has not made an answer easy. Yesterday I had to listen to a series of speeches from our own Back Benches on the Hungarian crisis which were filled with all the blind passions of war propaganda. Only John Haire, who really knows Hungary, tried to discuss a most complex situation objectively, and his speech was received almost as though it was an act of disloyalty to suggest that there could be two sides to the case. Ernest Bevin was far more moderate and restrained than most of his supporters. And to cap all this, a Conservative MP came up to me in the Lobby and said: 'Today's debate has provided the basis for a really national foreign policy. Now we are all of one mind on this vital issue. We accept the division of the world into two blocs.'

All of one mind? Certainly the House seemed to be all of one feeling. But minds are supposed to think, to weigh evidence and to assess national interest. What seemed to me lacking yesterday was precisely this sober assessment of British interests. The House seemed to be possessed by the passions of an anti-Communist crusade without caring a rap what would be the consequences to our country.

I suppose it is natural enough that you should accept with disappointment but with equanimity a two-bloc world. I cannot do this. As you know, the Labour Movement has always been anti-Communist in the sense that we believe democratic Socialism to be a far better thing than Communist dictatorship. We know the Communists better perhaps than you since we have had to fight them in the Unions and in the Party, and we have always believed that you cannot defeat Communism by force but only by offering people something better.

That is why in the past the Labour Movement has been suspicious of anti-Communist crusaders. Last November, when I moved the amendment to the King's Speech, I argued that both the Communist and the anti-Communist ideologies were a menace to Britain because if they were permitted to dominate world politics they would divide Europe into an American and Russian sphere of influence, and by dividing every country in Europe would squeeze out genuine democracy. What we needed was a United Europe planning its resources and trade in co-operation, and friendly both to the New World and to Russia. This was the idea which we developed further in *Keep Left* where we argued the need for Anglo-French leadership to prevent Europe from drifting apart.

You seem to think that we agree with Robert Boothby and want a Western bloc. Nothing is farther from our thoughts. Western Europe is a highly industrialised area with a food deficit. If it is separated from Eastern Europe economically, it must become dependent on the New World for its food supplies. Since America neither needs nor is prepared to take our exports in large quantities,

this would mean either bankruptcy or becoming pensioners of the USA. Our whole case is based on the need for the economic co-operation of Western and Eastern Europe. In the past, Britain has relied on the Baltic States for a large part of its timber, bacon, eggs and so on. We can only regain our independence by restoring our trade with this area and expanding it to the Danube countries. Equally, they can only get ahead with their plans for national reconstruction if they can trade their food and raw material surpluses for the industrial equipment which we can provide and Russia can't. To accept the division of Europe and of the world into two blocs is to accept the inevitability of the slow but deadly paralysis of Western European life, including that of these islands.

That is why I was as much delighted by the Foreign Secretary's response to the Harvard speech as I was distressed by yesterday's debate. The Harvard speech was not an offer of American assistance but a suggestion that American assistance should be conditional on Europe working together. It did not exclude Eastern Europe and Russia but expressly included them. It was not ideologically anti-Communist but expressly repudiated the stupid crusading spirit of the Truman doctrine. It provided the opportunity—and pray God we take it—for precisely that Anglo-French initiative in Europe which we advocated in *Keep Left*. That initiative will only make sense if Britain and France act as a funnel through which American raw materials and machinery can be poured not only into Western Europe but into Eastern Europe as well. If the Marshall offer merely ends in the formation of a Western bloc cut off from Eastern Europe, it may postpone catastrophe for a few years, but it will merely mean that we should take rather longer to die than we otherwise would have done.

You are right in saying that the world is already divided into two rival blocs. What it seems to me you overlook is that this division must prove fatal to us because it contradicts all the economic facts on which British recovery depends. I have often quarrelled with Mr Bevin about politics, but his economics are sound enough and I believe that he still recognises that sound foreign policy must be primarily based on economic needs. Our economic need, as we argued in *Keep Left*, is for a United Europe able largely to feed itself and so to reduce its dependency on the dollar.

Yours sincerely,
R. H. S. Crossman

My Dear Crossman,

I am afraid this still does not answer my question: how you think an independent foreign policy could work at the present time; and on this main issue, as on others raised by your letter, I am left as mystified by your views as before.

You complain that the House of Commons is 'possessed by the passions of an anti-Communist crusade', and imply that if we rid ourselves of these passions and treat Russia as a co-operative member of society, all will be well. But you then say that the only way to 'defeat Communism' is by offering people something better. If you yourself are out to 'defeat Communism', why complain that the House is affected with the passions of anti-Communism?

You go on to say that 'if the Marshall offer merely ends in the formation of a Western bloc, cut off from Eastern Europe, it may postpone catastrophe for a few years but it will merely mean that we shall take rather longer to die than we otherwise would have done'. I do not accept this defeatist view. But even if I did, I should, like everyone else not bent on early suicide, still feel in favour of postponing death for as long as possible.

But I do not accept the view that well over three-quarters of the people of the world cannot work out their own salvation together, and that any plans they may make will only stave off their extinction by a year or so. Indeed, if anybody faces ultimate catastrophe in a divided world, it is surely the East European countries. And I am sure that the only way eventually to bring the Russians and their satellites to heel is to let them feel for a while the chill of economic isolation from the West. In fact, it seems already that the satellites have an unpleasant apprehension about what is coming to them. What will they feel in a year or so's time? Even allowing for a Russian wheat surplus, gained incidentally at the expense of near-starvation in the Soviet Union, they will still be very short of food, and their industry will still be desperately short of raw materials and equipment that the West could have supplied. What, too, of Russia? Her potential may be enormous. But her immediate needs are as great.

Does not all this mean that if we, America and Western Europe go on alone, sheer economic necessity will achieve in the end what all the diplomatic approaches have failed to achieve—to force the East to co-operate with the West and so to restore the unity of Europe?

I am convinced that this is a far more likely way of bringing about that unity than sitting down and wishing for it and making no effort to save Western Europe lest we arouse suspicions in Russian breasts which have been there for many years. As far as I can see, all that your letter and *Keep Left* amount to is just such a policy of inaction and wishful thinking.

But you cannot still seriously believe in this after the Paris breakdown. You must surely realise that we should all remain hanging on the edge of the cliff for fear of creating a Western or Atlantic bloc. And, if so, what alternative do you see to our going on with America, and without Russia—hardly what you would presumably call 'an independent foreign policy'?

Yours sincerely,

ANTHONY NUTTING

MY DEAR NUTTING,

Events are moving so fast that it is difficult for our correspondence to keep up with history. Since you wrote your last letter, we know that we can expect no special autumn session of Congress and it is almost certain, as things are going at present, that our dollars will run out some months before any further assistance from America can be expected. So there does not seem to be much chance of your hope being fulfilled and three-quarters of the world working out a plan together. We have got to work on a plan with the other peoples of Western Europe, to pull ourselves out of the slough of despond by our ankle straps.

How extraordinary it is that the two of us who work in the same building for an average of eight hours a day, five days a week, find it so difficult to understand each other. It is not so much that we actually disagree on what should be done, but our approaches are so different that we constantly expect each other to disagree. You, for instance, seem to find it difficult to understand why, although I have been fighting Communists and opposed to Communism all my life, I regard the anti-Communist crusade as dangerous. Well, during the war, in just the same way I was one of the unpopular minority who regarded Vansittartism as a dangerous passion. I prophesied at the time that a people who had swung from an extreme pro-Germanism to an extreme anti-Germanism would be in danger of swinging back again into unreflective sentimental feeling for the Germans. Frankly, I dislike policy based on passion, whether it is anti-German or anti-Russian passion, and I have observed that popular feeling in this country is always swaying between dangerous extremes. In the war it was unreflectively pro-Russian and anti-German; now it is the reverse.

The trouble is that such pendulum passions obscure our national interests. Of course, having applauded Bevin's initiative in transforming the Harvard speech into a Bevin plan; having acclaimed his wisdom in specifically pressing that Russia and Eastern Europe should be included in the Paris conference, I also feel that we have no alternative but to go ahead in Western Europe leaving the door open for Eastern European participation. Where I think I differ from you is in my estimate of the amount of help we can reckon on receiving from America. As a Socialist, perhaps I tend to emphasise more than you do the effect of internal economic affairs on American policy and I am probably more confident than you that sooner or later, probably later, there must come a disastrous slump in America. I have always felt that—for quite different reasons—we cannot rely *either* on America *or* on Russia. We have got to try to work with both, though both in their different ways are difficult and unreliable. In the last resort in the event of war, we should probably find ourselves on the side of America. But you will agree with me that our main object must be to reduce the chances of that ultimate disaster as far as possible.

You seem to feel that the world is now divided finally into a Russian segment and a free segment and that the free three-quarters are ready and able to work for survival. I think that this is an over-simplification. To some extent it is true that there is a Russian segment because the Russian dictatorship does impose a terrific discipline on its satellites. But the so-called free segment shows little signs of unity and coherence, and in my view it would be most dangerous to assume that our wisest policy would be to take for granted the finality of Molotov's 'No', and to try to organise the free world outside Russia.

I am sure that the Foreign Secretary realises after two years of negotiations with Washington that, whatever the desires and policies of a few outstanding Americans like Marshall, the American Constitution renders America incapable of a coherent and stable foreign policy or of giving the degree of economic assistance to Europe and to the rest of the free world which America's long-term interest requires. In my view American help is likely to be too little and too late. We must certainly be thankful for what little we get and I do not think we could pull through without it. But most of our reconstruction must be the result of our own efforts and that of the Commonwealth and of our fellow Europeans. I am inclined to agree that the Eastern European countries would have all liked to have come into the Conference. The rapidity of their reconstruction was largely due to UNRRA supplies of seed corn, tractors, lorries, etc, and they will regret being cut off from this American aid. But I do not agree with your estimate that they would feel the pinch of being cut off from us any more than we should feel the pinch of being cut off from them. To begin with, they are all countries with agricultural surpluses, and normally do not rely on imports of food in order to live. In the second place, their rate of recovery under drastic national planning has been remarkable. Not only Czechoslovakia but Poland and Yugoslavia can look forward with some confidence to creating, within ten years, very considerable industrial areas. Considering the devastation from which they started, their reconstruction, and I may add the energy which people have put into it, has been more remarkable than that shown in Western Europe or in this country. We score on civil liberties; they score on economic self-help.

I entirely agree with you that, since the break has come, European unity may be best achieved by each side going ahead, organising as best it can and then trading across the Iron Curtain. I am puzzled how you can continue to assert that the policy I propound amounts to 'inaction and wishful thinking'. In *Keep Left* we summarised the actions which we felt that the British Government should take. We at least dared to put our programme on paper, which is more than you have done.

But now the prime problem of British foreign policy is the dollar crisis. We know that our gap cannot be bridged by American dollars and I, at least, would not be willing that it should be so bridged even if it could be. In my view we have got to bridge it (1) by building up a system of mutual aid with the sixteen countries and with the Empire, even though this involves denouncing the non-discrimination clause of the loan and having a row with America over that; (2) by as much trade as possible with Eastern Europe and Russia so as to reduce our dollar expenditure; (3) by reckoning on a modest amount of American credit as our share of Congress's loan to Europe, say 150 million dollars a year for three years; and (4) by even more drastic reduction in imports and spending and a rapid reduction in the size of the Armed Forces, bringing them down during the course of 1948 to the level at present contemplated for 1950. If you look at *Keep Left* you will find that those ideas were all written down there. They are not a policy of inaction but a policy designed to make our foreign relations commensurate with our economic strength and to follow, along with the French and as many fellow Europeans as will go with us, a middle position between America and Russia.

Yours sincerely,
R. H. S. CROSSMAN

MY DEAR CROSSMAN,

You seek to undermine my argument in favour of closer economic relations with the USA by saying that we shall not get much help from America anyway, because she will sooner or later have 'a disastrous slump'. I am not so certain about this. But what I am certain about is that the surest way of bringing on a slump would be for the Americans to refuse dollar credits to this and other Western European countries at this critical moment.

Another factor you leave out of account is the very prevalent fear in the USA of the 'Communist menace'. Like you and me, many Americans realise that the answer is to be found in economics, that if Western Europe goes bust, Communism will result.

A great authority on the USA once described American public opinion as resembling an avalanche. Once it starts to move, nothing can reverse its course. American opinion has moved fast since Pearl Harbour, and present developments are hardly likely to reverse it. On the contrary, surely, their need of us and their fear of Communism engulfing Western Europe should encourage them to help rather than to abandon us.

But even supposing, for one reason or another, we don't anticipate getting much out of the Marshall offer, I see no reason for adopting the policy set out in *Keep Left*. For to do so would probably get us nothing at all. As a small boy I should never have been so unwise as to insult an uncle a week or so before Christmas. What sense then could there be in telling the Americans now that we wish to be independent of them because we regard their proffered help as intended merely to make Europe and ourselves a solid and reliable outpost for fighting the Russians? I know you claim that we should build up a system of mutual aid with our Western European neighbours. This may sound very nice on paper, but the degree of stress you lay on it only shows to my mind a dangerous overestimate of our capacity and that of Western Europe 'to pull ourselves out of the slough of despond' by our own efforts alone.

Let me now turn to the long-term problem of the division of Europe. I am optimistic enough to believe it is still possible to end the present division. But neither pretending that no such division exists today, nor pleading with Molotov to co-operate with us will to my mind be of any possible use. I believe that only a policy of 'sanctions' will bring the Slav group into line. I do not agree with you that by such a policy we should hurt ourselves as much as we hurt them. Once again I think you overestimate the capacity for self-help of a Europe broken by war. You speak of the energy of the Slav peoples and their drastic national planning, to which they have subjected themselves, contributing to a remarkable rate of recovery. But energy and planning are no substitutes for equipment and machinery and raw materials. And without these vital necessities the Czech and Polish and Russian dreams of 'creating very considerable industrial areas' are likely to remain mere dreams. If the Slavs could get on so well, if isolated from the West, why, then, their reluctance to refuse the invitation to the Paris Conference? Why, too, should they miss 'the supplies of seed corn, tractors, lorries, etc', to quote from your letter? What you have said only proves to me that the Slav group would feel sooner rather than later the discomfort of isolation.

I entirely agree with you that trade is the answer to all these problems, that trade will succeed where diplomacy has failed. But surely the realistic method of using the trade lever is not to keep up a trickle of goods between this country and Eastern Europe, but to let Eastern Europe feel, through isolation, their dependence upon the West for the means by which they can build up their trade, which is really saying the same as you—only more crudely—when you agree that 'we have no alternative but to go ahead in Western Europe. . . .'

Yours sincerely,
ANTHONY NUTTING

MY DEAR NUTTING,

I think the time has come for you to put your cards on the table and to state what foreign policy *you* propose.

(1) Do you really—as your last letter suggests—advocate a policy of deliberately letting Eastern Europe and Russia learn their dependence on the West by letting them stew in their own juice for a few years?

(2) If so, how is Britain to feed herself during this period? Is she to remain dependent for foodstuffs on a New World which does not need her exports?

(3) Do you argue that we should base our policy today on the assumption that the Americans will come across with sufficient dollars to get us out of our difficulties and to enable us to maintain our heavy military commitments in Europe and in the Near East?

(4) Do you exclude from practical politics the proposal which was the central argument of *Keep Left* for the formation of a European Union based on the Anglo-French alliance, including those nations of Eastern Europe which wish to join and our colonial dependencies in Africa?

Yours sincerely,
R. H. S. CROSSMAN

MY DEAR CROSSMAN,

In answer to your last letter, I will restate briefly my views on British foreign policy:

(1) The art of diplomacy is surely to attempt only what is practicable. I do not believe we shall for the time being get anything out of Russia and her satellites either in the way of food or of political co-operation. In the event we shall anyhow have to find some alternative source of supply for our food, or, if none can be found, tighten our belts once more and make the best of a bad job. This means, to put it crudely, letting Russia and her satellites stew in their own juice for a while.

(2) We may equally be disappointed by the amount we eventually get from the Marshall offer. But that we shall get something from America is certain. And the more we can do to help ourselves and Western Europe, the more certain that 'something' will be. (The Americans, like everyone else, don't like backing bad horses.)

(3) Therefore, I should naturally support any practical measures for economic co-operation between this country and Western Europe and especially between Britain and France.

(4) In short, we should make the best of a bad job and concentrate on saving ourselves and our European friends and neighbours by our own efforts and with the assistance of the United States.

Yours sincerely,
ANTHONY NUTTING

MY DEAR NUTTING,

I am delighted to find that this correspondence has at least achieved one thing. In your first letter to me you condemned all ideas of a Western Union as ignoring 'not only present world conditions but past practice as well'. Now you accept the central thesis of *Keep Left*, that we and the French should help ourselves by achieving the greatest degree of economic co-operation possible. Well, well, we advance.

But I fear that we are still a very long way apart. I take it that your failure to answer 'No' to my third question indicates that you are against any reduction of our military commitments, and that you hope that American dollars will enable us to sustain them. In the past we have, of course, paid other nations to fight our wars, but I am surprised that you should seem so ready to reverse the process.

Yours sincerely,
R. H. S. CROSSMAN

*Go and hunt for a Swan
and recapture the bliss
of having a pen
of perfection like this!*

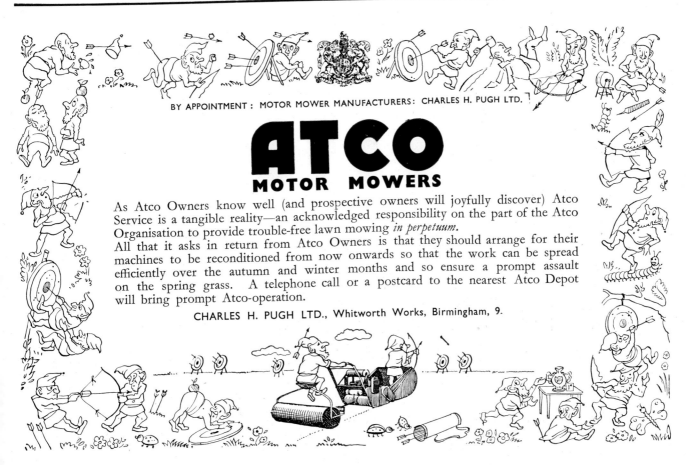

BY APPOINTMENT : MOTOR MOWER MANUFACTURERS : CHARLES H. PUGH LTD.

ATCO
MOTOR MOWERS

As Atco Owners know well (and prospective owners will joyfully discover) Atco Service is a tangible reality—an acknowledged responsibility on the part of the Atco Organisation to provide trouble-free lawn mowing *in perpetuum*.

All that it asks in return from Atco Owners is that they should arrange for their machines to be reconditioned from now onwards so that the work can be spread efficiently over the autumn and winter months and so ensure a prompt assault on the spring grass. A telephone call or a postcard to the nearest Atco Depot will bring prompt Atco-operation.

CHARLES H. PUGH LTD., Whitworth Works, Birmingham, 9.

Exide
THE LONG LIFE CAR BATTERY

Needs no handle to its name

He'd always been so careful . . .

(A TRUE INCIDENT IN A RESIDENTIAL DISTRICT THIS YEAR)

This motorist was busy talking. He was still talking when he opened the door.★

The bus slammed it shut, crushing his legs. He lost them both — and barely escaped death.

He had driven for years without an accident. At the hospital, he said he had never before opened his car door without looking back. . . .

Serious accidents so often happen to people whom most of us would call careful . . . but it takes only one accident to ruin a whole life.

The only way to make sure we shall never cause an accident to ourselves or to fellow-users of the road is to remember the Highway Code. Not vaguely, but accurately. Not just the parts everyone knows, but also the parts many have forgotten. And not just sometimes, but *all* the time that we are in a car or on a bicycle or crossing a road on foot.

A moment's forgetfulness can cost a fearful price.

KEEP DEATH OFF THE ROAD
LEARN THE HIGHWAY CODE

★ See paragraph 54 of the Highway Code

Issued by the Ministry of Transport

Letter from Azerbaijan

continued from page xiii

The numerous petty agents of the new power who, since they came from Soviet Azerbaijan, might have been expected to form a bridge between old and new, behaved like brigands, which they were. They despoiled the peasantry as no landlord had dared to do. When, by organised revolts all over the country, the Russians forced the resignation of the Persian Government in late 1945, they chose Qawam es Saltaneh as Prime Minister. They chose him because they believed he would act as their slave. No greater miscalculation could have been made. Qawam is a patriot. He is also one of the cleverest men in the world.

A strange figure, this elderly dandified gentleman who now took command and was to win back Azerbaijan for the Persian crown. His age is difficult to estimate because he dyes his hair and uses make-up very freely. He has a brain which works as quickly as a table of logarithms. Full of craft, he is absolutely sincere in his belief that Persia must contrive friendship with Russia and England at any price except that of her independence. After several meetings with him, of a formal unfruitful sort, when I was a member of our Embassy in Teheran, I retain an impression of exquisite politeness and polished humour, masking, but in no way pretending to conceal, a lofty pride such as most Persians feel in the ancient identity of their race.

Qawam set to work to strengthen his weak hand. He accomplished this with fantastic ingenuity. There was a tribal revolt in the south largely aimed against the Russian parties. Qawam (protesting to the Russians that his hand was forced) appeased this revolt by expelling Russian creatures from Ministerial office, and thus obtaining a united Cabinet. He then waited till that day in the autumn of 1946 when Mr Molotov made an anti-British speech at the New York Conference. In that speech the Russian chief delegate deplored the presence of English troops on friendly soil. Qawam made a speech a few days later applauding Mr Molotov's performance, recalling amid ecstatic expressions of gratitude the withdrawal, too, of the Red Army in Azerbaijan. He thus forced a choice on the Russians between New York (where Mr Molotov's speech had caused much satisfaction to many of the smaller nations), and Azerbaijan, guessing rightly that they would consider New York the more important prize. In Persia the Russians had meanwhile made another blunder. They had intimated to the leaders of the Azerbaijan Government that, unless they showed more aptitude, the Kremlin might feel obliged to side with the Shah against these rebels. This

continued on page xxiv

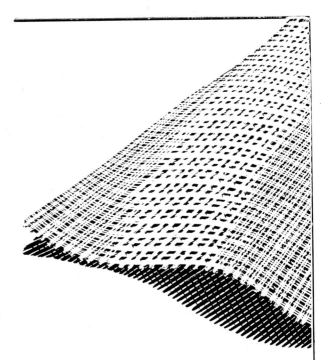

Letter from Azerbaijan

continued from page xxiii

naturally frightened the leaders out of their wits, and they attempted to treat secretly with Teheran. From this incident Qawam guessed, rightly again, that the Russians would not risk much, or despatch reinforcements, in defence of an experiment in which they had lost confidence.

In November 1946, the last chapter of this strange tale opened. An agreement between Teheran and Azerbaijan had been signed in October, and one of the clauses stipulated that the Khamseh province, south of Azerbaijan, should be handed over to the Teheran Government. This small province, which resembles Azerbaijan so closely that its separate existence is often forgotten even by Persians, had rather naturally become involved in the autonomous movement. The Azerbaijan troops withdrew and on November 16, the Persian army moved in amid scenes of hysterical joy. It had been supposed that the Teheran forces would be limited to small units of gendarmerie, but instead, a major part of the armed forces of the Shah arrived and took up battle positions along the whole length of the Azerbaijan frontier.

Qawam watched the Russians. The Soviet Ambassador delivered a formal protest against the new policy, and the radios of Moscow and Baku poured forth torrents of foul abuse of the Persian Government. But no Red Army soldiers appeared as reinforcements for the army of Tabriz, not even when fighting began in the Khamseh province.

Sincere efforts were made to preserve peace but excitement ran so high on the frontier that frequent clashes between patrols were inevitable. The Persian troops were joined by the wild Shahsavan tribes and their irregular cavalry made daily attacks on the forward positions of the provincial army. I saw one of these attacks, and as cavalry charges are rare spectacles today a brief description may be interesting. The attack (which occurred on December 4, 1946,) was on a small village called Rejin, north of Zenjan, which had been secretly occupied by Azerbaijan troops in the night. The attack came from the west and was delivered by a body of some hundred tribal horsemen. They rode very fast, not in line, but one behind the other, and though they rode into automatic fire they rode quite straight. On nearing the position they opened fire with carbines from the saddle. As far as I could see they did not charge directly into the position but rode twenty yards to the side of it, firing as they passed, and turning back in the saddle for a last aim after passing. This last manoeuvre, of course, is the Parthian shot whose tradition lives chiefly in the Persian technique of gazelle-shooting from horseback. The whole engagement which I witnessed was over in twenty-five minutes. One horse and horseman were killed, and seven of the defenders. The position was abandoned by the Azerbaijans.

continued on page xxix

The Central Library, Manchester

CITIES IN WHICH WE SERVE

MANCHESTER. The Romans named it Mancunium — the Doomsday Book calls it Mamecester. Between whiles it suffered a lot from the Danes. But by the 13th century it was a promising spot for making textiles. In Elizabeth's reign " it surpassed neighbouring towns in elegance." An 18th century visitor describes it as " the busiest village in England." The visitor today finds Manchester far from humdrum. There is an Austin Reed shop in St. Ann's Square.

BRISTOL. In Canute's reign it was an English slave market. John Cabot sailed from here in 1497 and discovered North America, claiming it for Henry VII. The king paid him £10 for the job. 116 years later, Bristol merchants gave Anne, James I's queen, a magnificent welcome. She left, owing them £800 for wines.

Bristol's prosperity grew with tobacco, slaves and general trade with America. In 1700 the city was second only to London in size and today is a great port and trading centre and ships sail into the very heart of the city.
There is an Austin Reed shop for men in Clare Street.

There are Austin Reed shops in Manchester, Bristol, London, Bath, Belfast, Birmingham, Bournemouth, Coventry, Edinburgh, Glasgow, Harrogate, Hull, Leeds, Liverpool, Norwich, Nottingham, Oxford, Plymouth, Sheffield and Southampton. Visitors are always assured of a friendly welcome.

JUST A PART OF THE AUSTIN REED SERVICE

The Suspension Bridge, Bristol

FROM THESE DEEP WATERS
COMES A WEAPON TO FIGHT DISEASE

In the deep-water seas of Greenland, Iceland and the North Pacific the halibut swims along the ocean bed. And scientists discovered that within the halibut are stored two vitamins which together form one of the most potent aids to health known to man. For halibut oil is a richly concentrated source of vitamins A and D, without which it is impossible for adults to maintain health or children to grow up with straight bones and strong teeth.

The Crookes Laboratories are proud to be associated with the work of these doctors and scientists — proud to supply them with the means to fight disease and to bring health and happiness into the lives of ordinary people.

CROOKES MAKERS OF VITAMIN PRODUCTS

THE CROOKES LABORATORIES LIMITED · PARK ROYAL · LONDON · NW10

Letter from Azerbaijan

continued from page xxiv

The Prime Minister who, during this period, remained blandly on the best terms all round, was fortunate in having two remarkable soldiers in the Persian service, Marshal Ahmadi as Commander-in-Chief, and General Razm Ara as Chief of Staff. These two men had carried through a brilliant programme of Army Reform. It was difficult for someone like myself, who had seen the pathetic remnants of Reza Shah's defeated army in 1941, to recognise the same army in the well-equipped force on the Azerbaijan frontier, in which high morale was infectious, in which relations between officers and men were comradely and exemplary, and in which the supply services worked with precision.

On December 10, the Persian army advanced. The campaign lasted one day. When they saw that the Russians did not intend to support them, the Azerbaijan leaders, many of the officers of the rebel forces, and almost all the agents from Soviet Azerbaijan, fled. Only two of the chief men remained behind: Dr Javid, President of the Council, and Aga Shabestari, Governor of Tabriz and chief of Cabinet. These two men behaved with dignity and courage. Having reached Tabriz on December 11, before the arrival of the army, I went to visit Aga Shabestari, whom I knew already, in the Governor's palace. It was an amazing interview. The whole town was in a state of disorder. No police services existed beyond volunteers led by nervous merchants. Shops were being looted. Arms were plentiful. The whole of Tabriz resounded with rifle and machine-gun fire. While interviewing Aga Shabestari, the din of machine-gun fire, approaching from two directions and sounding louder and more intense than I had heard it yet, seemed unmistakeably to herald an organised attack on the palace. I was conscious of claustrophobia and of that odd disposition to yawn which comes over one in moments of fear. One of the volunteer police rushed in and begged Aga Shabestari to take shelter, but the Governor, who had been conversing coolly throughout this scene, told the policeman that he did not feel inclined to move from where he was. 'Particularly', he added, with a polite bow to Mr Daniels of the *New York Times* and myself, 'while these distinguished guests are with us.' He was not going to show alarm in front of foreigners. The attack was beaten off. Five hours later the army arrived, and Dr Javid and Aga Shabestari, to the shame, as many people thought, of the Persian Government, were taken off under arrest. A week later the army was in occupation of the whole province while the frontier posts along the Araxes were crammed with terrified citizens of Soviet Azerbaijan and Armenia who a little before

continued on page xxxiii

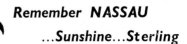

FEATURED:
Vanda coerulea, " The Blue
Orchid," nature's floral gem
from the forests of Burma.

Both equally exquisite...

IMPERIAL LEATHER
Toilet Soap for the discriminating

CHATER

Announcement of CUSSONS SONS & CO. LTD, 84 BROOK STREET, GROSVENOR SQUARE, LONDON, W.1.

Beau Brummell once said " I think that with a moderate degree of prudence and economy a young man might manage to dress on £800 a year." He probably said it in Covent Garden, a district that was for centuries famous as the home of the gay, the gifted and the well dressed. To-day, though Beau Brummell and his fellow-dandies have gone, Covent Garden's tradition of fine dress lives on at Moss Bros.

Letter from Azerbaijan
continued from page xxix

had played the tyrant under invincible Russian protection, and who were now fleeing to Russia in terror of their lives.

That is the end of that story. What can one make of it? I think the story proves this: that it is almost impossibly difficult to exert power effectively without regard to the claims of human dignity. Had the Russians accorded to Persia and the Persians some degree of respect, had they allowed them to feel confident that Russia had no wish to degrade them into servitude, then ultimately total Russian ascendancy could never have been challenged there. Nothing on this earth could have prevented Persia coming into Russia's sphere of influence. In 1945 the Persians were ready to accept this fate. As it turned out, Russian conduct so inflamed and embittered the Persians that in the end the army of this unmilitary nation marched into Azerbaijan prepared to do battle with Russia herself, while at the same time Qawam, by a series of brilliant diplomatic ruses, and supported by every class of the nation, virtually extinguished for a time the naturally vast influence of Russia in that part of Asia.

Letter from Hamburg

by Derrick Sington

HAMBURG to the German still means the sea and access to the outside world. But if you look out across the wide Elbe today you see only a desultory traffic. A river steamer passes, packed with people on excursions to villages further down the river. A freighter is discharging Swedish iron-ore for onward transportation to Czechoslovakia. A landing-craft, laden with Army lorries for repair, is steaming towards the sea. A tour of the port on a motor launch brings you close up to a score or so of unsalvaged wrecks, their decks awash just as they were when the bombs hit them three years ago. The great rusty hulk of the *Robert Ley* still lies in the Finkenwerder inlet dwarfing a group of fishing ships.

Town clearance work has at last got seriously under way. Large cleared spaces can be seen in the Innenstadt and in Altona, where a big site is being prepared for dock workers' dwellings. Eight stone-breaking machines are at work. Three others are idle for lack of labour and lorries to carry away the stones. Up to June 3, half a million cubic metres of debris had been cleared. So far so good—but there remains more than 39 million cubic metres of ruins, principally in Barmbeck, the industrial quarter.

Labour shortage has been a serious factor in

continued on page xxxv

Letter from Hamburg

continued from page xxxiii

Hamburg for some time. In June, for example, the loading or unloading of 23 ships was held up for lack of dock labourers. To remedy this, 2,500 workers had to be released from Control Commission employment or from German factories. At the end of July, Hamburg industries were short of 20,000 workers.

The shortage of manpower is, of course, in large part due to the deprivations of the war, but it is also closely linked to the disastrous shortage of food which has caused a fall in the workers' output of 40 per cent compared with prewar years. The black market, too, is undoubtedly claiming a considerable proportion of the able-bodied population. Pilfering, bartering, marauding expeditions into the country are surer methods of procuring more food than a full-time job which brings only enough money to buy the scanty rations which have been the Hamburg inhabitant's lot for many months now. When 1 lb of butter on the black market costs RM 250— or just 140 times the legal price—and 1 lb of sugar RM 80—or 200 times the legal price—there is little inducement to earn the 70 or 80 marks a week which are the normal wage.

Among conditions which are so often those of a primitive struggle for survival, it says much for the courage and character of many Hamburg people (as well as not a little for the amenities of the black market) that cultural activities are much in evidence. During the season which has just ended, there have been, for instance, plenty of productions well worth seeing at Hamburg's nine theatres. Contemporary French and American and, to a lesser degree, British dramatists have been well represented. But, as during the previous two years, there has been little or no sign of the emergence of a significant new German drama. The Schauspielhaus, now under the direction of Arthur Hellmer who, as Intendant of the *Deutsches Schauspielhaus* at Frankfurt before 1933 introduced Georg Kaiser's work to the German public, staged impressive productions of Giraudoux's *Undine*, Eugene O'Neill's *Mourning Becomes Electra*, and a magnificent production of Gerhard Hauptmann's drama of the Silesian weavers' revolt, *Die Weber*.

Earlier in the year a delightful pot-pourri of Gogol, Tchehov and Tolstoi 'one-actors' was put on at the Schauspielhaus. The Kammerspiele, which is a smaller theatre, with a more *avant-garde* flavour, is run by Ida Ehre, a Jewish actress, who has returned to the stage after 12 years' banishment. She has produced *Eurydike* by Jean Anouilh and Giraudoux's *The Trojan War will not take Place*. Probably the most popular of the Kammerspiele's produc-

continued on page xxxvi

tions, however, was Thornton Wilder's apocalyptic *Skin of Our Teeth*. At the Junge Bühne, a new theatre which is controlled by a young intendant, Answald Kruger, I found *Nun Singen Sie Wieder*, by the Swiss dramatist Max Frisch, a powerful and moving play. It handles the theme of Nazi Germany somewhat in the manner of Ernst Toller at his best. In July a stage version of the novel *On Borrowed Time*, by the American writer, Levis Watkin, was produced at the Junge Bühne. The two Thalia theatres, one of them recently repaired and re-opened, are now under the direction of Willy Maertens, a Hamburg actor of 25 years' experience.

At the Hamburg Staatsoper the outstanding event of the past season was undoubtedly the production in German of *Peter Grimes* which was sung many times to packed and enthusiastic audiences. Considering the shortage of materials of all kinds, the originality and, in some cases, even the magnificence of the decors of most Hamburg productions has been astonishing. Actors in Hamburg do not qualify for heavy workers' supplementary rations, but each theatre intendant receives certificates entitling 20 members of his company to get one meal daily at a Hamburg restaurant without surrendering coupons.

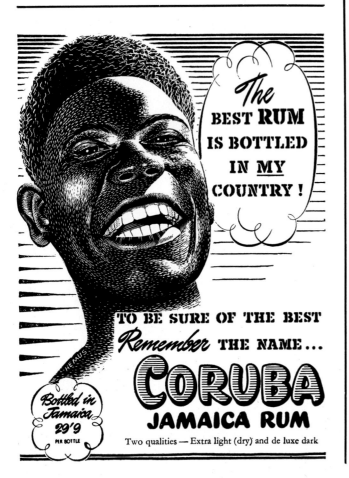

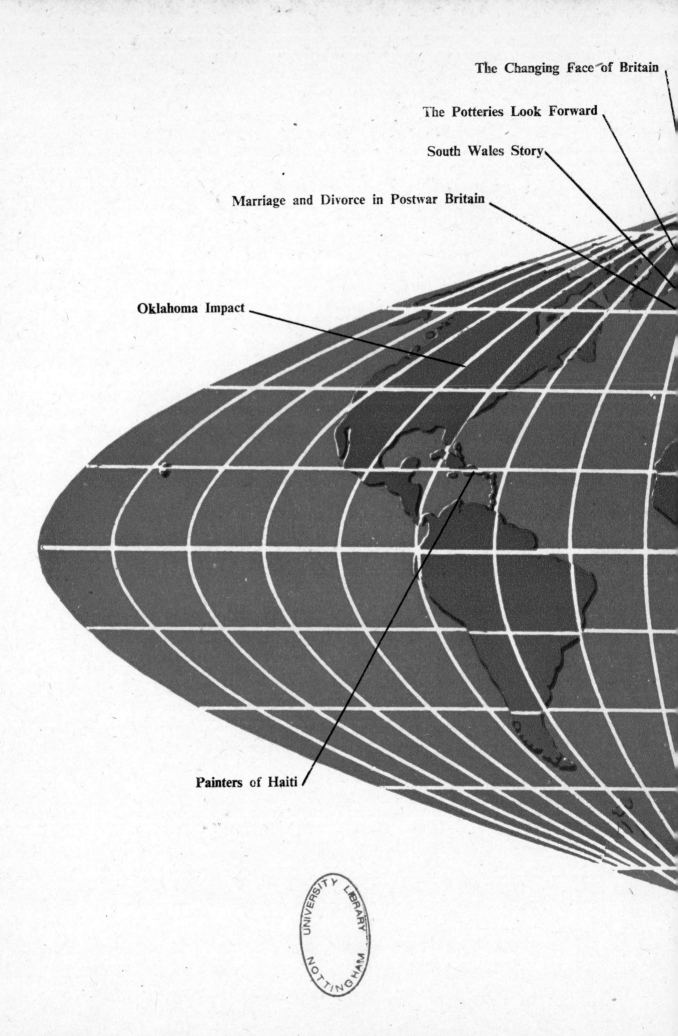

The Changing Face of Britain

The Potteries Look Forward

South Wales Story

Marriage and Divorce in Postwar Britain

Oklahoma Impact

Painters of Haiti